AF488674

Heavenly Flowers

Heavenly Flowers

Written by:
Frederic Baraga

Translated by:
Simona Stavbar

BISHOP BARAGA ASSOCIATION

Heavenly Flowers
by Frederic (Friderik Irenej) Baraga (1797-1868)

Originally published in Ljubljana, 1846

Translated by Simona Stavbar

Reviewed by:
Very Rev. Fr. Timothy Ferguson
Ms. Lenora McKeen
Rev. Monshau, OD
Dcn. John P. Vidmar

Published by:
The Bishop Baraga Association, Marquette, Michigan

ISBN: 9798218453121

Copyright © 2024 by The Bishop Baraga Association

Printed and bound in the United States of America. All rights reserved.

[Original Illustration from *Heavenly Flowers* printed in 1846.]

Nebefhke
ROSHE.

Friderik Baraga,

Mifijonar.

V' Ljubljani 1846.

V' salogi in na prodaj per *J. Klemensu*
bukvovesu na ftarim tergu. **Nr. 155.**

[Original Title Page from Heavenly Flowers printed in 1846.]

V' natif teh bukev fo miloftljivi Firfht,
GOȘPOD GOȘPOD
ANTON ALOJS,
Ljublijanfki Șhkof dovolili 30. profenza 1846.

[Original book dedication from *Heavenly Flowers* printed in 1846.]

Contents

I.

FEAR OF GOD

*"The fullness of wisdom is
to fear the Lord."*[1]

A humble and trusting fear of God is truly the beginning of wisdom. *"For the concern of the flesh is hostility toward God; it does not submit to the law of God, nor can it,"*[2] but the sacred wisdom "which makes God's servant faithful and attentive and then pleasing to the Lord."[3] *"Yet all good things together came to me with her, and countless riches at her hands,"*[4] all the wonderful Christian virtues.

Christian virtues are so beautiful on their own that every human honors them. However, there are a few who truly strive to demonstrate them faithfully in action. God-fearing and devout Christians are fortunate, but devotion (i.e., the essence of Christian virtues) must be real and firm, otherwise it is not salvatory. There are many who think they are devout Christians because they abstain from big, mortal sins. Others think they are devout because they abstain from some specific vices that are especially unpleasant in the behavior of a neighbor, although they carry many of their own vices that are even greater before God. Some think that a true devotion is if a person performs certain acts of worship, or some external good and penitential works, although this

---

1. Ben Sira 1:16.
2. Romans 8:7.
3. Matthew 24:45-47. In NABRE: Cf. Matthew 24:45-47.
4. Wisdom 7:11.

person's intentions are not always directed towards God and he or she is neglecting the duties of one's status.

All this is not a *Christian* but a *pagan* devotion as Jesus showed us in the example of the Pharisee who went to the temple area to pray.[5] Such devotion does not lead to life but, damnation. "*Sometimes a way seems right, but the end of it leads to death!*"[6] A true Christian devotion does not derive from the words and ideas of people but from the Word of God. A Christian has to serve God according to the will of God and not according to one's own will, if he or she wants to be pleasing to God. This is the true devotion this book will talk about.

The fear of God marks *the beginning* of true sacred wisdom, which is the essence of all Christian virtues. If a Christian faithfully listens to it, it leads him to reach *completeness* in the virtues because "*The fear of the Lord is glory and exultation, gladness and a festive crown,*"[7] i.e., the fulfillment of all sacred Christian virtues.

My dear Christian, fear God. "*See: the fear of the Lord is wisdom [...].*"[8] You should not be afraid of Him only because He is almighty and a harsh judge who will condemn a sinner to eternal suffering. Such fear does not hate sin because it is evil in itself and offends God, but only because it makes man eternally miserable. True and holy fear of God comes from the love of God and causes us to hate sin above everything else, to fear it more than a poisonous snake, and to avoid it because it offends God, and that we fear nothing in the world as much as offending God and thus losing Him forever. However, a Christian is also left to fear eternal suffering, which the righteous God has prepared for all those who live and die in sin.

---

5. Cf. Luke 18: 10-12.
6. Kohelet 16:25. In NABRE: Proverbs: 16:25.
7. Ben Sira 1:22. In NABRE: Ben Sira 1:11.
8. Job 28:28.

You should be afraid of God, my dear Christian, as a child fears his good father. The child is more afraid of losing father's love than of his punishment.

You should also fear Him as a servant fears his harsh master if this servant is lazy and negligent in his duties; this fear will always drive you to work diligently and faithfully for God who always and everywhere sees you.

You should, furthermore, fear Him as the evildoer fears his judge, because certainly and maybe even today, you will stand before His judgment seat where you will be judged harshly. And this fear must deter you from all that you will not be able to defend before the judgment of God.

You will also have to fear Him as your almighty God, according to the words of Jesus: *"I shall show you whom to fear. Be afraid of the one who after killing has the power to cast into Gehenna; yes, I tell you, be afraid of that one."*[9]

The fear of God is a beautiful and great gift from God. Ask God often for this gift and you will be fortunate. The more you are confirmed in the fear of God, the more you will enter into a covenant with God and God with you. The more you will fear God, the less you will fear the evil spirit and evil people. *"Whoever fear the Lord are afraid of nothing and are never discouraged, for he is their hope."*[10]

Consider here a fine example of fear of God. Since time immemorial, God has allowed His servants to suffer persecution, so that their piety and God-fearing can be shown as a beautiful example to others. To illustrate, during the time of the evil king Antiochus, who mercilessly persecuted the servants of God, Eleazar set a fine example of God-fearing. This king wanted to force the people of Israel to leave God's law and live in unbelief, and there were many who turned away from God

---

9. Luke 12:5.
10. Ben Sira 34:16.

for fear of suffering. This was not done by Eleazar who concluded that he would rather die than leave God and His holy law. The evil king wanted to force him to eat meat, which was forbidden to the Israelites by God's law. He did not want to eat it; therefore, he was sentenced to death. When his friends saw this, they felt sorry for him, but this mercy was unjust. So, they asked him secretly to let him bring such meat as was permitted for them to eat, so that he would eat it, and that the king would think that it was forbidden meat, and thus he would preserve his life. However, Eleazar did not want to do that and said to them: "*At our age it would be unbecoming to make such a pretense; many of the young would think the ninety-year-old Eleazar had gone over to an alien religion. If I dissemble to gain a brief moment of life, they would be led astray by me, while I would bring defilement and dishonor on my old age. Even if, for the time being, I avoid human punishment, I shall never, whether alive or dead, escape the hand of the Almighty.*"[11]

When King Antiochus saw that this steadfast servant of God would not be defeated, he ordered that he be led to suffering and death. In his suffering, Eleazar groaned to God and said: "*The Lord in his holy knowledge knows full well that, although I could have escaped death, I am not only enduring terrible pain in my body from this scourging, but also suffering it with joy in my soul because of my devotion to him.*"[12]

A truly beautiful example of the holy fear of God!

---

11.   2 Maccabees 6:24–26.
12.   2 Maccabees 6:30–31.

II.

LOVE OF GOD

*"You shall love the Lord your God with
all your heart, with all your soul, with all
your mind, and with all your strength."*

*"Remember your Creator in the days of your youth, before the
evil days come,"* says the Holy Spirit in the Holy Scripture.
Fortunate are those who begin to love the Lord, their
God at a young age and continue to love Him increasingly.

My dear Christian who is reading this, give your heart
to the Lord and conclude firmly to love Him alone
above all else. Would you be acting justly if you wanted
to give your heart first to the evil spirit, and then in old
age to God, if you are obliged to give it to him *immediately*? Would you be acting justly if you wanted to give the
best years of your life, *all* of which you owe to God, to
the sinful pleasures of the world and only the old, rigid
years to God?

Our heart is made for God. Only God can complete
our heart and make it truly satisfied and happy. Only
God is infinitely worthy of our love. If we could love
Him with *infinite* love, we would love Him as He is worthy of being loved. All kindness, all perfection, all beauty, and all goodness are united only in God.

The greatest joy and the essence of the salvation of
all of the elect in Heaven is to see and love God. And

the most terrible suffering of the damned in hell is never to see God and to hate Him.

My dear Christian, if you want to love God forever in Heaven, you must really want to love Him already in this world. "*We love because he first loved us.*" God loved us even before we were able to love Him, before we were in this world. It is precisely His love for us that made Him create us, in His own image, with an immortal soul, that is destined to rejoice with Him in Heaven forever. Oh, infinite love for such ungrateful things as we are!

But this was not enough for His immeasurable love. After we lost all right to the Heavenly Kingdom through our sins, He gave us His only begotten Son who saved us from eternal damnation, from eternal suffering. He did it in no other way than through His own terrible suffering and His bitter death on the cross. Oh, the un-imaginable love that completely forgets itself and does so much for its loved ones!

However, even this was not enough for eternal love. After the merciful God created us for Heaven and the Son of God saved us for Heaven, we are gifted with the grace of the Holy Spirit, who, so to speak, strives as much as possible to ensure our admittance for Heaven. Neither in this life nor in eternity, will we ever be able to fully understand how great God's love is for us!

Love Him as well, my Christian, and never stop loving Him, and love Him with all your heart. "*My son, give me your heart* [...]," God is saying to you kindly. Give your heart to Him then, and be glad that the eternal God de-sires such a poor gift as your heart, that He asks you to give it to Him.

Love of God must be shown in deeds. If a Christian does not live according to God's will and law, such a per-son certainly does not love God, even though this per-son might sometimes have certain sweet feelings of love in one's heart. Love is like fire. Fire warms and gives off light. If there is no light and no heat, there certainly is no fire either. It is the same with love. If there is no zeal in the service of God, no exemplary life, there certainly is no true love of God.

Our love of God has to transcend everything else, i.e., we have to be prepared to do everything for God, whatever He wants from us, even if it were really difficult. Prefer to give everything up rather than lose God's kindness; rather lose everything except God's grace. Endure torture and death rather than being separated from God by some sin. Our heart, our thoughts and all our intentions must be such that we can rightly say with St. Paul: "*What will separate us from the love of Christ? Will anguish, or distress, or persecution, or famine, or nakedness, or peril, or the sword?* […] *in all these things we conquer overwhelmingly through him who loved us. For I am convinced that neither death, nor life, nor angels, nor principalities, nor present things, nor future things,* […] *nor any other creature will be able to separate us from the love of God in Christ Jesus our Lord.*"

Without love we are nothing and everything else is of no use to us without it. Whoever does not first love God above all else and then, love his or her neighbor for God's sake and in God, ranks as nothing in God's eyes and will never see God in Heaven. Whoever dies in God's love will be eternally fortunate. Whoever wants to die in God's love must also live in God's love, so strive, my dear Christian, to truly love God above all else. Further, ask Him every day to kindle the fire of His love in your heart and to keep you in His holy love until the end of your life.

Consider the good example of love for God and imitate it. Two hermits begged God for a long time to let them know how they could truly love Him and serve Him completely. God heard these righteous requests and informed them that they should go to the city of Alexandria and find a man by the name of Eucharid and his wife Mary. They serve God more perfectly than the two hermits do.

Fortunate and grateful to God, these two hermits set out on their journey and spent a long time in the great city of Alexandria asking where Eucharid resides. However, nobody knew this poor man. Then they began to think that it was all a mistake and were already heading back towards the desert. But before they left town, they saw a woman standing in front of a low, poor house. They asked her if she knew where Eucharid lived. "My husband's name is Eucharid," the wife answered them, "and we live here. He is not at home now, but he will be back this evening."

Full of gratitude to God, they went into the house and wanted to see this holy servant of God as soon as possible.

That evening, Eucharid returned home driving the small flock of sheep he had been tending during the day. As soon as the two hermits saw him, they went to meet him, hugged him warmly and escorted him into the house. Eucharid was greatly amazed and could not understand why these two penitents were showing him so much kindness and honor. He was even more surprised when they started asking him to tell them exactly how he and his wife serve God, because they wanted to learn from them how to love God rightly and serve Him faithfully. "I am a poor and ignorant shepherd," Eucharid answered them, "and I do not love God rightly; I serve Him poorly. I ask you, venerable servants of God, to teach me to love Him the way the holy hermits love Him." Then they begged him even more and ordered him to tell them precisely how he lives.

To this Eucharid said: "I owe obedience to the servants of God. Therefore, I tell you that I started to serve God at a young age and to do everything out of love for Him. My mother was a God-fearing woman and taught me to love God at a young age. God gave me the grace to fulfill faithfully the teachings of my good mother. Whenever I had to suffer, I willingly suffered out of love for God. Whenever my parents ordered me to do something, I quickly did what I was told to do out of love for God. When I saw other children stealing sweets from their parents and eating them, I remembered God and out of love for Him I refrained from stealing. And as I learned to do in my youth, I always tried later to do everything for the sake of God and out of love for Him. I get up early in the morning out of love for God, do my prayer and dedicate the day to God out of love for Him. Then I go to work, and I work out of love for Him, because it is His holy will that I fulfill by tending to the duties of my status.

When I rest, I remember my Creator who rested after creating all things and out of love for Him I rest a little so that I can then work more diligently. I have a meal out of love for God, who created me, who sustains me and gives me everything I need. When I am hungry or thirsty, when I am cold or hot, when I suffer poverty or some illness, I remember Jesus who suffered all this for me, and out of love for him I willingly endure everything. When God sends me a long illness or a bad harvest, I gratefully accept everything from His hands out of love for Him.

I always live in peace and unity with my wife: what I want, she wants, and what she wants, I want. And as I live, so does my wife. This is all I can tell you about our lives.

Then the two hermits asked him if he had any property. And he answered them: "My possessions are small. I do not have much else besides this small flock of sheep. But the benevolent God always bestows His holy blessing on me, and I have enough of everything. I divide what I earn and produce into three parts. I give the first part to the Church, which is His house, out of love for

God. I give the second part to the poor and to travelers, out of love for Jesus. And in the image of the poor man, I see and worship the merciful Jesus. I keep the third part for myself and my wife, and I live in constant poverty, out of love for Jesus who chose poverty in this world and became poor out of love for us.

When I have bad food or when I lack food, I remember Jesus' hunger, which He felt many times out of love for me. I remember His favorite food was to fulfill God's will, and that a person lives not only from bodily food, but also from the Word of God. In this way, I bear my poverty willingly, out of love for God."

At the end, the two hermits asked him if he had any enemies. To this Eucharid answered: "Who in this world is without enemies? Jesus had them and the most holy friends of God had them. How could I, a poor sinner, not have them? It is true that I do not wish nor do any harm to anyone, nor do I speak anything bad about anyone; however, I have enemies who are jealous of me, but I feel mercy for them and love them. I sometimes go and visit them; and whenever I can do something good to them, I like to do everything for them, out of love for God. When someone says something bad about me or my wife, or when someone does something bad to me, I suffer peacefully out of love for Jesus who suffered much more for me. And my wife does exactly the same in all things. This is our poor life then, and we never do anything special or great."

The two hermits then returned home with great astonishment and heartily praised God for showing them such a beautiful and easy path to Christian perfection and heavenly salvation.

III.

IMITATION OF CHRIST

*"I have given you a model to follow, so that
as I have done for you, you should also do."*

Whoever wants to live a holy life must imitate holy examples. There has never been a more holy example in the world than the example of Jesus. Jesus is the Saint of saints, the greatest perfection of all virtues. St. Paul achieved such holiness because he always imitated Jesus. In the same way, all the saints always had the example of Jesus in front of them and faithfully imitated it.

This *"Good Teacher"* came from Heaven to this poor earth and became our equal, in order to teach us not only with His Word, but also with His life to fulfill God's will in all circumstances. Therefore, He became *a child* to teach children how they should behave towards God, towards their parents and towards all people. He became *a young man* in order to teach young men how to protect themselves from the dangerous and seductive world and to serve God while being still young. He became *a grown-up man* in order to teach grown-up people how to fulfil the duties of their status and how to endure all the difficulties of life.

Jesus gave young people *four* beautiful examples in particular, which they must imitate if they want to please Him.

1. The first example of Jesus in His youth was His quiet, humble, poor and hardworking life. The Bible

does not tell us much about Jesus' youth because His life was quiet and not known to people. Apart from His most holy mother and Saint Joseph, no one really knew Him in His youth. Only these two people knew that He was the only Son of the eternal God. A beautiful example of quiet humility, which God's son gave to young people who love to boast so much if they are of a slightly more noble birth, exalt themselves above others and despise those who are of low and poor status, and do not consider that there is no other excellence and highness before God than humility, because only the person who humbles oneself is exalted before God.

As the first teachers of the Church report, even though He was the Son of the living God, Jesus always worked diligently, even in His youth, and He set a fine example for young men and all people who are sinners and condemned to work by a righteous God.

My dear Christian, if you live in poverty and have to work hard, be content. Consider Jesus' poverty, His diligence and His effort. Out of love for Him bear everything as willingly as He did, and you will gain His liking and His love. Oh, happiness above all happiness to be liked by Jesus and to be loved by Him!

2. In His Youth, Jesus gave us a beautiful example of piety and zeal for God's service. Only twelve years old, He sets out on a long journey to Jerusalem with His parents. When He arrives at the temple of God, the house of His Heavenly Father, He is so joyful to be in this holy place that He cannot leave it. He never gets tired of listening to the teachers explaining God's law, although He is their "Teacher," and He fills them with His eternal wisdom. Imitate, my dear young man, this beautiful example. Where does your laziness in God's service come from? Why are you so negligent about listening to God's word? Why do you find the teaching of God's truths so boring that you doze off or think of other things

when teachers are explaining God's law? The reason is that you neither think about nor imitate Jesus' example. Rise then, oh Christian, from your pernicious slumber. Consider the example of Jesus and imitate Him. Be grateful to God because He always gives you the opportunity to listen to God's truths and salvatory teachings; to know God's law and Christian duties more thoroughly and more accurately.   Recognize this great grace and happiness with a grateful heart. How many there are, especially in this wild country where I am writing this, who never have this grace to hear the word of God because there are too few preachers of God's truths here. If they had the same opportunity you have, they would have converted to God and be saved. But you let your soul starve in all the abundance of God's word, you sit by the fountain of living water, and yet your soul dies of thirst!

3. Another beautiful example of the loving young Jesus is His faithful obedience to His most holy mother and to his foster father. He was completely obedient to them and subservient to them in all things, and not only to His own mother, but also to Saint Joseph who was not His real father but only His foster father and guardian. A truly fine example of obedience! Consider this well, my dear Christian, and imitate Him. Jesus is the Son of God, the eternal Son of the eternal Father. And yet, according to His human nature, He submits to men who are His things. Jesus is the eternal Wisdom and infinite Holiness. His providence and His will rule Heaven and earth and all created things. And yet, He completely surrenders His own will to the will of His mother and His guardian father, and always faithfully fulfills what they tell Him to do.

How then, my Christian, will you endure at God's judgement if you do not follow the example you have in Jesus? You are smaller than are your parents or superiors and you have less insight, wisdom and experience than they do. Consider that the same Jesus will judge you who gave you such a beautiful example of a humble obedience.

4. The fourth beautiful example of Jesus that we find in the Bible is that Jesus advanced in age, in wisdom, in grace and in favor before God and people. Jesus, who is God and at the same time is man, possessed all the highest perfections, even in His young years, but they were not recognized by the people in the beginning. Jesus revealed more and more in His actions and in His life, as He grew, in the same way as the sun itself is always the same, but does not seem as bright and warm in the morning as it does later when it rises higher, and especially at noon.

You can also learn from this parable, my dear Christian, that a person must *always* strive to advance on the path of Christian perfection if he or she wants to be saved. If a person strives only *sometimes* and then ceases again, this person is like a boatman rowing in running water diligently for a while and progressing a little, but then stops rowing and is swept back by the water, then begins to row again, but hardly gets as far as the first time, and stops rowing again. This person again loses his or her way and effort, and never gets very far.

Then, my dear Christian, be diligent on your way to Heaven and follow Jesus' example. How sad it is to see, especially among young people, that instead of becoming more and more wise, God-fearing and pious, they become more and more licentious, indecent and wicked, and more and more negligent and careless in the fulfillment of their Christian duties. They withdraw their hearts, which they owe entirely to God, from Him and give them to the seductive world and the wicked enemy. They turn their minds, which are just beginning to understand God's truths, into conceited worldly thoughts and sinful desires, and they subject their will, which God created as free only so that they would willingly bind it to God's will, only to the distorted ways of the world and to their wicked mockery. This does not lead to greater growth in wisdom, grace and pleasantness before God and before people, as Jesus did in the examples He set for us in His youth.

Not only in His youth, but during His entire life, Jesus gave us the most beautiful examples, which we must always imitate if we want to be liked by Him and saved. Throughout His life, Jesus lived in the denial of His godliness and in the spirit of penance. He lived this way not for His own sake, because His infinite holiness did not need penance and suffering. He wanted to do enough for us and to give us an example. Even in the spirit of prayer, in the spirit of obedience and love for His Heavenly Father, He set the most beautiful examples before our eyes. His whole life, especially when He began to teach, was full of love and mercy for His neighbor, not only for His friends, but also for His enemies, for whom even in His last hour He sincerely asked His Heavenly Father.

Our greatest honor and infinite happiness is to follow Jesus by faithfully imitating His example. To leave Him and to take another path would bring about our sure and eternal destruction. Jesus walked on a narrow and thorny path and had to *"suffer these things and enter into his glory." How will we then* be able to get to that very place if we always want to walk along the wide and smooth path of worldly pleasures and suffer nothing out of love for Jesus? St. Paul teaches us *"For those he foreknew he also predestined to be conformed to the image of his Son* […]."

It is very good to follow the example of Jesus at a young age and to grow with Jesus. He grew in years, as well as in wisdom and piety. *"It is good for a person, when young, to bear the yoke* [of the Lord]." The yoke of Jesus is especially sweet and pleasant and Christians should prefer to examine themselves in the mirror of His example at every opportunity rather than in the mirror of worldly vanity. And parents should teach and remind their children at every opportunity to act as Jesus did in His youth on such occasions.

We have the beautiful example that three pious souls provided for all parents, teachers and children. There was a poor and God-fearing widow who had a daughter, Dorothea. This girl was terribly restless and worldly in her early youth. Her mother was afraid for her and feared that she would grow more and more corrupt, following the example of worldly women. Although she was poor, she handed her daughter over to a good and pious female teacher, and she specifically asked her to teach her daughter to live a Christian life and follow the example of Jesus.

Dorothea, who was ten years old at the time, stayed with her teacher for two years, and saw and heard nothing but the holy words of God and Jesus' examples. God gave her the grace to keep all these beautiful teachings in her heart and she firmly concluded to act according to them for the rest of her life.

When she came back to her mother, the pious widow was heartily pleased of her beloved daughter. It was really nice to see how this girl was humble, patient, meek, and obedient to her mother in everything. She was always content and kind, never grumbled, never gossiped, nor used any other bad words or wanted to listen to them. She thought more than she spoke and her greatest joy was thinking of God, praying, and going to church.

This beautiful Christian life pleased her mother as well as all the other Christians of that place as well. Only the envious people could not stand her, because envy is the saddest and most hateful when it sees a neighbor in honor, happiness, or grace. Envy is terribly ugly and a great sin; in fact, it is the source of all sins, particularly, gossip and slander. Some jealous women tried very hard to ruin the good name of this pious girl by claiming that all her beautiful life was nothing but hypocrisy and hidden wickedness. Dorothea heard how evil they spoke about her, but she willingly suffered everything following the example of Jesus and out of love for Him. She never said anything bad about her enemies; rather, she always spoke the truth about them and encouraged them. The good Christians soon realized that her piety was not fake but true and heartfelt.

Her spiritual shepherd was particularly pleased about her beautiful life. He praised God for all the graces with which He so abundantly endowed this soul and for the good example and good teachings she gave to all the girls of his parish. He wanted to know exactly how she lived, so he called her to him and asked how she lived and worked, and how she behaved in all the circumstances of her life.

To this, she answered: "Dear Father, it seems to me that I do too little if I think about how my teacher taught me, and as I now hear your sermons and teachings, I often remember especially the teaching that my good teacher gave me, that in all my work, in all inconveniences and difficulties, I should strive to act according to the example of Jesus."

"When I get up in the morning, I remember Jesus, who from His young age offered all His days to His Heavenly Father. Following His example, I offer myself to God, I make a holy cross through which I plan the thoughts, words, actions and suffering of my entire day, and I ask Him that He may protect and preserve me according to His infinite mercy. When I pray, I think of Jesus, how heartily and humbly He prayed to His Heavenly Father. I conclude my weak prayers with His most holy prayer and therefore offer them to God. When I work and struggle, I remember that Jesus worked even harder in

His poor life in this world out of love for me. And this thought makes all the problems and all the effort much easier for me. Whenever my parents delegate me to do something, I remember how Jesus was submissive to His parents and immediately I obediently merge my will with His and do what I am ordered to do. When I am ordered to do something really difficult and annoying, I remember Jesus' obedience to His Heavenly Father, because He was obedient to Him until His death on the cross. Then, it seems easy to fulfill what was commanded to me. Out of love for the crucified Christ, I thoroughly complete everything. When someone says something nasty or insulting to me, I keep quiet, because I remember that many more insulting words were said to Jesus completely unjustly. However, I am a sinner and deserve to be despised. Since He remained silent despite all the insulting words, it is even more my obligation to do the same. When I have a meal, I remember that Jesus lived poorly in this world, that He often had poor food, and only ate as much as was necessary to maintain life and health, so that He could serve God and His neighbor. And I strive to follow this example."

Her spiritual shepherd was amazed when he heard this and said to her: "Dorothea, you are truly fortunate and rich. God gives you great blessings and great joy to your soul." To this she replied: "It is true that I find much joy and comfort in the service of God. However, the problems and inconveniences that I have to endure sometimes are occasionally great. Sometimes, my female friends look down on me and make fun of me. Occasionally, I have terribly evil temptations and I am in great danger of offending God and losing Him."

Then the priest asked her again: "What do you do to happily overcome all your temptations and difficulties your soul is facing?" She replied: "When I face temptations, I remember that Jesus also had them and that

He wanted to have them to show His servants that no person in the world can be without temptations, and to show us how we should overcome them. Following His example, I strive to overcome the evil tempter with a word of God. When facing difficulties of my soul, I think of Jesus on the Mount of Olives, how sad He is and how terribly He is suffering and sweating a bloody sweat. Or I imagine Him on the cross, abandoned and without all comfort and relief. And then my heart is soon lighter and happier, and I say these beautiful words of Jesus from my heart: *"not my will but yours be done."*

Full of holy joy and gratitude to God for this pious soul, the priest further asked her about whom she had been talking mostly with her companions. She answered this: "That is what I prefer to say to them, which is what I have been saying to you now. I tell them that they should strive to follow the example of Jesus in all things. That they should remember Him in their prayers, in speaking, in working, in eating, and in all physical and mental problems. That they should think about how He acted in all these circumstances, and that they should strive, out of love for Him and in unity with Him, to act in the same way. I tell them that my good teacher taught me just that. And I realize and understand more and more that there is nothing better we can do in this world than to imitate our Lord and God and serve the good Lord faithfully.

Then the priest recommended her to always act like this for the rest of her life and to try encourage her friends to live like this as well.

All those who faithfully imitate the example of Jesus out of love for Him are fortunate already in this world and will be eternally in the one to come.

IV.

LOVE FOR NEIGHBOR

*"'You shall love your neighbor as yourself.' [...]"
"[...], and to love your neighbor
as yourself' is worth more than all
burnt offerings and sacrifices."*

Love for one's neighbor is the principal virtue for a Christian, because Jesus clearly said that loving God above all and loving one's neighbor as oneself is the essence of everything that God has ever commanded people to do through the Law of Moses, the prophets and the Holy Gospels.

Although this virtue is highly important, it is only rarely found in its perfection among Christians. Most Christians only love their relatives, their friends, and acquaintances, and at most their benefactors, as long as they show themselves benevolent. For other people, especially strangers, they feel no inclination, no love, and often even no mercy, and they hate their enemies as much as they are hated by them. This is not called loving your *neighbor* as yourself, but only loving *yourself*.

Parents are mostly to blame for the fact that their children grow up lacking true love for their neighbor, and that only a few of them then come to this beautiful Christian virtue. I do not say that they are taught by *words* to love their friends and benefactors exclusively and to hate those who do something bad and nasty to them. Parents give their children this destructive lesson by their action and example. There are many Christian parents, who, in the presence of their children, prefer to talk about the transgressions, evil works and indecent life of their neighbors, and especially their acquaintances, as well as about the injustices and damages that their neighbors do to them out of envy or wickedness. They are furious or angry, and they speak very badly against their enemies, against all those who do something bad or abominable to them. And many times, they also speak in this way against people of authority and against their priests. They say all this in front of their children who grow with this bad example. How could a holy Christian love for one's neighbor take root in their hearts? These evil conversations suffocate all the spirit of Christian love that is in them. Afterwards it is difficult to capture that spirit, because the first understanding and feelings that a person learns in his or her youth are ingrained and rooted deeply in one's heart, and there are only a few who are able to uproot them later on and fill their hearts with things that are the opposite of those already mentioned.

These foolish and hypocritical parents do not consider how evil and destructive the examples they set for their children are by speaking like this, and that precisely because of this, there is so little true Christian love for one's neighbor among people. What follows from this is that people respect and honor each other very little, while despising each other all too much. From this come hateful thoughts and returning evil for evil to our neighbor. The result is that many people simply tolerate each other and nothing more. They like to grumble. That they are so towards those who are poor. This is at the root of so much jealousy, so much quarreling and so much gossiping among people. All this is opposite of true Christian love for one's neighbor, which is offensive to God and risks eternal destruction for souls.

Therefore, my dear Christian, beware of all this and, with God's grace and help, get on the right path and stay on it until the end. If you have children, beware of discouraging them with words that distract from love for one's neighbor, and see that by word and deed you revive and preserve the spirit of holy Christian love in their hearts.

But if you are still young, my Christian who is reading this, think again, if you too, after the foolish and unchristian conversations you have heard, have not absorbed the distorted worldly spirit, which is so much the opposite of holy Christian love for your neighbor. With the help of God's grace, truly strive to cleanse and purify your heart and fill it with true love for your neighbor, *which is more pleasant than all sacrifice.*

To be able to do this as fatefully as possible, consider these three things:

1. Consider *who* your neighbor is. Your neighbor is every person, i.e., whoever or whatever this person happens to be: rich or poor, good or evil, known or unknown, friend or enemy. This is what Jesus teaches us in the Gospel, in which He talks about a man who went from Jerusalem to Jericho and fell into the hands of robbers.

The duty to recognize and love one's neighbor in all people is so great and certain that whoever does not fulfill it, will not be saved, because "[...] *no one who fails to act in righteousness belongs to God, nor anyone who does not love his brother* [i.e., one's neighbor]." "*We know that we have passed from death to life because we love our brothers. Whoever does not love remains in death.*" If you, my Christian, would love all the people in the world and hated only one, that would be enough for your eternal damnation, because "*Everyone who hates his brother is a murderer, and you know that no murderer has eternal life remaining in him.*" So great is the Christian duty to love all people without distinction.

2. Think further, my Christian, *why* you must love your neighbor. The reason why you must love your neighbor is that this person is a child of God, created in His image, just like you, and has exactly the same Father as you, so he is your brother. St. John the Apostle, whose heart was full of holy love for God and for his neighbor, always writes in his Gospel and in his letters about *a brother* instead of *a neighbor*, i.e., "*anyone who does not love his brother is not righteous.*" Through this, he wants to remind us that we must always recognize our neighbor as our brother and love him accordingly.

Furthermore, you must love your neighbor also because he was redeemed from the slavery of the evil enemy with that infinitely precious woman, just like you, and Jesus shed His most holy blood on the cross for him as well. Consider that God, our Father, loves us infinitely, and that He wants and commands you to love your neighbor as your brother. Think about how Jesus loved all the people He called his brothers, and that He gave His life for them. Would it then be right and just if you would fail to love those whom Jesus loved more than His own life? That is why St. John says that whoever does not love his neighbor is not of God and is as great a sinner before God as a murderer.

3. Consider as well, my dear Christian, *how* you must love your neighbor as your brother. If you want to love your neighbor properly and in a Christian way, you must never wish him anything bad, but only good, and not only in words, but also in your heart. This refers not only to your friends, but also to enemies, that is, to those who wish or do something bad to you.

Be kind, meek and benevolent to all people. Have tender compassion for the afflicted, the unfortunate, and the poor. Do not be jealous toward those who are richer and more prominent than yourself. Love all those who are good because they are good, and love evil people so that they might become good. Wish that good people would remain persistent until the end and that the wicked would choose true penance. If you see an evil, sinful man, hate his sin, which is man's work, but love the person who is God's work.

However, it is not enough to desire and wish your neighbor all the best; you must strive to do as much good as possible to him or her because St. John says: *"Children, let us love not in word or speech but in deed and truth."*

The good things that we can do for our neighbor are threefold, namely, those that affect *the temporal things* of this world, those that affect *the honor and the good name* of our neighbor, and those that affect one's *soul*.

1. Be faithful and honest in all things that concern your neighbor. Whoever takes something from his neighbor or does him harm, does double harm to himself, because this person has a sin and, in addition, also has the duty to repay everything. Theft is not only rude, but it is also a terribly dangerous sin. A person who makes a small habit of theft reaches the point where he or she does not know how and when they have stolen and that slowly progresses from one to the next level, making one's own conversion more and more difficult and one's judgment more and more terrible. Through no other sin can a person cheat oneself or harm his eternal life as much as with small thefts to which this person has become accustomed. Such a person thinks that he or she sins little or almost not at all because he or she steals very little at a time. However, if this person could see all that he or she has already stolen during their lifetime, they would become terribly angry and realize that he or she is a great thief. However, everything is already obvious before God and at the Last Judgment that we will face immediately after death, whatever good or bad we have done in this world will be made obvious in our presence. Whoever sins in some other matter can obtain

forgiveness for this sin, according to the infinite merit of Jesus Christ, by truly repenting, confessing and improving oneself. But in the case of the stealing done by a person to his neighbor, this is not enough; the wrong must be corrected completely, i.e., as much as possible. How many people perish at the judgment of God, during which everything comes to light, especially if it is against love for one's neighbor. Jesus teaches us that everything we do to our neighbor will be counted as if we had done it to Him.

Think this through thoroughly, my dear Christian. If you have done any harm to your neighbor, repay everything and do not delay it, because perhaps the day of your final judgment is near and then you will not be able to repay anything and your injustices will rise up against you and will destroy you forever. Repay, therefore, while you still have time, confess, repent, and improve. And do according to the commandment of St. Paul: *"The thief must no longer steal, but rather labor, doing honest work with his [own] hands, so that he may have something to share with one in need."*

First of all, my dear Christian, strive to never do your neighbor any harm in temporal matters, and then do him as much good as you can, and you will be truly fortunate, because "[…] *It is more blessed to give than to receive."*

A truly beautiful Christian virtue is to have mercy with the poor! How fortunate is the person who can say with Job: *"Mercy has grown with me since my youth."* Whoever shows mercy to his neighbor will receive mercy from God, in life, in death, and in eternity, because the just and merciful God will eternally repay him with exactly the same measure with which this person gives to his neighbor. And Jesus receives all the good things we do to our neighbors, just as we would do this to Him.

2. As for the honor and good name of your neighbor, know that it is worth more than all possessions. The

Bible says: "[…] *A good name is more desirable than great riches.*" Beware of saying anything about your neighbor that is against his or her good name. Do not speak ill of your neighbor, even if this person is truly wicked and has done many evil and unjust things to you. Talk about this person only as much as it is necessary for the honor of God and the salvation of your neighbor. Beware of gossip and slander. Never prefer listening to this and do not immediately believe what you hear. If someone spreads gossip about your neighbor when you are present, stop the gossiper if you can and you will do a good deed. However, if you cannot stop this person completely, out of love for a neighbor, do as much as you can. When you know, or at least think, that a loved one did not really do what he is being reported to have said, stand up for him or her wholeheartedly and do not let anything bad be said unjustly about this person. But if this person is truly guilty, defend him or her as much as you justly can. Say something good about him or her, talk about his or her good qualities, and then see that you turn the talk into something else and so stop gossiping. However, if you cannot do anything for your neighbor despite all your efforts, at least show with your words and actions that it is hard for you to hear this gossiping.

Consider that at the Last Judgment we will be severely judged, especially for our words. Consider the words of Jesus: "*I tell you, on the day of judgment people will render an account for every careless word they speak. By your words you will be acquitted, and by your words you will be condemned.*" How terrible are these words of the Lord! Let us think them through! How little we think of our words, and yet by our words we shall be justified and saved, or condemned and destroyed!

3. What is most valuable is what concerns the soul of a neighbor, because the soul is immortal. Everything else passes, but the soul remains forever. The greatest

love for a neighbor is shown by those who do good to the neighbor's soul. The happiness of the soul is living a beautiful Christian life in this world, and eternal salvation in the next. Whoever wants to love his neighbor properly, must therefore help his or her soul reach this happiness as much as possible.

My dear Christian, strive to show your neighbor not only physical and temporal benefits, as much as you can, but also spiritual ones, which are even more valuable than physical ones. These benefits for the soul are threefold:

1. Pray for your neighbor every day. Pray especially for all those for whom you are responsible and for whom you will have to answer at the Last Judgement. Pray for your parents, your superiors, spiritual and worldly, your benefactors, friends and foes, and for all the souls in the purgatory. "[P]*ray for one another, that you may be healed.*"

2. If you see that your neighbor is in dangerous situations and has sinful habits, *kindly warn him or her* and try to save this person from danger. You will do this person an infinitely great favor by doing so. "[…] *whoever brings back a sinner from the error of his way will save his soul from death and will cover a multitude of sins.*" Do not be negligent in this part of Christian love, and do to your neighbor at least as much for his or her eternal life as you would do for his or her temporal life, if you find the opportunity. If you saw your neighbor falling into the water, you would certainly do everything you could to save this person from danger, so do exactly the same when your neighbor's soul is in peril.

3. At every opportunity give your neighbor *good advice* and *good teaching*, and especially *good example*. "A good advice from a friend, is sweetness to your soul." "*For lack of guidance a people falls; security lies in many counselors.*" In order for your good words to go to the heart of others, you must live rightly yourself and set a good example in everything you do. If you give good teachings to your

neighbor, but you live a sinful life, you are like a mason who builds with one hand and breaks down with the other, and thus builds nothing. So even you, with your most effective warning, will accomplish nothing if you do not do as you teach others. Whoever lives well makes a double profit: he saves *his* soul and also helps his *neighbor* to be saved.

Strive, my dear Christian, to show these threefold benefits to your neighbor as much as possible out of love for God and your neighbor, and never out of love for yourself. Be kind and benevolent to all people, because every person is your neighbor, but especially to your friends, your family and everyone around you.

In addition, a Christian must also show love for his or her neighbor by putting up with this person when this person is upset or wicked, because: "*Love is patient, love is kind.*"

A Christian must also defend his neighbor's misdeeds as much as one can justly do. And a Christian must not judge his or her neighbor's actions too harshly, but must consider that sometimes an action seems evil to us, which before God, who sees into the heart, is not evil, because of the good intention that a person has with it. Love "[…] *does not brood over injury, it does not rejoice over wrongdoing.*"

A person must not immediately believe what he or she hears against the neighbor. Everyday experience teaches us that those who like to speak ill of their neighbor add many things and tell a different story than is true. And even if what is being said badly about a neighbor is true, the best thing is to let it go and forget, and to tell no one what one has heard against a neighbor. However, sometimes a person is obliged to listen to what is being said against one's neighbor. For example, parents and superiors have a duty to listen to the bad things that are being said about their children or subordinates. And then they are obliged to warn them. However, this requires a lot of caution and wisdom. It is never good to warn somebody immediately when one feels great anger and resentment, as the superior must first make sure that the subordinate is really guilty. Because if the superior is wrong and warns the subordinate person harshly, he does more harm than good. But when he is really convinced that the subordinate person is guilty, the superior must warn this person calmly, wisely and benevolently, and must make this person feel that the warning is not made out of hatred, but out of love, so that the subordinate person may improve and be saved.

The epitome of love of neighbor can be found in these words of Jesus: "*You shall love your neighbor as yourself.*" This beautiful word of Jesus is explained with these words of the Holy Bible: "*What you wouldn't want someone to do to you, don't do it to others.*" "*Do to others whatever you would have them do to you.*" These words are so clear that any man can understand them. Moreover, they are also so elevated and perfect and mean so much in themselves that no worldly sage has ever uttered such words. If *every person* treated his neighbor in all things as he would like people to treat *him*, how beautiful and pleasant life in this world would be!

Great examples of love for one's neighbor can be found in the Bible. The example of Tobit is particularly beautiful. This holy man truly and sincerely loved his neighbor and showed this love in action at every opportunity. When he and his people were taken into slavery, he distributed everything he had and everything he could get continuously to the poor. In addition, he also gave them good advice, warm consolation and salvific teachings. After the king, who held the Israelites in slavery, began to hate and persecute them, Tobit went every day to visit all his acquaintances and friends, comforting them he gave to each of them as much as he could from his possessions. He fed the hungry. He clothed the poor who had no clothes and buried the dead.

Just as the pious Tobit was full of love for his neighbor, he recommended this love to his son as well. *"Give alms from your possessions. Do not turn your face away from any of the poor, so that God's face will not be turned away from you. Give in proportion to what you own. If you have great wealth, give alms out of your abundance; if you have but little, do not be afraid to give alms even of that little. You will be storing up a goodly treasure for yourself against the day of adversity. For almsgiving delivers from death and keeps one from entering into Darkness. Almsgiving is a worthy offering in the sight of the Most High for all who practice it."*

This is how this holy man taught his son to love his neighbor from a young age, and in this way he especially set a fine example for all Christian parents.

V.

LOVE AND RESPECT
FOR PARENTS

"Honor your father and your mother […]."

Wisdom itself teaches us that it is our duty to love and honor those who (according to God's will and providence) gave us life and so lovingly took care of us in our youth, when we could not help ourselves.

Even more, the Bible teaches us that it is our certain and sacred duty to love and respect our parents. God commands us distinctly: *"Honor your father and your mother […]."* The Bible states as well: *"Those who fear the Lord honor their father, and serve their parents as masters."* And we have a promise in the Bible that *"Those who honor their father will have joy in their own children, and when they pray they are heard."*

Indeed, those who love and fear God will never be disobedient to their parents nor will they despise them, because God terribly punishes those who sin against His commandment. Listen, my dear Christian, how God's Spirit speaks in the Bible: *"Whoever mistreats a father or drives away a mother, is a shameless and disgraceful child."* *"Those who curse father or mother—their lamp* [i.e., his life] *will go out[a] in the dead of night."* *"The eye that mocks a father, or scorns the homage due a mother, Will be plucked out by brook ravens; devoured by a brood of vultures."* *"Those who neglect their father are like blasphemers; those who provoke their mother are accursed by their Creator."*

How terrible are these words of the Bible! God grant that all young people, and especially all Christians, who still have their parents and do not respect them, would only think about these words and take them seriously.

In addition to this, consider, my dear Christian, how the Lord God has spoken in the Old Testament against those who do not want to be obedient to their parents. This is how it is written in the Bible: *"If someone has a stubborn and rebellious son who will not listen to his father or mother, and will not listen to them even though they discipline him, his father and mother shall take hold of him and bring him out to the elders at the gate[a] of his home city, where they shall say to the elders of the city, "This son of ours is a stubborn and rebellious fellow who will not listen to us; he is a glutton and a drunkard." Then all his fellow citizens shall stone him to death. Thus shall you purge the evil from your midst, and all Israel will hear and be afraid."*

God's Law is harsh against disobedient and stubborn children who do not respect their parents. And if today no one is condemned to death because of being disobedient to their own parents, there is still that very God among us who in ancient times gave this law. And just as He despised disobedience to one's own parents in the past, so does He now: *"For I, the Lord, do not change."* It is certain that all those who do not respect and listen to their parents will be miserable in the next world if they do not convert and truly become better.

Christians should not respect and obey their parents only out of fear of God's judgment, but much more out of love of God. Whoever loves God and wants to serve Him alone does not want to know more than that it is good, just and pleasing to God, to fulfill faithfully one's duties towards parents. This person will always fulfill them and will strive to fulfill everything exactly the way his parents command him or her because this person will recognize God's will in the request of his or her parents as well as *the fulfillment of God's will*. This is the greatest joy of all souls who love God, just as it is the eternal joy of the chosen ones in Heaven. Oh, most holy will of God! How good, how gracious You are! Be known and adored, loved and fulfilled always and everywhere – as on earth, so in Heaven. The main duties that those who still have their parents have to fulfill towards them are: *love, respect, obedience,* and *help.*

1. *Love* is the first duty, my dear Christian, that you have towards your parents. You must love them with a special and tender love, and not only in the way you are obliged to love your neighbor. How many there are who do not love their parents even as much as they are obliged to love every stranger or unknown people! Firstly, the love for parents has to be a *grateful love. "Remember, of these parents you were born; what can you give them for all they gave you?"* Always be grateful to them for the loving care they gave you in your childhood and for the great difficulties and inconveniences they endured for you then. Secondly, love for parents must not only be by nature, but must be Christian love, for God's sake; that is, you must love your parents specifically because God commands you to do so. And this love must be shown in a Christian act toward them: you must love to serve them, you must love to make them happy, you must willingly put up with them if they are annoying or act strange, you must have mercy on them when they do something wrong, and pray for them every day.

2. Further, it is your duty to your parents to *honor* and *respect* them as long as they live. Beware of ever scorning them, although they are old, annoying, and strange. Do not despise them in your own thoughts, and even less show by words or actions that you do not honor them. Accept with patience and willingness their warnings and their teachings, even though they repeat these ideas to you many times. The Bible says: *"Hear, my son,*

*your father's instruction, and reject not your mother's teaching."
"A wise son gives his father joy, but a fool despises his mother."
"With your whole heart honor your father; your mother's birth
pangs do not forget."*

3. Be *obedient* to your parents and act willingly according to their will, if they do not command anything that
is against the will of God, as we must always be more
obedient to God than to people. (*Obedience in general*, and
more specifically obedience to parents, will be discussed
at a later point.).

4. The main duty of children towards their parents is
also that they must *help* and *serve* them, especially in sickness, in poverty, in old age and especially in all mental
and physical needs. Consider often, my dear Christian, if
you still have your parents, how they served you and how
they took care of you when you were a child. Out of love
for one's neighbor, it is every person's responsibility to
help strangers in their needs, and even more one's own
parents. According to your judgement and according to
the teachings of the Bible, you have a special duty to
take care of your relatives, your family *"to make recompense
to their parents* [for their good deeds and their care], *for
this is pleasing to God* [...]." *"Anyone who does not provide for
their relatives, and especially for their own household, has denied
the faith and is worse than an unbeliever."* If you have been
taking care of your parents and helping them for a long
time, beware of thinking or saying that you have already
repaid them for everything they have done for you. You
will never pay them back, even if you take care of them
for a hundred years. You are only *saving* their lives with
your worries, but they *gave* it to you through God's providence. With what you give them, it is like paying an interest on the capital they deposited when they gave you life
and maintained it with their care, with God's help. And
you know that a debtor, if he pays just interest, even for

long and faithfully, does not pay off the principal, and still owes everything that was imposed on him.

Ingratitude is an ugly and a great sin. Ingratitude to parents is especially a terrible sin. To leave one's parents without help in their old age and need is a sin that cries out to Heaven for vengeance. Already in this world, the ever-righteous God punishes such ungrateful children and He certainly will not receive them kindly in the next. He who is justice and love and also demands justice and love of us. Indigenous people, who do not know God, have the habit of leaving their parents in their old age, when they can no longer look for food in the forest, to die of hunger. This often happens in this wild country, where I am writing this, among the nonbelievers, who have not yet converted to the Christian faith. However, when a Christian acts like this, this person is not worthy of the venerable name he or she has and is worse than a nonbeliever before God.

My dear Christian, in order to fulfill your duties towards your parents even more consistently, consider some of the examples found in the Bible. Firstly, consider how disobedient children were rejected by God in this world and died sadly. The two sons of the high priest Heli lived a life lacking any moral restraints and did not want to obey their father. Heli was sad to see his children like this, and he warned them. However, he did not warn them enough and he treated them too kindly. His two sons, who were also priests, listened less and less to their father and became more and more wicked, so that finally God punished them and both of them were killed at once by their enemies.

Another sad example of a disobedient, wicked and ungrateful child is Absalom, son of David. King David loved this son very much. However, he was not worthy of this love because he did not want to listen to the good teachings of his God-fearing father and always turned his thoughts and desires as well as his actions toward evil. He finally went so far in his wickedness and ingratitude to his good father that he rose up against him, drove him out of Jerusalem and his royal house and rebelled against him. However, God has shown how disgusted He was with the disobedience and ingratitude of children toward their parents. When, during a battle, Absalom was mounted on a mule while riding speedily through a forest, the mule passed under the branches of a tree and his hair caught fast in the tree. He hung there while the mule under him kept going. Then Joab, a high-ranking solder of David came, and taking three pikes in his hands, he thrust for the heart of Absalom.

Think as well, my dear Christian, about the most beautiful example of a good, obedient, hardworking and loving child that the loving Jesus gave us in His youth. The Son of God, eternal Son of the eternal Father, almighty Lord and God, and Creator of all things, because *"All things came to be through him, and without him nothing came to be."* becomes subject and obedient to His parents who are His creatures! What a wonderful example of humility and obedience, these two most beautiful virtues, which bind us most closely with God. Because obedience makes us subject to God to those who exercise God's authority over us, and humility towards God elevates us, He promised to elevate those to heavenly honor who will truly humble themselves.

Jesus is obedient to His parents and honors them, so that by His example, He can teach all those who still have their parents to respect them and, above all, faithfully to fulfill all duties towards them. He, from whom we all have life, submitted to His own parents in order to clarify how evil it is when a poor thing, such as man, exalts himself and refuses to be subject to those who brought him into the world and took care of him.

Consider further, my dear Christian, how you must behave toward your parents while you have them, and also toward your male or female masters if you are working.

Never forget that your soul is on their conscience. At the Last Judgment, they will have to answer for you as well as for themselves. Have mercy on their souls and on your own. When they order you to do something, act according to their order. Do not resist them at all, do not answer them back at all. Fear God; fear God's judgment. And never make God's judgment even harder and more terrible for yourself and them than it already is. *"Obey your leaders* [parents and masters] *and defer to them, for they keep watch over you and will have to give an account, that they may fulfill their task with joy and not with sorrow, for that would be of no advantage to you."*

Your parents or your masters, my dear Christian young man, are obliged before God to warn you and to forbid you everything that is contrary or dangerous to the salvation of your soul, for example: spending nights out, playing games, being drunk, having evil and dangerous company, etc. It is your duty before God to listen to them and obey them without answering. If they do not warn you because of your sinful and indecent life, due to carelessness, neglect or disbelief, they have a great sin. And you also have a sin because your own conscience warns you and reminds you to reject all these sinful opportunities. But if they warn you and you neglect their warning and remain in sin, your sin grows bigger and bigger and you will be judged more harshly.

In the same way, you too, Christian girl, are obliged to listen to your parents and superiors when they forbid everything that is, based on your circumstances and status, dangerous for your salvation, i.e., your behavior, your visits, your associations, your clothing, your speaking etc. Your own judgement, the Christian faith, and your own conscience teach and admonish you to avoid all dangers because "[…] *those who love danger will perish in it.*" If even those who are obliged before God to teach and warn you would not do their duty, you would still have the obligation to protect your soul from all dangers. But if they do their duty and you answer back, insult them and refuse to obey them, know that you answer back to God and that your sin is terrible. Remember that *"those who neglect their father are like blasphemers; those who provoke their mother are accursed by their Creator."*

Think carefully and take to heart, my dear young Christians, what I am going to tell you now, and do not listen to those empty excuses that worldly people predominately express, because they prefer to live by their own distorted will rather than by the holy will of God. Sometimes your parents or masters forbid you to go to a certain house or to be with a certain person, even though your conscience does not blame you for doing or hearing anything bad when you go to that house or when you are in the company of that person. However, you have a duty before God to be obedient to them, because the commandment of your parents or guardians, when it is not contrary to God's will, must be sacred to you and must apply to you as much as God's commandments, because God commands obedience to parents and superiors in the first place. And only when it is impossible to fulfill their command or when it is contrary to the will of God, are you not obliged to fulfill it, not simply when you *think* that you do not need to listen to them.

Consider now a fine example of obedience to parents. Being obedient to parents is a beautiful virtue for a Christian. Even more beautiful and greater is the virtue of the Christian who has unhappy, unkind, sinful and ungrateful parents, but who nevertheless loves them for God's sake and does them as much good as one can. A young man, Joachim by name, was this virtuous. His parents were poor and at the same time wicked and sinful. Such parents would not be able to raise their son in a good and God-fearing manner. However, by God's providence, Joachim found a good and caring confessor in his youth who faithfully taught him the law of God and especially recommended to him that he always fulfill his duties toward his parents and to be faithfully obedient to them, even though they themselves did not live a Christian life.

When he was fifteen years old, his father told him that he had to go to work because they were very poor. Joachim, as was his custom, immediately did what his father commanded him. By God's providence and goodness, he found a good and God-fearing master, Eugene. Just as Joachim was used to being obedient to his parents and serving them, he behaved in the same way toward his master. In addition, he always took care of his parents and gave them everything he earned.

When he had already been working for eight years, his sisters married and his parents were left alone. His father then ordered him to leave his job and come home. Joachim immediately promised his father that he would do that. Although he was pleased with his work serving such a good master and was better off than at home with his parents, he decided, according to God's commandment, to obey his father.

His master was saddened to lose such a good and faithful servant and promised to pay him more if he remained working for him. But Joachim replied that obedience to parents is worth more than the highest salary in the world and that now they cannot be without him because their daughter got married. Then the master said to him: "Do not worry about it. Whatever your parents need, I will give them if you stay and continue to work for me. And if you think about it, you will realize that your parents are not worthy of leaving a good job for them, because they live such a sinful life and because they treated you so badly when you were still with them. Joachim answered: "All this is true, and yet I do not want to leave them in old age and need. Although they are not good Christians, they are my parents and I am their child. God commands me to respect them and help them."

When Eugene heard this, he heartily rejoiced at the piety of this holy Christian. He would have liked to keep Joachim with him so much, but he said to him: "You are right, my dear friend, to honor your parents in this way. God's grace and His holy blessing will always be with you because you are an *"obedient child."*

He came to his parents and faithfully served and helped them. There are no words for how much trouble it was to support them and to get them everything they needed. The payment for all his effort, all his obedience, and love for his parents was that he was insulted and cursed at every opportunity. He nevertheless suffered everything willingly out of love for God and never answered them back. His consolation was that the less payment he would receive on earth, the more he would receive in the next world if he remained faithful in doing good to the end.

However, God already awarded him in this world to some extent. When he planned to get married, God gave him the grace to find a good God-fearing Christian woman who, in addition to God's love and a beautiful Christian life, also had temporal possessions and wealth. In unity and in Christian peace he lived with his wife long after the death of his parents, and the benevolent God gave them good and obedient children.

When Joachim was on his deathbed, he called his children to him and, before he died, he gave them this lesson: "My dear children, the greatest consolation and joy that I have known in my life, and which even now I feel in my heart is that I have always respected my parents out of love for God. That is why God has given me grace and happiness already in this world. I firmly hope that He will show me special grace in eternity as well. As I have always recommended to you, I also now recommend to you for the last time that you always keep God in front of your eyes, that out of love for him you work hard and willingly endure all hardships, and that you especially obey your mother faithfully for the sake of God. Keep this advice close to you and God will never leave you."

Then he died peacefully in the Lord and his children remained good and obedient.

It is indeed a great duty of a Christian to respect and obey his parents, and also his masters and superiors, as long as they do not command anything that is against God's law. However, when the truly sad thing happens, that parents and masters command something that is sinful and therefore contrary to God's will and law, then children and subordinates must not obey *them*, but *God*. They must resist, but nicely and decently, not with ugly and insulting words.

It is just as sad when parents and superiors set a bad example for their children and subordinates and corrupt them with their sinful, impure words, with their arrogance, with their indecent lives, with theft, anger, cursing, etc. Jesus used terrible words against them: "*Whoever causes one of these little ones who believe in me to sin, it would be better for him to have a great millstone hung around his neck and to be drowned in the depths of the sea.*"

Beware of imitating their actions, my dear Christian. Pray for them every day and ask God to grant them grace so that they would truly convert.

Even if they set a corrupt example with their actions, your duties to them do not stop. When they command you to do something that is just and good, you are still obliged to obey them. When they give you good teachings and advice, you are obliged to receive them and act on them. What Jesus taught about the Jewish priests who lived sinfully, He also commands us if we have wicked and scandalous parents, masters or superiors, namely: *"Therefore, do and observe all things whatsoever they tell you* [according to Christian law], *but do not follow their example. For they preach but they do not practice."*

However, if you allow yourself to be seduced into following their bad examples, even though you know and recognize that they are sinful, you are sinful and truly unhappy as well. You make your parents and superiors even more miserable than they are, because they will be judged harshly because of you. And you also make yourself miserable by imitating examples that you know are sinful.

Therefore, never imitate these examples, but try much harder, especially for your parents, to bring them on the path of salvation. Always pray for them, warn them very nicely and set good examples for them with your behavior. Perhaps you will finally have the great joy of leading your parents from the path of sin and destruction to the path of penance and salvation.

My dear Christian, never say anything bad about your parents or your masters and do not spread anywhere else whatever is spoken and done inside the house. This is a terribly ugly, evil, and harmful habit. How much scorn, how much hatred, how much sinful talk starts from this!

Never complain to other people about your own people if they are unkind, unjust or hostile to you. Endure calmly out of love for God and for your neighbor, following the example of Jesus who had to endure so much hostility and injustice from the Jews and also from his own relatives, and never complained, never spoke badly about them, and never stopped sharing goodness with them and praying for them. Realize that you are happy if, following the example of Jesus and out of love for Him, you suffer willingly. That is when you really suffer with *Him*. And happy is he who partakes of Jesus' suffering in this world, because he will be glorified with Jesus in Heaven.

Do not take anything secretly from your parents. And do not think that you only sin when you steal something from other people. Consider what is written in the Bible: "*Whoever defrauds father or mother and says, "It is no sin," is a partner to a brigand.*" Realize then that this is a great sin and never commit it.

My dear young Christian, when your parents threaten you or beat you, consider that they have the right and even the duty to discipline you if you deserve it. Listen to what the Bible says: "*Whoever spares the rod hates the child, but whoever loves will apply discipline.*" "*Do not withhold discipline from youths; if you beat them with the rod, they will not die.*" "*The rod of correction gives wisdom, but uncontrolled youths disgrace their mothers.*" These words from the Bible show how important it is for parents to discipline their children when they deserve it. If you do not want to be beaten, respect your parents and always be obedient to them, and you will not give them the opportunity to fulfill this duty.

Unreasonable parents who love their children only by nature, but not by faith and for God's sake, feel too sorry for the child when they should discipline it, and they do not threaten the child. The child soon realizes this and is no longer afraid of the parents, even if they warn him or her extensively. And so, this child grows fearlessly in its own evil will. Such mercy is not a true mercy, but is worse than killing before God. Such parents mostly kill their children's souls because they help them to eternal destruction. They think they love their children, but they truly hate them.

Childhood and youth are a threatening time for a child, before evil habits take root and become entrenched. A man would strive in vain to straighten a grown-up tree if, while it was small, it was allowed to grow crookedly. In the same way — without the miracle of God's grace — it is impossible to lead an adult man, who has grown up in his wickedness by his own will, on the path of Christian justice and eternal salvation. Such children cause shame to their parents as is written in the Bible: Now all the people who see them realize that their parents have not fulfilled their duty to them. When these children grow up, they themselves realize that their parents were not faithful and just to them because they let them grow up without threatening them and according to their own will. Now they curse their parents and sometimes even send a terrible curse to the grave after them. It often happens that such unfortunate people, when they are finally caught by the hand of the law of the country because of their wickedness, utter these sad words while being under the gallows: young people, learn from my sad example to respect and obey your parents. And you, parents, learn to hold your children in Christian fear. If my parents had justly threatened me in my youth, I would never have come to the state in which you see me now.

It is indeed a great and sacred duty of parents to threaten their children justly, out of love for God and for them. And it is the duty of children to bear threats willingly and to realize that it is a great blessing and happiness for them if they are threatened and beaten as they deserve.

If it happens, my dear Christian, that your parents or possibly your masters beat you too badly or even unjustly, do not say anything bad to them, but bear it willingly, in the spirit of penance, and consider that you deserve to be beaten even worse from God because of the large number of sins you have committed so far. Remember how the benevolent Jesus was unjustly beaten and suffered so willingly, but did not speak a single word.

Therefore, my dear Christian, fulfil all your duties to your parents: love them, be obedient to them, do not insult them in any way, respect them, help them in all their needs as much as you can, and pray for them every day until the end of your life, whether they are still in this world or already in the next. If you have a certain status or are of progressed age, or if you still have your father or your mother in this world, God's fourth commandment nevertheless binds you according to your circumstances. Because God did not say only that children should respect their parents, but He commanded to respect them in general; if you faithfully fulfill this fourth commandment, you will certainly deserve God's blessing for yourself and for your children. Possibly already in this world, but certainly in eternity.

In addition to these teachings, read here also the examples of two children, how they fulfilled the fourth commandment and what they deserved from God.

A noble lady had two sons. Their father died when they were still small. The firstborn, who was ten years old at the time, had already begun to use the obscene and sinful words he heard when his friends were talking. When his mother heard this, she warned him and said to him: "What is this? How dare you say such nasty words when I am around? When do you hear me say such words? These are sinful words. All good Christians hate them and guard against them. Only morally corrupt and foolish people talk like that. I hope to never hear you say such words again."

He improved as a result of this warning so much that he no longer used bad language when around his mother. But when he was with his friends, he still used it. When his mother found out about this, she warned him again and said: "You don't use any improper words when you are talking to me. However, when I am not around, you still use improper language. What do you think? Are you not ashamed? Do you not know that God hears you everywhere? You do not dare to use bad language in front of me, but you dare to use it in front of God? Fear God more than all men. He is your creator and He will judge you. And because of your sinful words he will judge you especially harshly as He says this to you as well: *"By your words you will be acquitted, and by your words you will be condemned."* Leave this sinful habit completely, my beloved son, and never say such ugly words again. I also strictly forbid you to enjoy the company of such friends who have a habit of using sinful words.

After being warned, this obedient child completely abandoned all sinful language and was more and more obedient to his mother. He thereby gained God's grace in such a way that he also became more and more perfect in humility and in all other Christian virtues. Finally, God gave him the grace to leave the world and enter the monastic life, where he reached a high level in piety and learning, became a great preacher and concluded his life in the spirit of penance and in the love of God.

His brother, on the other hand, was quite different and lived more and more licentiously and wickedly, and yet his mother especially loved him. This sad thing often happens, that parents love one of their children more than all the others, although this child is sometimes the worst and least worthy of love. When she saw his wicked life, she warned him, but she treated him with all due care. He listened to his mother less and less, mocked her and always sought the company of sinful friends who distorted everything in him, as they only talked about worldly happiness and discouraged him from all intelligent reflection, from work, from learning and from respecting his mother. His mother always wept and mourned heartily, but did not cease to warn him. However, all that did not help now. She should have threatened him from the beginning and kept a strict grip on him before sinful habits took root in his heart.

As he was used to being disobedient to his mother in all things, so he was disobedient to her when he thought of getting married. He married a girl against his mother's will who was just as worldly and foolish as himself. He even started to fight legally against his mother and forced her to give him his father's wealth. However, the righteous God did not allow him to enjoy this wealth for a long time. Shortly after the wedding he went for a walk with his wife. When they reached the city gate, he tripped and fell under a wagon that was just passing by. He died a terrible and sad death without penance and without receiving the holy sacraments.

Consider, my Christian, how God often punishes wicked and disobedient children and casts them out of His presence. He repays the good and obedient and makes them fortunate; His grace as well as His righteous anger will be even more evident in the next world.

My dear Christian, these teachings and examples should deter you from evil and confirm you in good so that you too will be happy here and in the next world.

VI.

SINCERE HUMILITY

*"Humble yourself the more, the
greater you are, and you will find
mercy in the sight of God."*

My dear Christian, after you have thoroughly considered the love of God, the love for your neighbor, and especially love for your parents, consider some other beautiful Christian virtues, which are truly heavenly flowers, because Jesus brought them to us from Heaven, planted them in our hearts with the holy faith that He gave us, and always nurtured them with His example, His word and with His grace. He will give us their fruit to enjoy eternally in Heaven if we keep them faithfully in our hearts until the end and show them in our actions.

Think first of the most loving humility, this heavenly violet. As the violet blooms quietly and always remains hidden and low in growth, it smells most beautifully among all flowers. In the same way, humility also hides from the eyes of the world, preferring to be quiet and low. However, before God it is highly revered and is the pleasing spirit of Christ to God because Christ was humble from the heart during His entire life in this world.

Jesus Christ, our most loving savior, gave us most beautiful examples of all the virtues, but especially in humility. Humility was truly the most pronounced virtue of Jesus in this world. This is the reason why He tells us to learn to be humble from Him, because His humility was extraordinary. The spirit of humility, with which the spirit of poverty is united, was the spirit of Jesus' life, from beginning to end. That is why He chose a poor and humble virgin as His mother, and why He wanted to be born in the poorest place. And that is why He first announced His birth to the poorest of people. All His life He lived in poverty, silence and hard work, unknown to others. And when He began to teach, He chose twelve poor, ignorant and, in the eyes of the world, worthless disciples. With them He travelled around Judea and preached the Gospel to the poor. He had nothing of His own in this world. *"He came to what was his own, but his own people did not accept him."* He was the almighty Lord of all things; however, He lived so poorly out of humility that He had nowhere to rest his head. He had not even as many possessions as birds of the sky and foxes in the woods had. With heartfelt humility He always willingly endured the most despicable and vicious words and actions from His enemies and opponents. And as He lived in humility and in poverty, so He died. Hanging between Heaven and earth on the despicable wood of the cross, unclothed, crowned with thorns, He handed His most holy soul into the hands of His heavenly Father amid the arrogant mockery of His enemies!

Oh, the wonderful, unimaginable humility of the Son of God! Ah! How ashamed we will be before Him at the Last Judgment if we do not live in humility according to His example! Therefore, let us be humble, let us be humble from the heart! God humbles Himself, why should people exalt themselves!

A true Christian humility is the source and guardian of all other virtues. Pride, on the other hand, is the enemy of all virtues and quickly banishes them from the heart into which it enters. A humble person is just and merciful to all people. Such a person keeps a firm grip on himself and judges himself harshly. A pretentious person is unjust to himself and his neighbor. In good things, such a person measures himself with too large of a measure, and his neighbor with too small of one.

In order to better understand, my dear Christian, how kind humility is and how shameful vanity is, place a vain person next to a humble person, look at them carefully and consider:

1. A vain person values *oneself too much*, always thinks of oneself, thinks fondly of oneself and looks so at oneself. Such a person prefers to talk about oneself and when this person does some (outwardly) good deed, he or she announces it everywhere. Such a person does not consider one's neighbor too much, and when he or she hears somebody talking about the good deeds of his or her neighbor, this person is quick to say something that diminishes or weakens the merit of those good deeds, truthfully or not.

A humble person hates him- or herself according to the teaching of Jesus, despises him- or herself, and is only surprised that God is putting up with such a poor and bad thing for so long in this world. Such a person prefers to think of God and prefers to talk about Him. This person always wants to do something good out of love for God, and when he or she really does something good, one's right hand does not know what the left hand is doing. When some good work that was done by this person becomes known, he or she seems ashamed as if he or she had done something wrong. Such people always respect and honor their neighbor more than themselves, namely in thoughts, words and in action. They truly think that their neighbor is better than they are, that is, if their neighbor would receive as many graces from God as they would, the neighbor would turn them all more faithfully to God's honor and the salvation of their soul than they would. Such a person honors the neighbor with words at every opportunity. This person's words are not just on the tip of his or her tongue; they come from a humble heart. All actions and behaviors toward others are kind, decent and respectful. This person always interprets the actions and intentions of their neighbor positively and they are reluctant to believe what he or she might hear about their neighbor's evil deeds or bad intentions.

2. If a vain person has some good qualities, this person values them *too highly*, shows them to others at every opportunity, and attributes them to him- or herself without giving honor to God. Accordingly, the good qualities of this person lose all value before God. Such a person does not see or recognize his own faults and bad qualities, and they carefully guard themselves against seeing and recognizing their own faults. This person does injustice to a neighbor as he or she undervalues the neighbor's good qualities and lowers them as well as degrades them as much as possible. He or she never talks about the neighbor's good qualities and also does not like to listen when others talk about them. This person prefers to talk about the bad qualities of a neighbor and about the neighbor's transgressions and weaknesses, be they real or invented, and presents them mostly in an exaggerated way.

Those who are humble judge themselves with severity, not admitting their own good qualities, or if they do admit them, they humble themselves before God even more, because they acknowledge that whatever they have that is great and beautiful has been assigned to them by God; however, they have not used those gifts well to God's honor and the salvation of souls. This person never speaks of one's own good qualities, except out of love for God and neighbor to set a good example for the neighbor and to give honor and praise to his or her heavenly Father according to the teaching of Jesus. Just as this person is poorly aware of his or her good qualities, so does this person recognize and see one's own faults in detail. And even if this person only sometimes commits a small sin, he or she truly considers himself to be a great sinner before God and sincerely asks Him to have mercy and not to remove him or her from His presence. This person judges a neighbor differently than him- or herself and chooses to recognize the neighbor's merits, his good qualities and good works, and is heartily glad of them. This person's joy is to speak of the good works of a neighbor, but rarely in front of him, because he or she understands that this is dangerous to the humility of his or her neighbor. This person never gossips or judges the neighbor because he or she considers oneself a great sinner and is afraid that by judging one's neighbor, one would pass his or her own judgement. When this person hears gossip about a neighbor, he or she defends the neighbor as much as one can, or at least does remain silent.

3. A vain person does not want or seek *honor and praise* for God, but for himself. Everything that such a person has in his possession or that reflects upon him is only there for his own honor and praise, as if everything resulted from him- or herself and was not received from God. Through clothing especially, this person seeks a conceited worldly honor and dresses as much as possible like a very self-absorbed person. Whoever praises him or her without shame and flatteringly is this person's best friend. If this person is famous and rich, he or she has a flock of such friends around. However, these friends are the greatest enemies who do immeasurably great harm to this person, because they keep him or her in one's own deception and in his or her sinful presumptuousness. And a cloud of incense of their worldly praise completely obscures *"the sun of justice"* for this person, so that it never warms and enlightens his or her heart. He does not praise his neighbor even when the neighbor

deserves praise. Nothing hurts this person more than to hear someone praise somebody else for good work. If possible, this person says what he or she thinks will dishonor a neighbor. It also rarely happens that someone praises one's own neighbor in front of him or her. This person's friends who know him or her well prefer to say dishonorable things about a neighbor and keep quiet about what is praiseworthy.

A humble person, however, does not seek honor and praise for themselves, but for God, because: "[…] *the only God, honor and glory forever and ever. Amen.*"

Even if this person finds something worthy of praise in him- or herself or does something good, this person realizes in his or her heart and in words that all this is an undeserved gift of God, and that the more a person received from God, the harsher he or she will have to answer at the Last Judgment, if one does not turn everything to God's honor and to the salvation of souls. Such person is never quite satisfied with all the good works one does and thinks that what he or she does is not sufficient and that all the good works done by this person are deficient. This person is more offended than pleased if he or she receives praise because of the heartfelt realization that all praise and honor belong to God alone. This is how a humble person thinks in his or her heart, although it is permissible to praise a good Christian in God and for God's sake. However, because a humble person truly thinks that he or she is not good, all the praise that someone gives him or her seems unjust before God. This person nevertheless likes to praise his or her neighbor, but not in his presence. All honor and praise in regard to the neighbor, however, is only given to God, from whom all good gifts come, because without Him we can do nothing but sin. This person also likes to listen when someone praises his or her neighbor because of his beautiful life, and is cordially and truly grateful to God for all His graces and goodness as was St. Paul when he heard something good and praiseworthy from the first Christians.

4. A vain person hates nothing so much, and nothing stings and hurts him or her so much, as *admonition*, even though it is right and deserved, and this person always thinks that one is wronged, because he or she does not recognize one's own bad qualities and transgressions, and does not want to. This is a terribly dangerous state of soul, because whoever hates the warning is on the path of transgression and destruction. When this person is warned, he or she never realizes and does not admit that he or she is guilty, but makes excuses, obstructs, conceals, swears, and endeavors as much as they can to show that he or she is not guilty. And when this person dares, he or she reproves a neighbor well, who showed such great love to him or her, that he warned him or her, and who wanted to open his or her eyes so that he or she could see one's own faults and improve. His or her friends, who know him or her, guard themselves not to warn such a person. Therefore, this person remains in sin and in disobedience and does not recognize himself until the Last Judgement when it is already too late. A vain person sees his or her neighbor differently than he sees himself. To find some fault in a neighbor and reprimand the neighbor harshly is this person's greatest joy. In this instance, this person feels superior to his or her neighbor; although he or she might have bigger sins, he does not see them.

A humble person realizes that creation is a great goodness and is grateful to a neighbor for this work of Christian love. Even if this person is severely reprimanded, he or she is still grateful, and does not talk back. The humbler he or she is, the more gladly this person receives severe and harsh reproof and does not look for excuses. This person does not diminish a transgression for which he or she is blamed, though this person had the right to do so. A humble person is truly joyful to suffer unjust accusation with Jesus, and he or she is humbly silent as Jesus was silent when He was shamed and denounced. This person also has a habit of asking one's own friends to warn him or her immediately when they see him or her doing something wrong. This person, therefore, recognizes himself more and more, judging himself harshly so as not to be judged by God. A humble person judges his or her neighbor kindlier than him- or herself and prefers not to warn him or her. Warning occurs because he knows that it is one's duty to warn our neighbor about sin for God's sake. However, this person warns a neighbor with a timid heart and with such love, kindness and humility that the neighbor, if he is not too presumptuous, cannot blame this person for being warned. A humble person says that he or she is a greater sinner than the neighbor who is being warned. However, a humble person is afraid to abandon the duty of love to God and to his neighbor if he or she would remain silent; therefore, this person kindly warns one's neighbor.

5. A vain person does *not like to obey anyone*, because being willingly obedient always means being humble, as disobedience means vanity. Such a person always thinks that he or she is wiser than other people and prefers to act on one's own. This person is obedient only when he or she cannot act otherwise, and therefore his or her obedience loses all merit before God. In every disobedience, that is, in every transgression of God's or man's law, there is more or less arrogance. The first sin, the disobedience of the angels in Heaven, was committed purely out of pride. Similarly, the first sin on earth, the disobedience of the first parents, was primarily caused by pride. If we consider this sad event, we see that from the beginning Eve did not want to break God's commandment and eat the forbidden fruit. However,

as soon as the evil tempter persuaded her that her eyes would be opened if she ate of the fruit, that she would know all things as God does, pride filled her heart and she broke God's commandment. The more pride there is in one's heart, the less willing one is to be obedient. A vain person always wants to control their neighbor; therefore, such a person longs for greatness and power. And when this person says or asserts something, he or she cannot stand for someone to contradict him or have different thoughts than he or she does. This person likes to fight and does not want to give in to anyone. He or she commands one's subordinates harshly and opposes obedience when it should have been shown by him- or herself, however, he strictly demands it from a neighbor, and disobedience greatly offends him, as can be seen in the example of the conceited king Nebuchadnezzar who was never more offended than when his subjects refused him obedience.

A humble person, on the other hand, loves obedience and hates his or her own will, so this person likes to submit not only to his superiors, but also to his subordinates as much as is possible. St. Francis de Sales, for example, was obedient to his subordinates in timely matters. Just as pride is the source of disobedience and of all sins, so do willing obedience and a holy life derive from humility. A humble person cannot live without obedience, and even small everyday tasks are done out of obedience. Humility is that *sweet and pleasant yoke* of a humble person which Jesus calls *His yoke*, and when a humble person is not obedient, he or she is sad and is feeling bitter. A humble person does not like to command a neighbor. Therefore, this person fears and avoids higher positions. Only when he or she is forced and when his or her conscience no longer allows this person to stop, he or she takes some high and honorable office and authority over the neighbor. When a humble person has something to command, he or she asks much more than commands, and it is visible that he or she recognizes and feels that one who is obedient is more fortunate than the one who commands.

6. A vain person does not want to humble him- or herself *before* God. Similar to the Pharisee that Jesus spoke about, this person prays a presumptuous prayer, because through it a vain person does not humble him- or herself before God and does not recognize Him. If this person would recognize him- or herself before God, he or she would soon improve. A vain person does not like to go to confession, and when he nevertheless goes, he does not truly humble himself in the confessional, either. Although a person should only go to confession in order to show him- or herself to the confessor as he or she truly is before God, a conceited and arrogant person strives carefully to always appear better than he or she really is. Therefore, he or she minimizes and beautifies his sins as much as one can, makes excuses, keeps silent about certain circumstances and sometimes also keeps silent about a sin because this person wants to preserve his or her honor before the confessor and show one-self better before him than he or she is before God. In doing so, this person commits a great sin, a sacrilege. If a confessor is somewhat harsh with this person and warns him or her about pride or other sins, he or she is soon offended and seeks another confessor who does not know this person. A vain person judges and accuses a neighbor even before God and in God's things harshly, similar to that Pharisee in the temple. Therefore, even in confession, this person prefers to denounce a neigh-bor rather than him- or herself, and strives to justify oneself by throwing blame for all his or her sins on a neighbor. And that is the reason why this person leaves the confessional just as little exonerated as that Pharisee left the temple.

A humble person deeply humbles oneself especially before God, before whom the angels in Heaven humble themselves and realize that they are absolutely nothing before Him. A humble person is ashamed before God because of his or her sins, especially because of ingratitude. In his or her prayers and through meditation, this person always asks God for the forgiveness of sins for the sake of Jesus' merit. And the more this person humbles him- or herself before God, the more God exalts him or her in grace. Confession is this person's greatest comfort in spiritual troubles. A humble person thanks God many times for this holy Sacrament, in which the merciful God forgives us all our sins after a humble confession if we are truly sorry that we have sinned and if we firmly resolve to improve. A humble person accuses him- or herself faithfully and prefers to say more than less. This person is not afraid of being recognized and warned by the confessor, as this is exactly what this person wants. Because a humble person loves humiliation, he or she humiliates himself and favors to see others humiliate him or her. A humble person has a positive opinion of a neighbor and considers him to be a better person than him- or herself. A humble person also does not have the habit of thinking and reviewing the life of his or her neighbor and paying attention to his or her speaking and behavior. Therefore, it never occurs to this person to denounce the neighbor at a confession, but he or she only harshly blames him- or herself and puts all the blame on him- or herself.

Humility is therefore a truly beautiful, loving, God-pleasing virtue, and Jesus' special virtue. Vanity, however, is an ugly, shameful sin, terribly abhorrent to God, a truly satanic sin because through this sin an angel of Heaven became Satan.

My dear Christian, "[…] *in arrogance there is ruin and great instability. In idleness there is loss and dire poverty, for idleness is the mother of famine.*" Truly strive to acquire a truly heart-felt humility and not that hypocritical humility, which shows itself in pleasant and humble words, but not in actions. "*Humble yourself the more, the greater you are, and you will find mercy in the sight of God.*"

Humble yourself always and on every occasion before God, and endeavor to contemplate His infinite, immeasurable greatness, omnipotence and holiness, and then remember your poverty, your weakness, your wickedness, and that you are absolutely nothing before God. Prefer to consider in the humility of your heart, the blessings you have received from God so far and that you still receive from He Who is your greatest benefactor, your creator, your savior, your sanctifier, your everything. Also consider as well that until now you have not shown Him enough gratitude for His great favors and that you did not turn them enough to His honor and to the salvation of souls, although He gives you everything only with the purpose that it would serve His honor and for the salvation of souls. Consider also that you will have to answer for all this and that your judgment will be all the more severe the less you humble yourself before Him.

It is easy to humble oneself before *God.* Who would not humble oneself before the eternal God if he or she gets to know Him only a little! Only Satan and those who, through arrogance, have become his equal, do not humble themselves before God. However, you also have to humble yourself before *people*, my dear Christian. It is not as easy to humble oneself before people as it is to humble oneself before God. But you have to humble yourself before them at every opportunity if you want to please God and be saved. Some people have *a higher status* than you, others have *a similar status*, and others have *a lower status* than you.

1.   Treat your superiors with respect and reverence, and be submissive to all who have authority over you. Remember that "[…] *there is no authority except from God, and those that exist have been established by God. Therefore, whoever resists authority opposes what God has appointed, and those who oppose it will bring judgment upon themselves.*" Be especially respectful of old people. This is pleasing to God. Beware of mocking them, imitating them in speech, in walking, or in any action. There is a sad example in the Bible of how God punished the children who mocked an old man. The prophet Elisha was bald. When the children of the town of Bethel saw him, they mocked him and called him "*baldy*". Then God sent two bears out of the woods who tore forty-two of the children to pieces.

2. Even to people who are of the same status as you are, behave humbly. Never brag in front of them for the sake of some fame or qualities you may have, or for the sake of your knowledge and learning. Self-praise is a sign of a worldly and presumptuous spirit. If you are of a slightly more distinguished status than others, consider that this is no real honor before God, but only an imaginary worldly honor. Only a beautiful Christian life in humility is worthy of true honor, and only those who humble themselves are honored and exalted by God.

People who live together as a family must be especially meek and humble toward one another in order to remain in unity and peace, which is so recommended for all Christian families. Therefore, they must humbly help each other, make each other's work and problems easier, bear with each other patiently in their human weaknesses and help each other in sickness. They should especially carefully avoid all fighting, arguing and yelling. A person who is truly humble prefers to stop and be silent than to argue with his or her neighbor. The humbler the people who live together are, the fewer quarrels and fights between them. They must especially guard themselves against envy, which comes from hidden pride and is, like pride, Satan's sin.

Family members, especially young family members, must be patient and hardworking. They must willingly and quickly do what they are told. And when they know what they must do, they must not wait to be ordered, but must themselves willingly fulfill their duty, and then help others with their work. They must not judge if others do enough work or not, they must only look to themselves to do as much as they can and do even more than is their duty; and all for the sake of God. Whoever acts in this way is truly humble and pleasing to God.

Strive to act in this way, my dear Christian, and you will be fortunate. God will love you and people will love you as well. This is how Jesus acted in His youth and throughout the whole time He was with His most holy mother and with His foster father, St. Joseph. That is why we read about Him in the Gospel: "*And Jesus advanced [in] wisdom and age and favor before God and man.*"

3. Be humble even to those who are of lower status than you are. If you have servants and subjects, be kind and benevolent to them and think that they are your brothers and sisters, just like Jesus who always called His disciples brothers and friends. St. Paul advises masters to treat their servants kindly for the sake of God, because God is the Lord of masters and servants, and only works and behavior are important not the condition of a person. And he writes to Philemon that he should kindly receive his converted Christian servant Onesimus not as a servant, but as a loving brother, for God's sake. Be therefore good to your subjects and speak kindly to them. Have mercy on them because they are poor. And think often how you would like to be treated by your master when you too would have to serve, and treat your servant accordingly.

Be especially good and kind to poor people and love them. This is humility as well. That is why Jesus loved the poor so much, preferred to be among them and favored to preach the Holy Gospel to the poor, because He was humble from the heart and wanted to provide the best examples of humility in all things. Be merciful with the poor and help them as much as you can. By doing so, you will humble yourself and honor God. "[…] *happy the one who is kind to the poor!* […] *those who are kind to the needy honor him.*" "*Whoever mocks the poor reviles their Maker* […]" When you see poor people (who are often despised by the world), do not despise them, but remember that perhaps they have a higher status before God and are more fortunate than you, because they are perhaps among those of whom Jesus says: "*Blessed are the poor in spirit, for theirs is the kingdom of heaven.*" If you are wealthy and living in abundance, consider that the riches of this world are deceitful, and that perhaps you too will become poor and will need the mercy of your neighbor.

My dear Christian, if you want to live in a truly heartfelt humility, you must humble yourself not only before *God* and before *people*, but also before *yourself.* Humble yourself in your mind and in your heart. If you have frivolous, pretentious, and presumptuous thoughts, you are already greatly offending God. The arrogance of the angels in Heaven was only in their minds, however God threw them out of Heaven and into hell. Do not exalt yourself in your thoughts above others because of your beauty, your clothes, your mind, your knowledge, or for the sake of your wealth. All these things by themselves are worthless before God. And perhaps precisely because of these things you will be renounced by God at the Last Judgement if you do not turn them to His honor and to the salvation of souls. Whoever seeks his own honor in these things and exalts himself above others for the sake of it, is not humble and is unjust to God as all these are God's gifts and to God alone goes all the glory for them.

You offend God even more if you exalt yourself above others for your virtues and for your piety because piety is truly God's gift. He who begins to boast of his piety will surely soon lose it. If someone thinks that he or she has beautiful virtues and therefore elevates him- or herself in their thoughts over others, undermines and tears down all the true virtues in him- or herself, because he or she takes away their foundation, that is, humility. All true Christian virtues are namely firmly based in heartfelt humility. However, if there is no humility, all virtues are hypocritical. *He who thinks that he is quite valid, is valid only a little. But whoever thinks that he is much valid, is valid nothing.* Consider these thoughts thoroughly.

Do not rely too much on any virtue you may have, but consider how many there are that you do not have. And always strive to gain them. Do not rely on what good you have done so far and do not think that you have reached completeness. Rather consider "*forgetting what lies behind but straining forward to what lies ahead.*" Consider that a single sin, especially a sinful habit, is enough to destroy you eternally. One virtue alone will not win you Heaven. Humble yourself before God for your good works because "*We have all become like something unclean, all our just deeds are like polluted rags*".

In order to increase your humility, consider the words of St. Bernard: "If a man thinks carefully about himself, he finds within himself enough opportunities to humiliate and despise himself. His conception was in sin, his birth in difficulties, his life is full of troubles and inconveniences, his death is certain. And after his death, nothing else remains but stench and rot, dust and ashes. This afflicts his corpse in this world. But his soul, as soon as it leaves the corpse, must undergo the Last Judgement.

There, God will judge whether it will be eternally fortunate or eternally unfortunate. And this Last Judgment will be terrible to the holiest man!"

Behold then, oh human, oh you vain and sinful thing! Look and think about what you are. Why do you boast and exalt yourself? Only those who do not know themselves as they truly are, boast and exalt themselves. But the one who knows him- or herself and reflects, humbles oneself, and the more someone knows himself, the more he humbles himself.

VII.

FAITHFUL PERSEVERANCE

*"By your perseverance you
will secure your lives."*

The life of a person, especially in this world, is *"full of troubles and problems."* Special hardships, however, are endured by those who strive to live a Christian life. St. Paul says: *"In fact, all who want to live religiously in Christ Jesus will be persecuted."* Jesus told the Christians aforehand that they would suffer a lot because of him: *"Amen, amen, I say to you, you will weep and mourn, while the world rejoices [...]."* He further stated: *"Blessed are you when they insult you and persecute you and utter every kind of evil against you [falsely] because of me.*

Since our life is full of problems and disagreeableness, it is true what St. Paul says: *"You need endurance to do the will of God and receive what he has promised.",* i.e., to gain what God has promised you, namely eternal life. Without perseverance, it is not possible for us to live and be saved according to God's will, because God, in His infinite wisdom and providence allows many difficulties in this world to befall us. It is also His will that we willingly suffer them following the example of Jesus, that we walk behind Him with the cross on our shoulders, and that we go to Heaven along the path that *He* showed us. There is no salvation without a consistent Christian perseverance, which is why Jesus tells us that we will preserve our souls for eternal life only with perseverance.

The infinitely wise and benevolent God does not allow our lives to be so full of disagreeableness and difficulties without a good intention. God, our heavenly Father, loves us more than the best father in this world could love us. If He allows us to suffer at times in this world, He certainly has the purpose to give us the opportunity to gain something better than all the joy and indulgence that the world can give us. This is why St. Paul says: *"I consider that the sufferings of this present time are as nothing compared with the glory to be revealed for us."*

Since perseverance is such a necessary virtue, think about it well, and strive diligently, with God's help, to acquire it, and to demonstrate it faithfully in actions until the end of your life. In this way, you will preserve your soul.

Think first, my dear Christian, about the source of true and God-pleasing perseverance. Your perseverance must come from the faith in God's word. If it comes from this source, it is Christian, it is for the honor of God and the salvation of your soul. If it comes from other sources, it is natural and not a Christian virtue. We can read in the accounts of ancient times that there were worldly sages who were extraordinarily perseverant in suffering. We can see even today that sometimes people who live only in this world and not in God, show great and constant perseverance in certain difficult deeds and in great unpleasantness. However, it is easy to realize that the *source* of all their steadfastness and perseverance is worldly honor before people, the desire for temporal goods or the desire to act according to their own will. Such perseverance is not Christian and is without merit before God.

If you think about it, my dear Christian, you will find that the most holy virtues, *God's virtues* originate from true Christian perseverance.

1. A firm Christian perseverance comes from *faith*. Faith teaches us that God is the master of the whole world, that nothing can happen without His will or permission. Then, all abominations and problems come to us only from the hands of God. Anyone who firmly believes and truly considers this can willingly endure anything. Faith teaches us that the benevolent God does not punish us out of hatred, but out of love, out of infinite love. Is this not truly the infinite love of our merciful God, that for our wickedness, infidelity, ingratitude, with which we have already earned hell many times, He strikes us with a whip of short suffering and, if we willingly suffer, redeems us from the eternal suffering that we have deserved? Whoever thinks this again in firm faith will surely be confirmed in perseverance. Faith also teaches us that temporal goods and riches are dangerous for salvation and that God sometimes takes these temporal goods from us in order to grant us imperishable heavenly goods in eternity if we surrender ourselves completely to His holy will. Whoever recognizes this well and firmly believes will despite all losses utter the beautiful words of St. Job with a perseverant heart: *"The Lord gave and the Lord has taken away; blessed be the name of the Lord!"*

2. True Christian perseverance comes from firm *hope*. Whoever has true Christian hope relies as firmly on God's promises as if he or she had seen everything that God has promised us in the next world. A person who has such hope does not attach one's heart to anything in this world, and longs only for union with God. Therefore, this person can persevere when someone despises him or her, because he or she does not want and does not seek the honor of this world, but wants to receive the *"crown of life"* from the merciful God. This person also willingly perseveres when God sends him or her sickness or poverty, hard work, persecution, or any other difficulties, because this person's heart is

not attached to the joy of this world, but only wants to "*share* [your] master's *joy*." Why did the holy martyrs have such firm and wonderful perseverance in unspeakable suffering? Because they were not attached to anything in this world, but all their hope, all their thoughts and desire were turned only to Heaven. One can also read about what great and invincible perseverance the saints had during long and difficult illnesses. From their great trust in God and in His holy promises came their faithful perseverance. They trusted that "[…] *this momentary light affliction is producing for us an eternal weight of glory beyond all comparison.*"

3. As faith and hope are, so is *love* the source of Christian perseverance. That is why St. Paul says: "*Love is patient* […]." Or, as love is "*the bond of perfection*", so does love make one fully patient. Love is not only the source of perseverance, but it brings it to its highest level. Whoever has a great and ardent love for God is not satisfied to willingly suffer all the disagreeable and difficult things that human life offers, but they want and seek to suffer even more, and they find their joy in suffering. That is how the Apostles were. They wanted to suffer. And when they suffered, they were happy. As soon as they began to preach the teachings of Jesus, they were persecuted and beaten by the adversaries of faith in order to stop them from spreading these teachings. However, we can read in the Holy Scripture that they were not afraid or dissuaded, but were "*rejoicing that they had been found worthy to suffer dishonor for the sake of the name.*" And how much the holy Apostles had to suffer because they preached the holy faith throughout the world. They suffered everything with joy and wanted to suffer more and more in order to become more similar to their Lord and Teacher, until they all shed their blood for His holy faith. St. Paul expresses: "*I rejoice in my sufferings.*" He suffered greatly and much. He further says: "[…] *I am filled*

with encouragement, I am overflowing with joy all the more because of all our affliction." This joy in suffering and this holy desire to suffer more and more came from the great love that the holy Apostles had for God. This is exactly what is written about other saints. Saint Teresa, for example, possessed such a burning desire to suffer. She always had this request on her tongue and in her heart: "*Oh, Lord, let me suffer or die!*" Her heart was so full of love for Jesus, who suffered for us, that she could no longer live without suffering. About St. John of the Cross is written as well that when Christ asked him what kind of payment he wanted for so much work, he answered: "*Oh, Lord, I want to suffer and be despised for your sake!*"

Oh, holy perseverance that comes from such holy sources! Endeavor then, my dear Christian, to acquire this holy virtue so necessary for every Christian, and to always demonstrate it in action on all occasions. Get to know it well and think about it carefully so that you will love it more and more. Then consider *why* a Christian should be perseverant. You should be perseverant, my dear Christian in order to

1. *Fulfill God's will.* Our greatest happiness in this world is to fulfill God's will. And that should also be our greatest joy. This is precisely the greatest joy of the chosen in Heaven. It is God's will that our life be full of abominations, difficulties, and afflictions. Moreover, it is His holy will that we should willingly suffer all things for His sake. Whoever is perseverant in difficulties fulfills God's will. Whoever is unwilling acts against it. Do not say, my dear Christian, that you cannot believe that all the troubles that befall you come to you by God's will, because you see that they sometimes come from the wickedness of your enemies. It is true that it is not God's will for someone to hate and persecute you, to harm you and to cause you injustice. This truly only comes from the wickedness of people, and God does not want

people to be wicked: *"This is the will of God, your holiness: that you refrain from immorality."* Whatever befalls *you*, you must receive everything from the hands of God, not from the hands of hostile people. God leaves the sinner to one's evil will, thereby giving them the opportunity to suffer something disagreeable and to earn eternal salvation through perseverance. In the Holy Gospel Jesus tells us that the landowner did not allow his servants to pull out the weeds immediately when they appeared, but told them to let everything grow together until the harvest. This means that God leaves wicked people in the world and does not destroy them immediately when their wickedness is revealed in order to give them time to recognize their mistakes and convert, and to give His servants the opportunity to show perseverance when evil people persecute them and do them injustice and harm. God allows evil and hostile people to do something disagreeable to you too, and it is His will that you endure everything with perseverance. Holy King David showed us this truth beautifully through his example. When he was being pursued by his son Absalom, the wicked man Shimei cursed him and spoke to him so terribly that the king's soldiers wanted to kill him on the spot. But David stopped them and said to them: *"What business is it of mine or of yours, sons of Zeruiah, that he curses? Suppose the Lord has told him to curse David; who then will dare to say, 'Why are you doing this?'"* This means that the righteous God did not want to perform a miracle to convert the sinful Shimei, but left him to his own evil will, by which he then cursed his king. And the penitent David accepted and suffered this abomination as willingly as if it had come directly from God. You too, my dear Christian, accept all your abominations and troubles from God and not from sinful people, bear them with a faithful perseverance and *"[…] do the will of God and receive what he has promised."*

2. Be perseverant in *imitating Jesus and following Him*. Following Jesus, that is, imitating His beautiful example is so necessary for us that without it we cannot hope to get to Heaven. He distinctly commanded us to imitate Him. If we do not imitate Him, we do not fulfill His commandment and we will not be saved. He specifically commands us to imitate Him in faithfully bearing all crosses and difficulties that He sends us. Consider carefully, my dear Christian, His holy words: "*Whoever wishes to come after me must deny himself, take up his cross, and follow me.*" "*[A]nd whoever does not take up his cross and follow after me is not worthy of me.*" Behold, my Christian, Jesus will give up on you if you will not be perseverant. But if you are perseverant, you will be worthy of Him, you will be worthy of being His *disciple* and even His *friend and brother*! Oh, holy perseverance, to what honor you raise a Christian! My loving Jesus further says: "*Whoever serves me must follow me, and where I am, there also will my servant be. The Father will honor whoever serves me.*"

Look then, if you want to serve Him, you must follow Him *with a cross on your shoulder* in this world, but in the next world, you will be where He is *crowned with the crown of life*. Oh, most beautiful, infinitely valuable perseverance which, after a short suffering, wins eternal joy for us, and, oh, the unimaginable goodness of Jesus who prepared *a cross* for us only for a short lifetime, and *a crown* for an endless eternity!

Jesus' apostles teach us as He did to imitate Him in His suffering. St. Peter writes in His first letter: "*Christ also suffered for you, leaving you an example that you should follow in his footsteps.*" St. Paul teaches us: "*[…] if only we suffer with him so that we may also be glorified with him.*"

Think thoroughly about this, my dear Christian, and take to heart that when you willingly suffer, you imitate Jesus, you hang with Him on the cross, you become pleasing to Him, and if you remain faithful in your perseverance until the end, you will be in eternity with Him. This thought will give you wonderful strength in suffering.

3. Be perseverant, my dear Christian, *to preserve your soul for eternal life*. A Christian earns much more before God if he or she willingly endures suffering than when he or she does not have anything for which to suffer. That is why saints wanted to suffer, and why the benevolent God prefers to send sufferings to His chosen ones, so that He forms them in perfection from stage to stage.

A good example of this can be found in the book of Tobit where it is written that because this holy man was pleasing to God, God tested him by inflicting suffering and difficulties upon him, and through this he showed himself even more righteous. Through suffering, the Lord God puts His servants to the test, that is, to give them the opportunity to show Him that they love Him faithfully, and that they only *love Him for His sake*, not for the sake of various timely things, for the sake of the goods or joy that He gives them in this world. That is why God sometimes takes it all away from them. Then the faithful servant of God shows the extent of pure love to which he or she loves God. The book of Job states that Satan wickedly judged this servant of God and said that he only serves God because God gives him abundant goods and joy. For Job's sanctity to become known and his merits to increase, God allowed that Job lost everything and became the poorest man in the world, besieged with suffering and problems. However, it was exactly then that his sanctity showed itself most beautifully through his faithful perseverance, and he earned more before God in a short time by persevering in his suffering than in his previous life with prayer and offerings. As gold is purified in fire, so is the soul purified in suffering if it willingly endures it. And just as gold is tested by fire, whether it is real gold or not, so can the soul be best tested in suffering if it has true love for God or not. "*For in fire gold is tested, and the chosen, in the crucible of humiliation.*" Suffering, if willingly and perseveringly endured, is a great and special grace from God, as St. Peter teaches: "*For whenever anyone bears the pain of unjust suffering because of consciousness of God, that is a grace.*" Jesus tells us clearly: "*By your perseverance you will secure your lives.*" With willing and firm perseverance, a person earns great merit for his or her soul and preserves it for eternal life. Be perseverant, my dear Christian, in this short lifetime, which is the time of sowing, so that you will harvest perpetual happiness in eternity. And what the royal Prophet writes will be fulfilled in you too: "*Those who sow in tears will reap with cries of joy. Those who go forth weeping, carrying sacks of seed, Will return with cries of joy, carrying their bundled sheaves.*"

4. Be perseverant so that *you will live in the spirit of penance*. Penance is important to us all according to Jesus' teaching: "[…] *if you do not repent, you will all perish as they did!*" However, there are many who are negligent in penance, who even neglect to perform those penitential works that the holy Church commands us all to do, namely the obligatory fasting. Christians in general do not do enough penance for their sins. Merciful God, who does not want the death of the sinner, but wants the sinner to repent and live, according to His infinite grace, often gives us the opportunity to do penance, that is, He sends us some disagreeableness and difficulty, e.g., illness, poverty, loss, persecution, contempt, injustice, etc. His benevolent intention is that we should receive all these difficulties in a spirit of penance. That we should realize with a humble heart that we still do not suffer enough for our sins. That we should link our suffering with the suffering of Jesus and offer it to God. That we should bear everything willingly, without grumbling, without evil thoughts toward our enemies who persecute

us or do us harm and injustice, but that we should pray much more for them, and that we should seek to do them something good and return evil with good. This is the intention of the merciful God when He sends us suffering. Fortunate is the person who acts in this way. Therefore, act in this way, my dear Christian, and you will be pleasing to God, you will live in a spirit of penance and you will gain much for Heaven. However, if you are unwilling, but you still suffer as God has intended for you, you lose all your merit, because you are acting contrary to God's purpose, God's will. Moreover, you live without penance and are in great danger of dying and being doomed without penance. Jesus says clearly that whoever does not do penance will perish. If you will not be doomed because of not being perseverant, then you will certainly extend your time in purgatory. Willing perseverance in difficulties has so much merit before God that for the short suffering that we perseveringly endure in this world, He will greatly shorten our suffering in purgatory. The suffering there is unfathomably great, so great that all the suffering of this world is nothing compared to the suffering in purgatory.

All this, my dear Christian, may, with God's grace and help, awaken a firm will in your heart, to endure everything with perseverance, whatever God, in His infinite grace and providence, sends you to endure. And do not make excuses and do not listen to the tempter, so that he does not fool you and lead you away from the merit of perseverance.

Consider now the *excuses* of the impatient Christian, and you will see how empty they are, and how you must guard against them.

1. My suffering is too great, I cannot bear it willingly. Oh, my Christian, never ever say this. Anyone who speaks in this way sins against the infinite wisdom, providence and goodness of God. After all, only God sends us suffering. We are in His hands, and without His will not a single hair falls from our head. The greater the difficulty that He sends us, the greater is the grace and help that He gives us to bear it willingly. As the benevolent God said to St. Paul, who found himself in trouble, so He says to us when we are in some kind of suffering: "*My grace is sufficient for you.*" Who suffers *too much* in this world, if we think about it? Are we not all sinners before God? A single mortal sin is already so great before the Almighty, eternal God that all the suffering of all people would not be enough to cleanse it. If a person commits only one mortal sin in his or her entire life, this person already deserves to burn eternally in hell, if God, by His great grace and by the infinite merit of Jesus, would not spare him or her. Even if a person suffers so much in this world, all this evil is nothing against what he or she has already truly deserved to suffer.

2. My suffering is too long, my perseverance has already left me. Consider, my Christian, that only God is the master of all things and also of our lives. And only He knows when and how long it should happen to us this way and when and how long it should happen differently. Surrender yourself completely to His holy will. He did not promise us to be with us for a while and protect us, but to remain permanently. To every person who believes and trusts in Him, He says these loving words: "*Can a mother forget her infant, be without tenderness for the child of her womb? Even should she forget, I will never forget you.*" Why would a person consider his or her suffering in this world *long* if their entire life is *short*? And yet no one suffers continuously throughout their lives. Only the suffering of the damned in hell is long because it has no end. Perhaps you have already deserved this suffering, my dear Christian. And you complain that you suffer here so long? Recognize the goodness of God, submit to His most holy will, trust in Him and He will never leave you, be faithful until death and He will give you the *"crown of life"*. *"But the one who perseveres to the end will be saved."*

3. I am innocent, but I suffer. All my suffering comes from the evil of my enemies. My dear Christian, are you not glad that you suffer but are innocent? Be pleased, truly pleased and praise God! Oh, how fortunate you are if you suffer innocently and bear everything willingly! You can never become more like Jesus than if you suffer innocently and willingly. It is the greatest happiness and the greatest honor for a Christian to be equal to Jesus. Jesus tells us all: *"Blessed are you when they insult you and persecute you and utter every kind of evil against you [falsely] because of me. Rejoice and be glad, for your reward will be great in heaven."* Oh, how comforting these words of the benevolent Jesus are for all Christians who suffer unjustly, yet willingly. He promises them the eternal reward in Heaven for their short suffering. Therefore, believe in Jesus and be fortunate when He gives you the opportunity to suffer innocently as He did. Consider also what St. Peter writes about this: *"For the eyes of the Lord are on the righteous and his ears turned to their prayer [...] Now who is going to harm you if you are enthusiastic for what is good? But even if you should suffer because of righteousness, blessed are you."* Fortunate is a Christian who suffers innocently if he endures everything with perseverance. Then, my dear Christian, do not prevent your happiness. Recognize it with a grateful heart. Take all bitterness and disagreeableness from the hands of your heavenly Father like Jesus did on the Mount of Olives. Conclude your little suffering with His unspeakable misery. Submit with Jesus completely to God's will and you will be truly fortunate. The more you suffer innocently, the more fortunate you will be, and Jesus will really love you because He will have seen how you have striven to equal His example. He will lovingly invite you with His grace to Him, saying: *"Come to me, all you who labor and are burdened, and I will give you rest."* If you take this truly to your heart, my dear Christian, your soul will gain such holy strength that you will be fortunate in the midst of suffering and will only want to suffer more.

4. I have no help in my suffering, nor do I know how I can be helped. "These are the words of a Christian who only trusts in him- or herself and other people and not in God. *Thus says the Lord: Cursed is the man who trusts in human beings, [...] whose heart turns away from the Lord.*" My dear Christian, never give up in suffering, but the more you suffer, the more firmly trust in God. If *you* do not have any tools to help you in your problems, *God Almighty* has them. Trust in Him, ask Him and He will help you. "*Then call on me on the day of distress; I will rescue you, and you shall honor me.*" If it is His holy will that you continue to suffer, or that you lose your whole life and everything, let this be your consolation, that God's good will happen to you. Do not be in suffering and in difficulties like the unbelieving, stubborn, and ungrateful Israelites about whom you read in the Books of Moses. They saw so many miracles that the benevolent and almighty God had done to save them from the Egyptian slavery and from all other problems, but at every opportunity they gave up and grumbled against God. With this, they often earned severe punishment from God. Try to resemble the holy servants of God who were "*hoping against hope.*" God never abandoned them but helped them when it was His holy will. Endeavor to have a confidence as firm and perseverance as steady in all troubles as King David had, and say with him: "*The Lord is my light and my salvation; whom should I fear? The Lord is my life's refuge; of whom should I be afraid? [...] Though an army encamp against me, my heart does not fear.*"

Consider as well, my dear Christian, *on what occasions* you especially need to be perseverant.

1. In gossiping, scorn and slandering. Personal experience teaches us how insulting are gossiping and scorn, even if they are deserved. Even more offensive is unjust slandering. When a person hears that someone has spoken unjustly against him or her, one's perverted nature and the evil tempter quickly instill evil thoughts in this person. And if this person listens to them, he or she will be angry with the person they were slandered by. This person will immediately tell everything bad about the person who behaved unjustly toward him or her and would want to commit more harm. As for you, my dear Christian, if this occurs, do not listen to your nature and the evil tempter, but listen to the wisdom and the grace that speak though your conscience and tell you to be silent and to willingly suffer. You may find it hard to keep quiet and bear it, but remember: "[…] *the kingdom of heaven suffers violence, and the violent are taking it by force.*" Also remember that God's grace will help you. With its help, you will overcome everything bad if you really want to strive. You can find beautiful examples of perseverance in the face of slander in the life of Jesus and in the lives of saints.

2. In persecution due to pursuit of justice. "[T]*he whole world is under the power of the evil one.*" It can be often observed that wicked people, who are enemies of God, enjoy great happiness and honor before people. The righteous, however, who love God and strive to serve Him only, are despised and persecuted. This offended the servant of God, King David, so much that he had great temptations and almost strayed from the right path because he saw "peace and happiness of sinners and persecution of the righteous." The infinitely benevolent and wise God allows this for good purposes (as was said before), namely, He gives the righteous an opportunity to show perseverance and deserve Heaven. If you too, my dear Christian, come to such an opportunity that you have something to suffer for the sake of a good and righteous deed, thank God that He gives you such a beautiful opportunity to earn the heavenly crown and bear everything willingly and calmly with special perseverance.

3. In poverty. Poverty is the source of problems and suffering. A poor person has to work hard to survive. Such a person suffers cold and heat, pains and hunger. A poor person has poor food, bad living conditions and inadequate clothing. And all this often makes him or her reluctant and dissatisfied with the status in which God's providence has placed him or her. However, if a poor person had properly considered his or her condition according to the teachings of the holy Christian faith, he or she would have been pleased about it, would have thanked God for it, and would have endured all problems with a steadfast perseverance. Poverty is more valuable to God than wealth, which is why Jesus chose poverty in this world and taught that the poor will be saved if they endure the problems of their status in the Christian spirit. If you, my dear Christian, live in poverty, consider the beautiful opportunity you have to earn the heavenly riches if you willingly suffer your troubles. Be content in your poor state, out of love for Jesus who became poor out of love for you. *"For you know the gracious act of our Lord Jesus Christ, that for your sake he became poor although he was rich, so that by his poverty you might become rich."* Consider that there were many saints who were of noble and wealthy status. When they really began to love God, they left the worldly excellence and all wealth and lived in great poverty to imitate the poor Jesus and became rich through His poverty. Look, my poor Christian, you do not have to seek poverty because you are in it by God's providence. Just try to willingly endure the problems of your status out of love for Jesus with a certain amount of perseverance and you will be fortunate.

4. In a long illness. Patients sometimes suffer much and for a long time. And there are many who do not bear their illness with true perseverance, but are reluctant or have harsh thoughts, no one can help them, every little thing offends them, and often they make their impatience known with sinful words. Such patients greatly multiply their suffering because they decline help or at least reduce the help of God's grace. But whoever willingly endures illness, suffers much easier because God's grace helps him or her. When the benevolent God sends you some illness, my dear Christian, receive it from God's hands with humility and endure it with perseverance, and you will earn much from God. If you suffer great pain, think that you are nailed to the cross with Jesus. And out of love for Him, suffer willingly, because He suffered even more out of love for you. This is especially the case if you are sick for a long time and if sadness and worries burden your heart. It is sad, however, that a person rarely accepts one's temporary misfortunes in this spirit. With impatience, with despair, with evil thoughts, a person does infinitely more damage to their own soul than all the misfortune and loss that have befallen him or her. My dear Christian, firmly believe, and faithfully keep in your heart and memory this truth, that there is no greater misfortune in the world than sin. By committing a sin, a person damages or even loses his or her soul. And this is the only true misfortune as everything else that a person loses can be regained or replaced. However, if a person loses his or her soul, he or she suffers eternal damage. This is why Jesus says: "*What profit would there be for one to gain the whole world and forfeit his life? Or what can one give in exchange for his life?*" It is precisely in this spirit that you can say: What harm does it do to a person if he or she loses the whole world to protect only his or her own soul? A soul is worth more than a thousand worlds! These are sacred and eternal truths. Consider them well, my dear Christian, keep them in your heart, and you will be able to endure everything with perseverance, no matter what happens to you in this world.

5. In the inconveniences of marriage. There are some times many inconveniences and problems attendant to this status. Great, constant perseverance is necessary for married people if they want to preserve their souls for eternal life. These inconveniences come from unpleasantness and annoyance or from the wickedness and sinfulness of a husband or wife. If you, my dear Christian, find yourself in these difficulties, make a constant effort, out of love for God, to endure everything willingly. If you have a wicked wife, be perseverant for the sake of God, and consider that the just and merciful God allowed this for the sake of your sins, to put this cross on your shoulder and that it is His holy will for you to bear it with perseverance to the end. Consider the examples of saints who found themselves in exactly the same difficulties and who suffered so willingly that they became saints. The righteous Job had a wicked wife, as we read in the Scripture. Similarly the righteous Tobit. However, they always willingly endured *"as for the seed that fell on rich soil, they are the ones who, when they have heard the word, embrace it with a generous and good heart, and bear fruit through perseverance."* If you have an evil and sinful husband, because of whom you suffer a lot, accept all this suffering with humility and in the spirit of penance from the hands of God, as all these problems come to you by God's permission. Think about the female saints too. How many holy women were there who had wicked husbands and had to endure many hardships. By being faithfully perseverant in these problems, they became even more holy. For example, St. Monica had an evil husband who cursed. Nevertheless, she always willingly put up with him, and she not only saved her own soul with her perseverance, but also saved her husband's soul, because her husband finally converted and died in God's grace.

My dear Christian, let this beautiful Christian grace be recommended to you on all occasions. May God give you the grace of perseverance in this life, and in eternity the reward that He has promised to all who are perseverant.

VIII.

CHRISTIAN OBEDIENCE

"Obedience is better than sacrifice."

Among the main virtues of a faithful Christian obedience ranks first. Obedience is so important that without it a Christian does not deserve the name Christian and he puts his salvation in danger. The path to salvation is difficult, narrow and full of danger. Whoever wants to walk it alone, risks getting lost and even condemnation. On the other hand, a person who submits to Christian obedience, remains on this narrow path and arrives at the narrow gate. Consider *"[How] narrow the gate and constricted the road that leads to life. And those who find it are few."* If you want to remain on this narrow path of salvation, my dear Christian, you should always live holy Christian obedience.

The beautiful virtue of obedience stems from humility and patience and is intertwined with both. A person who is heartily humble easily submits to the will of others, and the person who is truly patient endures problems that are predominately out of obedience, patiently.

My dear Christian, if you would like to be even more confirmed in this essential Christian virtue, ask first to *whom* a Christian should be obedient in the first place. The answer is to *God* who is the eternal Lord of All Things, to *spiritual shepherds* who are God's substitutes, to *parents* whom we should especially respect as God commends to us, and to all *superiors* and *rulers* whose authority comes from God.

God created all things and He preserves everything and keeps everything in his power. Therefore, He has every right to set our laws, and we have a great and permanent obligation to submit ourselves to His laws. This is not only our duty but is the source of our happiness as well. All God's laws are made this way, i.e., the more a person complies with them, the happier he or she is. The first people received God's laws so that they could recognize Him as their Supreme Lord. If our first parents would have fulfilled God's law faithfully, they would have made themselves (and us) happy. The world would be much different than it is today.

Think now even more thoroughly, my dear Christian, about why we always have to be fully obedient to God.

1. He is our Lord Most High, or even more, He is our *only* Lord. When God gave the commandments to his own people a long time ago, He explained this with following words: "*I am the Lord your God.*" And after proclaiming this, He introduced the Ten Commandments, which we are obliged to fulfill. By beginning in this way, He wanted to reveal His great right to impose commandments as well as our important duty to obey them.

2. His law is sacred and good. The Prophet David writes about this in the following way: "*The law of the Lord is perfect, refreshing the soul. The decree of the Lord is trustworthy, giving wisdom to the simple.*" (i.e., to the humble). "*The precepts of the Lord are right, rejoicing the heart. The command of the Lord is clear, enlightening the eye.*" Thinking about the holiness of God's law should encourage one greatly to always and everywhere fulfill it faithfully. If God's law were always fulfilled, His goodness and holiness would become even more evident. As Jesus said about His teaching, if a person wants to recognize whether the teaching is of divine or human origin, one only has to

attempt living according to it. He or she will soon recognize that its source is sacred and divine. One can rightly say about all God's laws and commandments that if all people would fulfill God's law, they would live as holy, as peacefully and as happily as the inhabitants of God's kingdom. The holiness of God's law fully reveals itself.

3. God's law is important for us because without it, real happiness cannot be achieved. The sin of the first people dimmed and blinded the human mind so that it cannot lead itself toward heaven. This is the reason why God gave us His law, His holy word, so that it would shed light on this path as King David says: "*Your word is a lamp for my feet, a light on my path.*" The more a person meditates and recognizes God's words and laws, the more he or she will become enlightened about the way to salvation. Therefore, a good Christian prefers to meditate on God's word and law and always asks God for the grace to recognize its truth more and more clearly and to grant him or her the grace to follow it faithfully according to the example of God's holy servant David who always asked God: "*Blessed are you, o Lord, teach me your statutes*" "*Lead me according to your law before your face.*"

To make your obedience likeable to God, it needs to have the *right qualities*. The qualities of a true *Christian obedience* to God are:

1. *Obedience* to God *more out of love than out of fear*. It is true that a Christian should fear God; the fear of God is a pleasant gift of the Holy Spirit and is the beginning of holy wisdom. A Christian should love God more that fear Him. As St. John puts it: "… *perfect love drives out fear.*" Love of God banishes the exaggerated *fear* a slave has of his harsh and ruthless master. The spirit of the law of the Gospels, which is taught by Jesus, is the spirit of love, and becomes the innocent spirit of a child and no longer the spirit of fear, as was the case in the Old Testament. Therefore, St. Paul writes to the

Christians: *"For you did not receive a spirit of slavery to fall back into fear, but you received a spirit of adoption, through which we cry, "Abba, Father!"* As a good child is obedient to his good father out of love, so should you always strive, my dear Christian, to be obedient to God.

2. Be obedient to God and serve Him much more because of Himself than because of the reward He promises. The thought of fulfilling God's law in order that He would *bestow happiness and blessing* upon you, and increase your work and your fortune, maintain you and your family's health, and ward off all misfortune from your house, should never reach your heart. There are so many who serve God only for this reason. However, God does not appreciate this type of work and obedience. And the evil spirit rightfully says about them what he wrongly said about Job, namely that *"he is serving God just because of his possessions."* Do not serve God only to come into *heaven.* Is it permissible to a Christian to remember often about the reward that God has promised in His infinite grace if we are faithfully obedient? Jesus tells us several times that we should not perform good deeds because of people, but because of God who *"will reward you."* However, a Christian should not fulfill God's law and serve God *just* to receive eternal award. The memory of eternal salvation should support us only in our weakness and comfort us only in unbearable difficulties. If a person serves God only to attain heaven, then he or she loves and seeks himself or herself more than God.

3. Serve God and be obedient to Him because of Himself and not because of people. Whoever serves God and obeys His law in order to be seen and praised by other people is not really God's servant but is also a hypocrite who is displeasing to God. Pharisees were this kind of people and the Bible describes them: their outward actions equaled the works of good servants of God. They prayed a lot, fastened a lot and gave abundantly to the poor. However, Jesus rejected them and their actions because they did everything to impress people and not to please God. Beware, my dear Christian, of such hypocritical service to God and such strange obedience toward His holy laws. Do good as much as possible, but hide, according to the teaching of Jesus Christ, your good deeds before people, so that they would only be visible to your Heavenly Father who sees all hidden things and deeds. Your good deeds should become known to your neighbor only as much as is necessary to set a good example to your neighbor. *"Just so, your light must shine before others, that they may see your good deeds and glorify your heavenly Father."* In the same way, do all your other work and your daily chores much more because of God than because of people. In this way, you will truly be God's servant. If you are at your workplace, do your work as faithfully as you can, whether your master sees you or not. Remember though that your real Master is in heaven. He always sees you and tells you to fulfill the duties of your rank with diligence. If you are not working for a man, you are nevertheless in God's service because you are a Christian. Remember always that God is watching you, therefore you should always work for Him diligently.

4. Your obedience toward God has to go hand in hand with self-restraint. Whenever God commands something that is close to your own will and inclination, it should please us to be obedient to fulfill His holy commandment. However, when He commands us to do something that is contrary to our distorted nature and our inclinations, there are only a few who would be completely obedient and faithful to Him. We immediately find an excuse to follow our own will rather than God's. Dear Christian, do not be obedient to God only when it is easy and pleasant for you to follow His command but rather show a firm and steadfast will to act according to His holy will, even when it is against your own inclination and your own will. Your obedience will then be Christian and immeasurable because it will come from faith and love, and will be of priceworthy quality.

5. *Be faithful and obedient to God in small things.* Many Christians err because they think that holy Christian obedience can be only shown through big and admirable works performed for God's sake. However, obedience to God is not only shown in such grand works, but in small and ordinary daily chores as well. Many saints in heaven performed ordinary works here on earth – similar to other people. Yet, they also surrendered to God's will and cultivated such good thoughts and intentions that they pleased God in all things and became saints. Jesus tells us clearly: *"Since you were faithful in small matters, I will give you great responsibilities. Come, share your master's joy."* St. Augustine says that Jesus told us to live according to His example when He said: *"learn from me."* He did not want to say to us to learn how to perform miracles from Him, but He wanted us to be meek and wholeheartedly humble as He was. This is more appealing to Him than the performance of miracles would be; everyone can do this and no matter whether this person if of high or humble birth, his goal should be to suppress his or her own will and submit it to God's will. My dear Christian, do not waste time then with empty wishes about opportunities to do something big and marvelous for God. Many times, these thoughts hide a very dangerous love for oneself. You should commit yourself with trust to God's providence for what lies ahead. Now, do thoroughly what God tells you to do within your own rank, unite your will with God's most holy will, honor your works with good intention and hand them over to God. Do everything to truly please Him. If you always act in this way, my dear Christian, you will surely be happy because you will live exclusively from good works,

you will be faithful in small things, you will please God and be His joy.

After God, a Christian should next be obedient to his or her *spiritual shepherds,* who are God's surrogates. Jesus gave His apostles and all His vicars the command and authority to preach His teachings to all people, saying: *"Go, therefore, and make disciples of all nations, baptizing them in the name of the Father, and of the Son, and of the Holy Spirit, teaching them to observe all that I have commanded you."* These are the words with which He requested spiritual obedience from all people to all those who preach His teachings. Jesus says further *that those who will not listen to the Church,* who will not be obedient (i.e., who will not be obedient to spiritual teachers in regards to salvation), will be treated *"as you would a Gentile or a tax collector."* With these words, He imposed a duty of spiritual obedience on all Christians, on all members of the Church. This duty is so significant that without it, a Christian does not have any more hope of salvation than the staunch unbeliever has. How would it be possible for a Christian to be saved if he or she does not want to listen to Christ? This is also the case when a Christian does not want to listen to his or her spiritual teachers and be submissive to them as Jesus said: *"Whoever listens to you listens to me."* Moreover, the obligation Jesus demands of us to be obedient to our spiritual teachers as well, is so pressing and so clearly defined that those who disobey are not worthy of this high honor either. We can understand this from the words Jesus used when He said: *"Therefore, do and observe all things whatsoever they tell you* (the spiritual teachers), *but do not follow their example. For they preach but they do not practice."* If you find yourself in these such sad circumstances that your spiritual teacher himself does not act according to Christ's teachings, my dear Christian, you are obliged before God and your conscience to act according to his good teachings, and not to the instructions of false teachers. Jesus himself, your Lord and God, teaches you and warns you through the mouth of your *spiritual teacher*, and you hear *Jesus' word* when you listen to your *spiritual teacher*. Recognize from Jesus' words that He will not judge you by the teachings of His assistants.

However, should it happen that a spiritual teacher would depart from the true Catholic and Christian faith and begin to preach false teachings, you should not listen to him any longer. Then, it cannot be claimed any longer that Jesus Christ speaks through his mouth.

You are especially obliged, my dear Christian, to listen to your confessor. In order to become more confirmed in obedience, remember how you call him, i.e., he is God's substitute because Jesus, our Lord and God has put preachers and confessors in His place as He said to all (in the person of His apostles): "*As the Father has sent me, so I send you.*" and "*Whoever listens to you listens to me.*"

When your confessor speaks to you about things that honor God and are meant for the salvation of your soul, do not think that a man speaks; it is God Himself! Be afraid of not being obedient to God. The confessor is the father of your soul. As God tells you to be obedient to your *biological father*, He tells you even more explicitly to listen and be even more faithfully obedient to your *spiritual father* whom He gave you in place of Himself.

As long as you are obedient to your good confessor, you are on the right path, on the path of penance, on the path of salvation. However, when you start to resist and answer back, when you do not do what he tells you and you grumble about him, you are being distracted by the evil tempter. If you listen to the tempter, you will be in danger of leaving the path of penance and salvation, and be doomed.

In addition, a faithful Christian has to be obedient to his or her parents as long as they are alive. My beloved

Christian, your obedience to your parents, if you still have them, has to be because of God. As St. Paul puts it: *"Children, obey your parents [in the Lord], for this is right."* If your parents command you to do something, remember quickly that it is God who does this. God really commands you through His fourth commandment to honor your parents. If you are obedient to them, you are obedient to God. Whenever you resist them and despise their commands, you despise God's commandment.

However, should the sad thing happen that parents command their children to act against God's law, i.e., to steal, to lie, to live impurely etc., then children should not listen to their parents, but to God. They should rather endure beating than commit sin.

When the command of the parents is such (for example, about the path of life) that their children cannot distinguish whether their parents' command is just and pleasing to God or not, they have to turn to God and consult with Him. In such an event, they should confer with their confessor or some other God-fearing and wise Christian and act according to their advice combined with their own conscience before God.

My dear Christian, be obedient to your superiors and rulers out of love for God. Obedience is a beautiful and redeeming virtue in itself. It keeps a person on the path of Christian righteousness. *"The heart of the just meditates obedience."* Therefore, beware of disobedience and be faithfully obedient to all who have a certain power over you *"for there is no authority except from God, and those that exist have been established by God. Therefore, whoever resists authority opposes what God has appointed, and those who oppose it will bring judgment upon themselves."*

A Christian will not remain on the path of salvation without obedience. Disobedience is the quintessence of all sins because all those who sin, do not do what God commands them to do, nor do they avoid what God forbids, i.e., they *disobey God*. Thus, if we think about it thoroughly, there is only one sin in this world, and it is *disobedience*.

Believe, my dear Christian, that you are happier if you fulfill the will of others (when it is not against God's will) than your own will. Fulfilling one's own will leads to peoples' damnation, especially that of young people. Whoever allows it to follow will mostly be led to the eternal abyss. *"Obedient person will talk about restraints,"* says the Bible, i.e., if you prefer to be obedient, you will beat your most dangerous enemies, namely your own will and evil inclinations. You will recognize that there is nothing causing you as much good as your own obedience because through it, you gain God's admiration and His blessing. *"Obedience is better than sacrifice, [...] and arrogance the crime of idolatry."*

Think also, my dear Christian, *why* you have to be obedient at all and what drives you toward a true Christian obedience.

1. First is *Christ's own example* of this wonderful virtue. He was obedient to all, obedient in all circumstances, and was obedient at all times until His death. He was obedient to *God,* His heavenly Father. This is why He came into this poor world; he took upon himself the image of a servant, performed many deeds, suffered for the salvation of the world and finally died on the cross. He was obedient to the *priests of His time who* lived in Jerusalem. Therefore, He faithfully fulfilled the law and the commandments of the Jewish priests when they were not offending God's will by their teachings. He advised His disciples and followers to be obedient to the priests, even to those who did not act as they preached. He was obedient to His *parents,* i.e., His Holy Mother, Virgin Mary, and His foster father, holy Joseph, whom He worked with and helped in all things, walked with them wherever they went and was faithfully obedient to

them while He lived with them, i.e., until he turned thirty and began teaching. He was obedient to *authorities and rulers*; therefore, He completely subjected Himself to all laws of the land and recognized that all their authority is given by God. He taught people to give back to Caesar what is Caesar's, that is, to fulfill all their duties toward their local authorities faithfully, especially obedience. Therefore, Jesus is truly the most beautiful and the most perfect example of the holy, God-pleasing obedience. This example should encourage you to the fulfillment of this holy virtue, my dear Christian. Follow faithfully the kind Jesus who was obedient to His death, even to His death on the cross. He cherishes obedience very much. If you want to be really acceptable to your Jesus, be obedient in a right way.

2. Example of God's saints. Saints were faithful imitators of Christ and were always imitating Him in obedience. They left us an example which we must follow if we want to walk on the path on which they walked and would like to arrive where they did. Whoever reads the lives of saints can see how these friends of God wholeheartedly wished to be obedient to God and because of Him, to all other legitimate authorities as well. It was precisely this spirit of obedience, which was truly the spirit of saints, that filled deserts and monasteries with God's servants, who lived in such holy obedience and were submissive to the will of their authorities that it might seem as if they had no will of their own. In general, all God's saints lived in the spirit of obedience because this is the spirit of Jesus and without Jesus' spirit, there is no holiness.

Following Jesus' example and that of His saints, involves being gladly obedient as well, my dear Christian. Be obedient to God and because of God, be obedient to all those who have some legitimate kind of authority over you. Always ask God to give you the spirit of obedience and strive to suppress your own will and subject it to the holy will of God. Ask Him to let you recognize His holy will in all things, so that you will be able to fulfill it. Ask Him with king's prophet: *"Teach me to do your will, for you are my God."* Ask God every day in your prayer with most heartfelt wishes to do His holy will as the apostle Paul said to Him: *"What shall I do, sir?"*

IX

HOLY PURITY OF HEART

*"Blessed are the clean of heart,
for they will see God."*

Purity is a beautiful Christian virtue. It is a heavenly lily and it is a special virtue of the most holy Heavenly Mother. This virtue is especially pleasing to Jesus. Because St. John always lived in the virtue of virginal purity, our Lord loved St. John more than the other apostles. When on the cross, Jesus handed His most pure mother over to him. Jesus recognizes all pure souls as His brides. No groom in this world can love his bride as heartily as Jesus loves a pure soul.

This virtue is not only meant for all those who are single, because every vocation has its own standard for purity. The one who lives purely according to one's status, out of love for God, is pleasing to God, and his or her soul is Jesus' bride. Just as purity is appropriate for every status in life, so it is for every age. However, it is especially necessary, beautiful and full of merit for someone young.

The virtue of purity is much more a heavenly virtue than it is an earthly one because it makes young people equal to angels, as the teachers of the Church write. And Jesus says that in Heaven they do not marry, but are like the angels of God.

According to St. Jerome, those who faithfully preserve their purity receive some of the same honor and merit as the holy martyrs do because, just as martyrs have to fight against the evil spirit and the persecutors of the holy faith (who are his servants) in order to preserve their faith, so must a Christian who wants to preserve purity, heartily and always fight with his or her enemies, that is, with his or her distorted nature, with seducers and with all those who give him or her sinful examples, and with the evil tempter, who always wants to lead a person into impurity.

St. Bernard says that besides the martyrdom for the holy faith, through which blood is shed, there is also the threefold martyrdom of Christians: firstly, temperance and the spirit of poverty in wealth and abundance, as we read about King David and Job in the Holy Scripture; secondly, wisdom and contentment in poverty, as the pious Tobit always had; thirdly, preservation of purity in youth, as Joseph of Egypt set a good example for all young people.

Purity is furthermore, according to the teachers of the church, *the greatest beauty of life, the honor of the body, and the source of holiness*. Indeed, this sacred virtue is so beautiful in the eyes of God and the good people that without it all other beauty is worth nothing: neither the beauty of speaking or behaving, nor the beauty of dressing or status. However, the one who faithfully preserves this heavenly virtue is beautiful and dear without all these other beauties.

Purity is also the true honor of the body. A pure body is venerable even in this world because in its heart dwells Jesus, the beautiful bridegroom of all pure souls. It is the temple of the Holy Spirit because *"Do you not know that your body is a temple of the holy Spirit within you* [...]" as long as it remains pure. However, when the idol of impurity comes into this temple, it drives out the Holy Spirit from it because *"the temple of God and the idols cannot be together."* A pure body will be honored in the next world even to a higher extent. It will rise from death venerably, it will shine like the sun, it will be more beautiful than all the beauty of this world. Jesus promised especially to those who keep a pure heart that their pure eyes will look at God forever.

Similarly, purity is truly the source of holiness. Holiness is manifested in beautiful and true Christian virtues. True chastity, however, must be rooted in the *heart*; it is not enough if it is only shown in beautiful words. But if the root is vile and impure, how will beautiful, holy virtues grow from it? You see, my dear Christian, that a pure heart is truly the source or root of holiness.

Strive always faithfully to preserve holy and God-pleasing purity. Not only virginal purity, but purity in general because every status has its own purity. If up until now you have been so unfortunate and have not lived in this beautiful purity, repent of your sins with all your heart and never despair. There is still *the purity of penitents*. It is true that it is not as beautiful as virginal purity, but it is pleasing to God and salvific to the soul. Consider the examples of St. Mary Magdalene, St. Augustine, St. Margaret of Cortona and other saints who from the beginning lived impurely in sins and then converted, repented, began to live in great purity and remained faithful in this virtue until the end. In this way, their souls became the brides of Jesus and their bodies the temple of the Holy Spirit.

Beautiful examples of purity can be found in the Holy Scripture. Young Joseph, the son of the patriarch Jakob, set a beautiful example of firm *virginal* purity to young people in particular. This holy young man was sold into slavery by his brothers out of envy and hatred and was taken to Egypt, where Potiphar, one of the highest officials of the pharaoh, bought him. Joseph was an amazingly good and handsome young man, and Potiphar entrusted him with all his goods and even with his house.

Potiphar's wife, however, was wicked and unfaithful and wanted to lead Joseph into sin. She tried many times to win him over with sweet words, but he always steadfastly resisted these dangerous temptations. And although he knew that in the end he would fall into disfavor with this powerful woman and that she would begin to hate and persecute him (as she then really got him into prison), he never wanted to consent to sin and was ready to undergo anything and even suffer death rather than to lose his virginal purity.

This is indeed a great example for you, my dear young Christian. But by what means did this holy young man preserve this beautiful virtue so faithfully? These means were faithful and humble prayer and a perpetual remembrance of God's presence. *"How, then, could I do this great wrong and sin against God?"* he answered this wife when she urged him to sin. Do the same, my dear Christian, and you will preserve this beautiful virtue.

Susanna, the wife of the prominent Israeli Joakim, set a fine example of *marital* purity and sanctity. This holy woman, according to the custom of the Middle East, was bathing in her garden and thought she was alone. However, two old men who were judges of the people of Israel were hiding there and as they saw Susanna alone, they came to her and wanted to seduce her into sin and threatened her with death if she would not consent. But she thought of God and decided to remain faithful to God and her husband and rather die than sin. She uttered these beautiful words: *"Yet it is better for me not to do it and to fall into your power* [i.e., to die] *than to sin before the Lord."* Then she began to shout at the top of her lungs and call for help. However, the two men also shouted against her. When the people came running, they testified that she had sinned with a young man who ran away. People immediately believed this testimony and Susanna was sentenced to death. However, God did not allow for her to be murdered, but enlightened the young man Daniel to convince these two old sinners that they had wrongfully accused the innocent, pure Susanna. And so she was saved, and her two suitors were led to die.

After you have considered, my dear Christian, how beautiful the virtue of purity is, consider also the tools by which it is most easily preserved, and make a firm decision to use them faithfully.

1. The first and best tool is to stop evil temptations and impure thoughts at the very beginning, before the evil spirit takes possession of your heart. If you are negligent from the beginning, and if you defend yourself only a little against evil thoughts, you will confirm yourself in an impure sin and perhaps you will never completely leave it again. Therefore, restrain from it from the start and you will easily and completely defeat it. Sin is indeed a disease of the soul. As a disease is most easily stopped and averted when the patient takes a proper medicine right from the beginning and treats the disease with it, the easiest way to ward off this sin is to resist these evil temptations with all your strength right from the start.

Fear, my dear Christian, this shameful sin more than death. Always watch over all your thoughts and all your feelings. Hate and quickly discard all obscene and impure images that the evil spirit sets before the eyes of your soul. Quickly think of something else and remember God who is always watching you. Also remember your guardian angel whom God gave you to bring you to Heaven. God always gives you His grace with which you can resist all evil temptations and keep yourself pure if you really want this. If you consent to sin despite all this, you are to blame for your own misfortune. Listen to what the teacher of the church, St. Bernard, says: *"Disregard an evil impure thought as soon as it comes to you. If you really disregard it, it will leave you. Or if it doesn't leave you, it will not defile you as long as you hate it. A thought that is not immediately disregarded begets liking. Liking begets consent. Consent begets action; from action comes habit. And from habit another nature, which further confirms the wretched sinner in wickedness and disobedience."*

When a person eats or drinks something poisonous, this person can save his life if he or she quickly takes some medicine to get rid of what is poisonous. In the same way, a person having evil impure thoughts, which are the worst poison of the soul, can protect themselves from sin, which is death to one's soul, by quickly disregarding and hating them.

Be faithful to God when you are being tempted and disregard the temptation immediately. Do not wrestle with temptation. If you listen to temptation and respond to it, it will seduce you like the serpent seduced Eve. If Eve had not talked to the snake, but had fled at the moment she heard it speaking against God's command, she would not have sinned. If you listen to temptation just a little, it will soon tell you something that will fool your mind and you will begin to think that it is not sinful if you only do this or that. That it is not a mortal sin. That you will confess, etc. Oh, how many souls has the evil infernal serpent already got into its power!

St. Jerome says that impurity is a poisonous snake. And just as a man steps on the head of a snake when he sees it, so must he do with unclean temptations. This snake tries to get into the heart and if it gets inside, it soon fills it with poison.

St. Gregory says that impurity in the heart of a thoughtless person is kindled like fire in straw. If it is not extinguished immediately, it is difficult to distinguish at a later point. A big fire sometimes comes from a single spark. The sparks of the fire of impurity are: a single willing evil thought, a single impure look, a single obscene word; an impure song, some secret conversation, etc. Remember, my dear Christian, that your heart is like dry straw. Do not willingly bring it near these dangerous sparks. And if one accidentally falls into it, shake it out and trample it. It is easy to extinguish a spark, but difficult to extinguish a great fire. In this way, even impure sin can be overcome easily in the beginning, but with terrible difficulty at a later point when it is already rooted and confirmed by some sinful attachment, some evil habit or some dangerous knowledge.

2. The second tool by which purity is preserved is *diligence* or *industriousness*. Laziness is the source of sins in general, and of impurity in particular. It opens the door to all impure thoughts and desires, accepts them and nurtures them. The lazy loiterer is surrounded everywhere by dangerous temptations, by those wicked enemies who pray for this person's soul. When loitering, many thoughts and desires come to a person, and specially a desire for worldly joy and enjoyment. And it does not stay long with the thoughts, because "*thought* (in the words of St. Bernard) *begets liking, liking begets assent, assent begets action.*"

The Bible gives us the following example. From the beginning, King David always went to battle himself and endured effort and hardship together with his soldiers. Later on, he began to live more comfortably and only sent soldiers to battle; he, however, remained in his buildings in Jerusalem. After lunch, he had the habit of lying down and sleeping, then walking around the upper room of his building, where he could see the whole city around him. It happened, however, while he was walking one day, that he saw a beautiful woman bathing in her garden. In his heart, which at that time enjoyed laziness, sinful lust awoke, from which came consent and then action. However, the king repented this sin before God his entire life and received complete forgiveness. Then, my dear Christian, if you wish to remain pure, beware of laziness and the conduct from which such unfortunate sins can arise. Never say: "If I sin, I will do penance as King David did." Sin is soon committed, but true and perfect penance takes time. King David has many imitators of his sin, but only a very few imitators of his penance.

3. Moderation in *food* and *drink* is a good tool for maintaining purity as well. Without this virtue, it is difficult or impossible to maintain purity. Therefore, it is written in the Holy Scripture: "*And do not get drunk on wine, in which lies debauchery* [...]." "*Wine is arrogant, strong drink is riotous* [...]" Especially young people will deeply submerge in the sin of impurity if they do not use this tool. Their blood is hot in itself and prone to these sins. But when it gets warmed up with wine, an impure fire ignites it quickly. Listen again to the teacher of the Church, St. Jerome: "*Mount Etna, Mount Vesuvius and Mount Olympus, which always throw fire themselves, do not burn with such heat as the blood of young people when it is inflamed with wine and immoderate food.*" He further writes: "*If one wants to receive good advice, if one wants to believe my own temptation, I warn and beg the soul that wants to live in the grace of Jesus Christ and preserve its purity, to fear wine as the worst poison. Wine is a powerful weapon of the evil spirit with which it often defeats especially young people. Wine and youth combined make a double fire of impurity.*"

4. The fourth tool is *to beware of bad and sinful company* and to avoid such places where purity is not regarded highly. An immoral companion is the most dangerous enemy of the soul. In the company of such companions, if you do not avoid them, you will hear many evil words and you will learn and see many things that will lead you to eternal damnation if you do not reject and hate them, and if you do not completely leave such company. Such groups are especially dangerous for young Christians. How many of them have lived in innocence and purity

for a long time? However, in some bad company they heard obscene talk, which they were ashamed of from the very beginning, but after hearing such talk several times, they got used to it and began to speak and live like their companions.

Impure words are like sparks, and the heart of a young man is like dry straw. And just as from a single spark often a great and harmful fire emerges, so does a single impure conversation sometimes ignite a great impure fire in the heart of a young man. Beware, therefore, my dear Christian, bad companions and hate all evil words because *"Bad company corrupts good morals."*

5. *Avoiding talking to people of the opposite sex* is also a good tool for maintaining purity. The beautiful virtue of purity is in the greatest danger in such a conversation, especially when there is no witness. People who have long struggled with all other temptations, and who have always successfully overcome them, have finally weakened and sinned due to such friendly conversations. One can read about saints and even about holy hermits who lived in such severe penance that they did not always ward off this danger. That is why it is written in the Holy Scripture: *"Do not let her reveal her beauty to any male, or spend her time with married women; For just as moths come from garments, so a woman's wickedness comes from a woman."* *"Never recline at table with a married woman* [who is not your wife] [...], *otherwise a fire will burst out* [i.e., the fire of impurity]."

Just talking to people of the opposite sex is dangerous to purity. How much more so is any other manifestation of worldly love, e.g., free and sweet words, special kindnesses, embracing, kissing, etc. All this gives opportunity to many impure thoughts and desires and leads directly and quickly to impurity. That is why St. Jerome says that all these things are *"the last sigh of the dying purity."*

6. A tool by which purity is preserved is the *protection of one's eyes.* The holy teachers of the Church repeatedly

say that the eyes are the door through which sin enters the soul. This is especially true of a sin of impurity. Impure looks are terribly dangerous and sinful because such looks are always connected with evil desires, most of which are mortal sins. This is why Jesus says that "[…] *everyone who looks at a woman with lust has already committed adultery with her in his heart.*" Even those thoughtless glances, in which there is no evil intention and no desire from the beginning, are terribly dangerous and you must guard against them, my dear Christian if you want to keep a pure heart. Worldly love and inclination to impurity come into the heart after such glances without even noticing when. That is why the holy servant of God, Job, says: "*I made a covenant with my eyes not to gaze upon a virgin.*" And that is why he expresses before God that no woman has ever seduced his heart. The Holy Spirit says further in the Holy Scripture: *Do not entertain any thoughts about a virgin, lest you be enmeshed in damages for her. […] Do not look around the streets of the city or wander through its squares. Avert your eyes from a shapely woman; do not gaze upon beauty that is not yours; Through woman's beauty many have been ruined […].*" These are beautiful and true teachings worthy of all contemplation! My dear Christian, imprint them deeply in your memory and in your heart. Carefully guard your eyes so that they do not lead you into sin. Do not turn them deliberately into something that you find dangerous to look at. And should your eyes happen to see something indecent, turn them away. Likewise, never look at obscene images because if you willingly look at them, they will soon awaken sinful thoughts in your heart and possibly even evil lust.

Christians, especially young people, who like to see something and who like to be seen, and therefore like to go someplace, come into great spiritual danger. This danger is even greater for girls than for young men. A terribly sad example of this is found in the Holy

Scripture. *Dinah*, the daughter of the patriarch Jacob, wanted to see the inhabitants of the town of Salem, so she went to walk around the town out of her own free will. However, these obscene desires, to see and be seen, led her to a great misfortune, and they also made many other people unhappy. For when Shechem, the leader of this region, saw Dinah, impure lust was kindled in his heart. He ordered her to be forcibly brought to his house and thus her virginal purity was lost. When Jacob's sons heard this, they were terribly angry, especially Simeon and Levi. They did not stop until they had killed all the inhabitants of the city and their ruler.

7. The seventh tool is *that a person refrains from secular joy*, that is, from everything that pleases worldly people who do not think much of God and do not love Him. All joy is not forbidden to Christians. Moreover, St. Paul tells us that we should always rejoice. "*Rejoice with those who rejoice [...].*" "*Rejoice always.*" and "*Rejoice in the Lord always. I shall say it again: rejoice!*" This is what the holy apostle writes on several occasions in his letters. Therefore, joy is not forbidden to us but recommended as a holy joy in God. Only the evil and sinful joy of worldly people, e.g., drunkenness, sinful games, dancing, staying out late and other worldly foolishness are forbidden to Christians. With all this, Satan rejoices and God grieves. To those who seek such amusement Jesus says: "*Woe to you who laugh now, for you will grieve and weep.*"

This joy is a dangerous net in which the evil spirit ensnares many souls. It is the same as a sweet poison, which tastes pleasantly; however, as soon as it is consumed, it brings death. And it is infinitely worse than poison, because poison makes the corpse miserable and kills it. Worldly joy, on the other hand, kills the soul, that is, it makes it lose eternal heavenly life and finally leads it to eternal misery. If you want to protect yourself from dangerous *worldly joy*, as is your Christian duty, do the following:

1. When you see a worldly thing and when you feel that indecent thoughts are rising in your heart, turn away your eyes, even if that thing is very beautiful and if people like it very much.

2. Completely and forever abandon all indecent pushing and pulling. Such occasions are often accompanied with much indecent laughter, many dangerous words, and dangerous action. All these are the sources of impure thoughts and often the beginning of an impure life.

3. Never look in the mirror too much and unnecessarily. The mirror will make you more worldly than you are, and you will revive many vain and even indecent thoughts in yourself. Let your mirror, my dear Christian, be the example of Jesus and look into this spiritual mirror rather than into the worldly one, and examine your conscience rather than your face.

4. Do not go for a walk in places where there are many people, not even with worldly companions, no matter how persistent they are with their invitation. Never go to any place of worldly pleasure, e.g., to a dance, to a comedy or to a pub without any real need.

5. When you meet a friend who is worldly and is telling you things about which it would be better for you not to know, leave him or her and prefer to preserve the kindness of God rather than the worldly one. Leave a friend who starts inviting you to *worldly places* and worldly pleasures. Do according to the teachings of the Holy Scripture: *My son, should sinners entice you, My son, do not walk in the way with them, hold back your foot from their path! [For their feet run to evil, they hasten to shed blood.]* [...]."

My dear Christian, if you are even a little God-fearing and shy, you will not go to these places and experience these terribly indecent opportunities because here the soul gets mortally wounded in no time, and shyness, that holy guardian of purity, does not last long in such places. St. Cyprian says: "*If you go pure to such places, you will come out impure.*" Comedies and dances originate from the old pagan times and are contrary and offensive to the holy Christian faith. Christians imitate them after non-believers and thus act in direct opposition to their holy baptismal promises, because in baptism a person renounces the evil spirit and all its vanity. However, it is this worldly joy that is truly the work of the evil spirit and its presumptuous joy, as it captures the most souls here. This is exactly what the teachers of the Church testify to. For example, how much did St. Augustine strive (as we read in his sermons) to turn his listeners away from worldly joy. He always reminded them of their Christian duties and baptismal promises and that a Christian who renounced the evil spirit must not return to those places where he is served with sinful worldly amusement.

The example of Christians whom you see walking into these dangerous and indecent places should not disturb you or lead you astray, but you should rather grieve over their blindness and the indecency they provide. They are truly blind because they do not see the sins that they themselves commit on such occasions; they are also guilty when others commit those sins. The holy teachers of the Church say that this worldly amusement is the "plague of Christians;" "mocking the holy Gospel," "obvious display of impurity and rudeness," "the rock on which the ship of youth gets broke," etc. The one who ventures into these perilous occasions seeks one's own destruction, his or her eternal misfortune because "[…] *those who love danger will perish in it.*" To seek one's unhappiness and even one's *eternal* unhappiness is a great folly and a great sin.

In order for you to believe more, my dear Christian, that there is much danger in these places and occasions of which we are speaking here, consider these two things:

1. *Only one dangerous look* caused King David, who was such a holy and wise man, to sin. How dare you, who are a bad person, to say and think that there is no danger for you when you go to a dance, attend a comedy, or some other worldly occasion, where you see and hear so many indecent and dangerous things? Is it not in itself dangerous and sinful to do what is disagreeable to God and the Church and what the Church and spiritual teachers have always forbidden? Is it not already a sin putting yourself and others in obvious danger?

2. Think carefully about *why* you participate in such occasions. Not for the love of God or your neighbor, that is for sure, but for the love of worldly joy, out of curiosity, the vain desire to see and be seen. And when a person is in such places, he or she is entirely different than usual. Such a person does not think of God there. His heart is wide open to worldly joy; indecent thoughts, which this person otherwise fears and avoids, no longer seem so dangerous to him there. One's conscience is no longer so timid and gets used to sin more and more.

This is all a certain truth, and everyday experience shows that this is indeed so. And so you can see, my dear Christian, that there is much danger in worldly amusement. Then, if you do not want to be lost, avoid danger. Believe Church teachers more than worldly companions.

Tertullian, who lived in the early days of Christianity, described in his writings that the Christians of those times never attended comedies, never went to a dance, or to any other place of worldly amusement. However, a woman was present among those Christians who was baptized but did not live faithfully according to the Christian faith and went to see a comedy. Suddenly, the evil spirit possessed her and she began to suffer terribly. The Christians quickly sent for the priests. And when they came and forced the evil spirit to confess why it possessed this Christian soul, it said: *"I had the right to possess her, because I found her in a place which is under my power."*

Be afraid of and shun such places, my dear Christian, that are under the rule of the wicked enemy. If you enter into his possession, you give him great authority over your soul. Everyone has more power over his own possession than anywhere else.

My dear Christian, in addition to these seven tools, I recommend three other tools by which holy purity is preserved and multiplied, namely:

1. *Prayer.* A heartfelt and constant prayer is in general a good tool for gaining God's grace and beautiful Christian virtues. Specifically, a person must sincerely ask God to maintain purity, otherwise it will be difficult to maintain it. Purity is a gift from God and God likes to give it to those who truly ask Him for it. Therefore, always ask God to give you this great gift. Ask Him to create in you that pure heart and to keep it as His pleasing abode. Recommend yourself often to the most pure Virgin Mary and your guardian angel whom God gave you to protect you on all your paths and bring you happily into Heaven.

2. *Frequent confession and Holy Communion.* This is also a particularly good tool for maintaining holy purity. If you wish then, my dear Christian, to preserve this most beautiful and God-pleasing virtue, go willingly and often to confession and receive Holy Communion (if you are allowed to), and always reveal to your confessor precisely all your inclinations, your thoughts, all opportunities, in which you find yourself and, in general, everything that is necessary for him to fully recognize you for how you are. If you reveal yourself to him frankly, he will warn you, he will advise you on what to do and recommend the tools that will be best for you according to your circumstances. However, if you hide from your confessor and do not let him know what you are like before God,

it would be better not to come to confession, because such confessions will not only help you do any good, but will multiply your sin, and you will be led into an ever-increasing danger of eternal damnation. An open-hearted and frequent confession is truly a great tool for maintaining purity because the confessor, if he cares at all for the salvation of the children who are dear to his soul, is especially sad when he sees that someone sins against holy purity, and does not leave this person behind, but strives to bring him or her back on the right path. After St. Augustine came to recognize himself and converted, he especially regretted that in his youth he had not chosen any spiritual teacher who would have led him away from his shameless vices onto the path of penance. St. Jerome writes about a priest who, with his wisdom, saved a young man from dangerous impure temptations and opportunities and led him onto the right path. Then he testifies that if this young man had not come into the hands of this priest, he would not have overcome his temptations and would have possibly perished forever. (More about receiving the holy sacraments more often will be discussed later in this book. You will learn more thoroughly about how good this tool is for maintaining holy purity.)

3. Meditating the eternal truths and reading sacred books. Meditating about the four last things is a good tool for keeping a person pure. If this person was so unlucky and has lost this beautiful opportunity, he or she will regain it and then always keep it after this reflection.

Death. There is not a more miserable death than the death of an impure sinner. This sin has a sad property of fooling and hardening a person, so that even on his or her deathbed this person does not confess and repent and he or she mostly dies as he or she lived, without the grace of God.

Judgment. How horrible will be the judgment of the unrepentant sinner! The judgment of the impure sinner will be especially horrible! The sinner is used to sin in this world secretly and knows to hide his or her shameless sins from people in such a way that sometimes no one knows this person for what he or she really is. At the judgment, however, especially at the Last Judgment, everything will come to light and all people will know what the wicked one has done. Where will this person hide from shame then? He or she would want the hills rolling over him or her and be covered together with one's shame. This person's trial will be horrible, especially at the Last Judgment where our bodies will be judged as well. This body, which this person served so faithfully, to which he or she allowed so much sinful joy, will now be condemned to burn for eternity in the fires of hell!

Hell. No sinner is burned so fiercely by the fire of hell as the one whose heart has been burned with impure fire in this world. Therefore, the almighty God, who could have punished the impure Sodomites in any other way, wanted to kill them with fire in order to let the whole world know that the impure sinners will suffer profoundly in eternal fire in the next world.

Heaven. As God shows us how impurity is abhorrent to Him and how terribly He will punish it in eternity, He also lets us know how highly He honors and loves purity and how unspeakably fortunate He will make pure souls in eternity. How much He loves and honors holy purity we recognize from the fact that He chose the purest soul as His mother. He loved the purest of his apostles, who is called *"the bridegroom of pure souls,"* the most and handed over to him His most holy mother while hanging on the cross. He will make the pure souls in Heaven very fortunate as one can surmise when He says that those who have a pure heart will see God, and only pure virgin souls will follow the Lamb into Heaven and sing a new song that no one else will be able to sing.

Contemplating other holy Christian truths and diligently reading good sacred books are good tools for maintaining purity, because reading and contemplating fill the heart with holy thoughts and feelings that drive away everything that is impure and worldly and bind it more and more with God and preserve it for Him.

Let this, my dear Christian, be heartily recommended to you. Use these tools faithfully and you will maintain beautiful holy purity. Recommend them to others, especially to young people, out of love for God and for your neighbor. If you help someone with God's grace to maintain purity, you grant him a greater goodness than if you gave him all the gold in the world, because purity is the *gold of the heart*. And the gold of this heart, which God created for Himself to be with Him forever in Heaven, is worth more than the gold of this earth, which will be destroyed with everything it has on Judgement Day.

X.

THE CHOICE OF A GOOD CONFESSOR

*"Tobiah went out to look for someone
who would travel with him to Media,
someone who knew the way."*

The way to heaven is difficult and dangerous, my dear Christian. There are many deep abysses on both sides of the way and there are many sideways which are pleasant to a person in the beginning, but lead to eternal ruin, and there are many who tempt people with false pretenses to enter these distractions. There are many enemies and bandits at all points on this way who are extremely dangerous, especially to all those who walk alone. Therefore, my dear Christian, you will need a faithful man who would accompany you on this dangerous way. A man who knows the way very well, who knows all the dangerous places, all the difficulties along the way and has the authority and power to ward off and defeat all adversaries and enemies.

Even on a less dangerous path, such as the path to salvation, a person is looking for a faithful man who would accompany and bring this person wherever he or she wants. It is written in the Holy Scriptures that the old Tobit suggested to his son before sending him to a distant land, to find such a faithful guide.

Jesus says that *"If a blind person leads a blind person, both will fall into a pit."* It is even more certain that a blind man will fall into a pit if he or she walks alone on an unknown path. *"But woe to the solitary person! If that one should fall, there is no other to help."*

Whoever relies too much on one's abilities in spiritual things, on his or her own smartness, caution, wisdom, and piety, will not remain on the right path that leads to Heaven for very long. As the Holy Spirit says in Scripture: *"Whoever trusts his own thoughts, acts sinful."* and *"Those who trust in themselves are fools."*

Therefore, do not only rely on yourself, my dear Christian, and do not walk according to what you think is the right path for salvation, but find a faithful man, i.e., *a good confessor* and ask him to lead you on this difficult, narrow and dangerous path, then submit completely to him and he will teach you the way of the Lord, show you the dangers you should avoid and duties you would have to fulfill. If you will step off the right path, he will lead you back onto the right way. If you fall, he will give you his hand and lift you. If your worldly friends want to lure you onto the wide and pleasant way they are pursuing, he will keep you on the good path with his good lessons, his abundant warnings and especially with his heartfelt prayer for you before God. He will teach you to love the narrow and thorny path of Jesus even more thoroughly and to detest sin as well as the wide and worldly path more and more. He will teach you to love Jesus above all, to do everything for Him and to suffer because of Him, out of an abundant love for Him and through His holy will, and to bond with Him so thoroughly that there is nothing to separate you from Him.

Look, you will find all this and much more if you find yourself a faithful and caring guide on the way to heaven. You will say with an unfamiliar happiness of your heart about him: *"You filled me with every good thing."*

When choosing a confessor, you should commend yourself well to God who knows all hearts. And, furthermore, you should trust in God's Providence. It is predominately your local spiritual shepherd who was given to you by God's Providence and is the holy man who will accompany you and lead you on God's path. Firstly, he has more opportunities to know you than other priests have because you are entrusted to his pastoral care. Secondly, he will be able to give answers about you before the Last Judgement; therefore, he will be able to take care of your soul more thoroughly than any other priest if he were to become your confessor. Thirdly, because he is your spiritual shepherd through Divine Providence, there is hope that God would give him more graces and enlightenment than any foreign shepherd to lead you on His ways.

However, if you think reasonably and conscientiously before God that it would be better for you to go to some other priest for confession, do not go *secretly* someplace else, but tell your spiritual shepherd that you are going to somebody else for confession. Explain to him that it is not because you dislike him, but that you are going to somebody else only because you truly believe that it is better before God to do so.

A good confessor is a great gift from God. God showed great kindness to the young Tobias when He sent him the archangel Raphael who accompanied and protected him on his way to the distant land. However, there is an even greater good which God gives to you, i.e., when he gives you the grace to find a good, faithful, and caring confessor.

The Archangel Raphael protected the young Tobias on his way so that no harm was done to him. When he went to wash his feet and suddenly a huge fish tried to swallow him, Raphael came to his rescue. A good confessor protects you so that the evil spirit, who always preys on your soul like a roaring lion, does not devour you forever.

The Archangel Raphael helped Tobias get the money his father lent to his friend. A good confessor helps you obtain the eternal heavenly riches that cannot be stolen by any thief and are worth more than everything on earth and within it.

The Archangel Raphael helped Tobias to get a rich and good wife and made him happy with her. A good confessor helps you transform your soul to become Jesus' bride. It makes the soul so happy that all the other happiness that ever happened on earth means nothing compared to the one happy soul which is Jesus' bride.

The Archangel Raphael made Tobias happy for the rest of his life with all the goods that were given to him by the will of God. A good confessor will make you endlessly happy through his holy effort. Not only for the entire time of your earthly life when he helps you maintain God's grace and live in the holy peace, but he will make you exceptionally happy for eternity with the help of God's grace if you are obedient to him.

Look, my dear Christian, at what a blessing a good confessor is. Ask God to provide you this blessing and to keep it. Strive to fulfill all duties toward your confessor faithfully. If you are not fulfilling your duties, there is no other confessor who could help you reach salvation. These duties are:

1. You should always honor and respect your confessor. Honor him like he is an angel from God. If you have a good confessor, then you have two guardian angels. One was sent to you by God from heaven, the other was given from Him in the person of a confessor. He is your spiritual father. Because you are obliged by God's command to worship and honor your *earthly* father, you have the duty to worship your *spiritual* father even more as the soul is worth more than the body. You should always speak respectfully about him. Talk with him humbly and reverently. Listen to him diligently and faithfully when he teaches you as if you would listen to your guardian angel speaking to you. If you hear secular people talking about him being too strict or too harsh, and suggesting that a person should not go to his confession, do not believe anything, but rather thank God in your heart that He gave you the grace to find a sharp and thoughtful confessor. He is the one who does not want to be condemned with you, but wants to walk with you on Jesus' thorny path that leads to heaven. And then love and honor him even more. Be careful though, my dear Christian, not to get too *attached* to your confessor. Such bond can sometimes cause a certain inclination disliked by God. If you develop such inclination toward your confessor, tell him honestly, explain to him thoroughly and follow his advice.

2. You have to place great trust in your confessor. This trust is so essential that without it, not even the best confessor can help you much. As people trust the captain of the boat and do not fear, even as the boat rocks heavily due to storm, you should trust the man of God who leads your soul over the dangerous waters of your life and you should not fear to drown and be condemned until you trust with him in God, although there is an abundance of danger around you. As does a patient trust a doctor in taking medicine even if it tastes bitter, so should you trust in your spiritual doctor and be fully confident that he wants to do you good, even if he gouges out your right eye or tears off your right arm: *"If your right eye causes you to sin, tear it out and throw it away. It is better for you to lose one of your members than to have your whole body to be thrown into Gehenna."* If a patient has some hidden disease or wound, he or she overcomes one's shyness. Both ailments are shown to a doctor whom a patient trusts to be healed. The more a patient reveals to a doctor, the easier he or she can be cured. You have to act in the same way toward your confessor and repent to him openheartedly as well as wish that he would know you thoroughly. If your trust is real, which is your obligation, you will open yourself up easily as does a child to its mother or father and a patient to his or her wise doctor. You will show your trust to your confessor by consulting with him in all things, especially if you want to change your status. Do as he suggests that you do to the best of your ability.

3. Obedience is an important duty you have toward your confessor, my dear Christian. All your confessions will be empty without obedience to your confessor, which derives from trust. If you have the right trust in him and if you want to be saved, you will be faithfully obedient (This book describes the topic of *obedience* and *confessor* in a previous chapter about *obedience*.)

4. Further, *faithfulness* is your great duty toward your confessor. Be faithful to your confessor and do not cheat on him in any regard. You could cheat him and he could cheat you as well, but God cannot be cheated. Be a faithful child of your spiritual father and a faithful sheep of your spiritual shepherd. Jesus says "*I am the good shepherd, and I know mine and mine know me.*" Therefore, my dear Christian, strive to be more thoroughly known by your spiritual shepherd. Never do what sometimes the unfaithful souls do who are never truly known to their spiritual shepherd, i.e., if you are so unhappy and commit some bigger sin, do not go secretly to some other confessor who does not know you, but to your regular one. Do you not want to be completely known to your shepherd? Did not Jesus say that a good shepherd has to know his sheep? If you act as mentioned, he will never know you and will always think that you are better than you really are because you only reveal some minor sins to him and bigger sins to somebody else. My dear Christian, do not act this way, but overcome your hidden vanity that is keeping you away from humility. "*To the spiritual man bow your head.*" and God who lifts the

humble will forgive you everything. "*It was good for me to be afflicted, in order to learn your statutes.*" Further, my dear Christian, if you want to be well known by your spiritual father, you have to regularly attend confession. If you only confess rarely, he will not get to know you for a long time and will never know you well. Be faithful to your confessor and never imitate those Christians who regularly change confessors. Do not leave your confessor. Leave him only when before God and before your conscience you cannot do otherwise. Choose your confessor in God and because of God and leave him in God and because of God.

5. It is your duty *to pray for your confessor.* As you are obliged to pray for your parents, you are even more obliged to pray for your confessor who is a caring father of your soul. Confessors need special graces from God in order to perform their sacred duties. It is true that they ask God themselves for the graces and commend themselves to Him every day. However, all their spiritual children are obliged to pray for them as well, and their joint prayer will achieve much before God because as Jesus says "*I say to you, if two of you agree on earth about anything for which they are to pray, it shall be granted to them by my heavenly Father.*"

My dear Christian, faithfully fulfill all these duties to your confessor, do them in God's grace and to the eternal salvation of your soul. The more you fulfill them, the more certainly you will be saved with help of the Almighty, merciful God and His substitute.

XI.

FREQUENT AND GOOD CONFESSION

*"If we acknowledge our sins, he is faithful
and just and will forgive our sins and
cleanse us from every wrongdoing."*

You can realize from what was said about a good and faithful confessor that a good confessor is truly a great gift and a special grace from God. However, you should make good use of this grace, my dear Christian, that is, you have to like to go to confession, you have to attend it regularly and you have to make a good confession.

Let this meditation encourage you to confess frequently. Although you can abstain from mortal sin for a while, you will not be able to keep it away for long if you do not often confess your venial sins.

1. Although you can restrain from a mortal sin for some time, you will not be able to stay away from it for long if you will not confess to your venial sins regularly. If you will be less and less afraid of them, you will hate them less and they will soon lead you into greater sins.

2. If you do not attend confession regularly, you cannot remember all your sins easily. Then, you are in danger of making a bad and incomplete confession out of your own negligence.

3. You will never know yourself well if you rarely go to confession. Confession is a mirror of your soul or a reflecting surface on which a soul can see itself as it

really is – with all its stains. However, a person who only rarely looks into this mirror forgets how one is and never gets to know oneself as well as the one who often examines oneself in it.

4. If you do not confess regularly, you will reaffirm yourself in bad habits and you will not even know when you commit them. You will choose dangerous opportunities and you will not be able to see the trap in which the evil spirit wants to trap you. If you go often to your confessor and show him faithfully how you really are, if you reveal all your circumstances to him, he will kindly warn you, teach you and show you the dangers you are facing that you do not know much about. He will help you tear out all evil roots from your heart before they become firm. A field of a careless farmer who rarely weeds and clears it grows more and more weeds and less quality grain.

5. The best tool to avoid these evil temptations and defeat them is a frequent and faithful confession. A person is surrounded by dangerous temptations from all sides. Especially temptations of impurity are terribly dangerous. If one is left to oneself and rarely hears the good teachings and recommendations of his or her spiritual father, it will be almost impossible to resist steadfastly the evil spirit and remain pure without sin. The best soldier would not be able to defend himself for long against the enemy without good and powerful weapons. The good teachings of your caring confessor are the best weapon for you because they come from God. *"Put on the armor of God so that you may be able to stand firm against the tactics of the devil." "Therefore, put on the armor of God, that you may be able to resist on the evil day and, having done everything, to hold your ground."*

How often one should go to confession cannot be said in one word. Some need to go more often than others. Go to confession at least once a month. If you want to live more purely and carefully guard even against small sins, go to confession more often. It is written about the saints that some of them went to confession every week and others even every day. It would be best for you, my dear Christian, to ask your confessor how often you should come to confession, then submit to his commandment with humble confidence.

Do not follow those who think that they should confess only when they commit some grave sin. Confession, especially frequently, is not only recommended for the forgiveness of sins; it is also a good tool to resist evil temptations and guard against sin. As doctors do not only have drugs that heal, but also drugs that prevent people from becoming ill, so do confessors, who are healers of souls, not only have tools and power to heal a soul when it falls ill, i.e., when it falls into a sin, but also healing tools, good teachings and advice with which they protect a soul and make it strong so that it does not sin, even though it falls into dangerous temptation, and to overcome them out of love for God. The Holy Spirit says: "*before you get sick, prepare the cure.*", i.e., take the kind of medicine that will prevent you from getting sick. The best drug or tool for the soul not to fall ill is a frequent and good confession.

Do not imitate all those, my dear Christian, who do not go to confession for a long time after they commit great sin. Some do not go out of false shyness or indifference. This gives them a chance to repeatedly commit this same sin or other big sins since they think: "I already have a sin. I will confess all these sins at once." Just as a man who is dirty is no longer as careful as he was before about keeping himself clean, so does the person in sin no longer guard the condition of his soul as carefully as he did before committing his first sin. If such person does not clean his or her soul with the help of the

Sacrament of Penance, this sin becomes more and more habitual and it seems less and less ugly and shameful.

Never act in this way, my dear Christian, but gladly go to confession and go regularly. Do not go to confession only when committing some big sin, but more often than that. Repent immediately if you are so unlucky and have committed a big sin. How will all those be able to answer before God at the Last Judgement if they take more care of their body than of their soul. If a person cuts or smacks oneself, he or she does not say "Oh, I will wait until I cut or smack myself again and will then go to a doctor who will treat both wounds at once." A person does not say so, but hurries to find a person to treat the wound and to bandage it. You can see a sad blindness of all those Christians who are more concerned for their decaying body than for their immortal soul created in the image of God.

Delaying confession and penance is very dangerous, especially if a person is living with a mortal sin because a person's life is like a drop of water on a branch. If such a person dies suddenly, he or she is eternally doomed. How terrible is the danger of living in a mortal sin. One can read in the past texts that a king wanted to show one of his friends how his life is permanently in danger. He asked to hang a sword on a piece of horsehair above his seat and then called his friend (who did not know that horsehair hangs above the king's seat), sat his friend on his seat and said that he will be king from now on. This person was extremely happy and thought this is the beginning of the happiest time in his life. However, when he was the happiest, he noticed a sword hanging from above his head attached only to one horsehair. He got so scared that he did not want to sit at the king's place any longer and preferred to leave all honor and grandeur behind than to remain in such danger. Look, my dear Christian, this is an image of a man who lives joyfully in this world, although he has a mortal sin. This person is in constant danger of losing not only his worldly, bodily life but also the eternal heavenly life of his soul and becoming eternally unhappy.

Recognize this well, my dear Christian, become at least as careful as was that king's friend. Run away and do not *"walk in the counsel of the wicked"*, run away from sin and into the arms of the merciful Heavenly Father who welcomes his abandoned son with endless love if this son truly returns to him, because *"I swear I take no pleasure in the death of the wicked, but rather that they turn from their ways and live."*

There is another great danger in delaying confession and penance that you must think about thoroughly, my dear Christian. If you delay for a long time, especially after committing a heavier sin, you are making yourself more and more unworthy of God's grace. If your conscience blames you that you have offended God and have lost His kindness, and you do nothing to reconcile with Him, although you know that you can reconcile with Him through the Sacrament of Penance, you evidently show that you do not love Him and do not care much for His kindness. How dare you say to God in your daily prayer: *"Our Father ... forgive us our trespasses ..."* if you do not want to do what God tells you to do for the forgiveness of your sins, your trespasses? God tells you to repent and to receive the Sacrament of Penance worthily, and He will forgive all your sins. However, you are turning away from this salvific tool more and more. This is not really loving God in spirit and in truth. My dear Christian, do not do so with the Almighty, Eternal God. *"Make no mistake: God is not mocked."*

The evil spirit, this enemy of all good, will place many obstacles in front of you in order to divert you from confession, especially from a frequent confession. If you will listen to the evil spirit, you will not like to go to confession and you will not go often. The evil spirit will sometimes give you the thought that it is too difficult to get in line, that you will have to wait in line for too long, that it is too difficult to prepare for confession, and that you are never too well prepared. Sometimes it will tell you that it is still not the time to go to confession, that you can wait a bit longer. Sometimes it will give you a thought that you are too busy, that you do not have time to go to confession. Sometimes, the evil spirit will maybe evoke that sad and sinful shame that you will be ashamed before the confessor, or that you will be ashamed to be seen in the confessional often as are some who are not ashamed of sinning often, however, they are ashamed of going often to confession.

Think good, my dear Christian, about all these troubles and hindrances which the evil tempter does to you and you will see how empty they are.

It the evil tempter diverts you from going to confession by suggesting that confession is always related to some trouble, recall that a good confession deletes your sins if it is a good confession, and makes you gain God's grace or confirms you in it if you already have it. Are these great spiritual virtues not worthy enough to gain them with this little effort? If you are afraid of these little efforts to make confession, what will be in the afterlife, considering you come only into purgatory? If you find it difficult to wait here a bit for your turn for the forgiveness of your sins, how will you be able to wait in the purgatory in great suffering for years for the forgiveness of only some minor sin?

When the evil tempter distracts you with this thought, making you unable to ever prepare for confession in a right way, and you always delay confessing, realize that he is really cheating you. Don't you see that delaying confession will divert you from preparing for it and confessing completely. If you go to confession often, you remember all your sins easily. If you go seldom, it will be difficult for you to remember all sins. And if you delay, you will certainly forget many and will not confess properly out of your own negligence.

Never listen to the evil tempter when he tells you that it is not yet time to go to confession. This is a dangerous temptation. Every human is a sinner and sins every day and *"If we say, "We are without sin," we deceive ourselves, and the truth is not in us."* If you do not have big sins, you certainly have small ones. It is good that you confess your small sins as well because if you are not afraid of small sins and do not avoid them, you will soon commit big sins without being aware of it. Think how a person acts in the case of bodily pain and illness if one is cautious. If a person feels ill, he or she does not wait until he or she almost dies, but calls a doctor and takes medicine even if it tastes bitter. Therefore, my dear Christian, be at least as cautious and caring for your soul as most people are for their bodies.

If the evil tempter distracts and diverts you away from a frequent confession with the suggestion that this is too much work, remember the beautiful words of Jesus *"There is need of only one thing."* Which thing is then so important? Certainly, no worldly errand, because when Jesus said these words He also warned Martha that she is taking too much care of worldly duties. He praised Maria who sat at His feet and listened to His teachings of salvation. Take these words of Jesus to your heart, my dear Christian, out of love for him, move slightly away from your worldly errands and worries, come gladly and often to the seat of mercy, and listen at the feet of Jesus' substitute about His teachings of salvation. In this way, you will be able to overcome your temptations more easily and will beat the evil tempter completely at the end *"I [Jesus] will give the right to eat from the tree of life that is in the garden of God."*

When the evil enemy distracts you with temptations of shyness, think how unclever it is to be ashamed of your confessor. A confessor does never disclose the sins you confess. Therefore, there is no danger of disclosing your sins to people after your confession. You also do not have to be ashamed before your good and caring confessor. He is your spiritual father and your spiritual healer. A good child opens up in all things to his or her father rather than to other people. In order to get better, a patient reveals his or her hidden illnesses and pains to his or her doctor as well. Therefore, reveal yourself to your confessor faithfully and overcome your shyness. He does not want to hear your sins in order to know them, but for the merciful God to forgive them if you really confess and repent. Think how infinitely good God is. You deserve evidently to be punished for your sins and to be disgraced at God's judgment before *all men.* However, God gave you the holy Sacrament of Penance through which you confess your sins to *only one person,* i.e., to your confessor, your spiritual father and your best friend. God will forgive you your sins and erase them so that you will not be disgraced at God's judgment. However, if you do not want to recognize this goodness of God and you are ashamed before your confessor, your sins will remain on your conscience and your shame will be infinitely great at the Last Judgment and for all eternity.

If you are ashamed to be seen near a confessional often, think about Jesus' words: "*Everyone who acknowledges me before others I will acknowledge before my heavenly Father. But whoever denies me before others, I will deny before my heavenly Father.*" Whenever you are ashamed to do what Jesus asked us to do for the salvation of your soul, when you betray Him before people and you are ashamed to be His disciple, then you are in danger that He will be ashamed of recognizing you as His friend before the Heavenly

Father because He said *"Whoever is ashamed of me and my words, the Son of Man will be ashamed of when he comes in his glory and in the glory of the Father and of the holy angels."*

You can see from all this, my dear Christian, that all those difficulties and all excuses that prevent you from going to confession often, are merely temptations, and terribly dangerous temptations, from the evil spirit. Therefore, do not listen to them. Go regularly to confession and strive always to make a good and God-pleasing confession.

In order to make a good confession, you need to prepare thoroughly. Three things are necessary, i.e., questioning of conscience, a heartfelt repentance of sins, and a solid firm decision not to sin again. All this needs to be done before you see a confessor. That is why it is called *preparation for confession.*

1. Questioning one's conscience. This is a difficult task if you want to make it right and even more difficult than Christians think. However, it is crucial for a good confession. Before you start questioning your conscience, ask God to enlighten you and give you grace to get to know yourself well. The latter is very difficult. People usually think they are better than they really are. A wise man from the past said that it was considered great wisdom to know yourself well. If you want to gain this wisdom, ask God for it. *"But if any of you lacks wisdom, he should ask God who gives to all generously and ungrudgingly, and he will be given. But he should ask in faith, not doubting [...]."*

Then think thoroughly about God's commandments and the teachings of the Church, capital sins and other sins, and the duties of your rank. If you have not been to confession for a long time, or if you want to make a *long confession,* you have to prepare thoroughly. In some prayer books, i.e., in the *Pasture for the Soul,* there is plenty of help for questioning your conscience.

Be sure to question your conscience thoroughly, my dear Christian; this is necessary for a good confession. Strive also to recall as many sins as possible. Beware that your own self-love does not make you blind. It is sad to see how our selfish love sometimes pushes its way into our best works, and sometimes it does so secretly so that it is difficult to detect. Our selfish love is like a worm that invisibly destroys a root of some herbal plant below ground and then this plant slowly dies and is not worth anything. So does our selfish love distinguish our best works and makes them unworthy before God. God wants us to do good works out of love for Him and not out of our selfish love. It is especially important, my dear Christian, to know when questioning your conscience if self-love is impeding your good intentions.

If you want to know yourself more thoroughly, question your conscience every evening. This was strongly recommended by all past spiritual teachers and was done by all saints. If you have not yet developed this good habit, my dear Christian, work now to gain this habit and keep it faithfully till the end of your life.

1. Heartfelt act of contrition. Whoever recognizes thoroughly how big and unfaithful sinner one is before God, and whoever loves God just a little bit, cannot but feel sorry for offending his or her generous and kind God so many times and so deeply after questioning one's conscience. The more one loves God, the more one is sorry to have treated God in such an ungrateful way. It is that heartfelt act of contrition that a sinner needs to have in order to gain God's absolution from sins. This contrition has to come from the love of God. There must not be much fear of hell, otherwise there is more selfish love involved than the love of God. It is true that we are allowed to mourn when we have lost heaven and earned hell with our sins. God left that to us because *we are heartless.* It is much better to repent from our sins only because we have offended our loving and infinitely good God by them.

In order to more easily regret your sins for God's sake only, my dear Christian, think often how God Himself is worth of all love and how merciful and benevolent He reveals Himself to you in all occasions. Not only when you are preparing for confession, but think often about God in this way, especially on Sundays. The more you think about Him, the more you will know Him and the more you know Him, the more you will love Him and the more you love Him, the more you will regret offending Him and you will be more careful not to offend Him.

An exceedingly comforting example of how God forgives all those who repent their sins out of love for Him is Mary Magdalene at Jesus' feet. She was sorry from the bottom of her heart that she offended her God so many times and so terribly with her sins. Her heart was so burdened that she was unable to speak and could only shed tears at Jesus' feet. She made a beautiful confession there, concluded with heartfelt contrition, not with words, but in her heart, because Jesus sees into the heart, and because he saw her heartfelt contrition, He uttered these kind and benevolent words: *"So I tell you, her many sins have been forgiven; hence, she has shown great love."*

2. A firm resolution not to sin again. When someone is really sorry to have committed something, they resolve firmly not to repeat that action. If a person does not make this resolution, this certainly means that he or she is not truly sorry. A firm resolution not to sin any more grows from a thorough act of contrition for sins as a plant grows out of its roots. These two things are so intertwined that one cannot be without the other. If there is a true act of contrition, there surely is a firm resolution not to sin again. If there is none, there is no true repentance. This firm resolution should not only be displayed in words, but in actions. It must produce fruit, i.e., "[...]

as evidence of your repentance," otherwise it is worth nothing. A plant producing nothing is worth nothing despite its beauty, but is worth only when it bears ears of grain.

What is this worthy fruit of penance that must come from repentance of sins and from a firm resolution to sin no more? This fruit is true conversion and improvement. A sinner must now hate and carefully avoid what he or she previously loved and love what he or she previously hated. This means that he or she must now hate sin and those sinful opportunities he or she previously loved and sought. Conversely, such person must now love modest acts previously shunned and complete them in action, and seek and do everything that points to them. If a sinner lived in animosity with his or her neighbor, he or she needs to forgive this person and reconcile amicably. If a sinner was ruthless and hard-hearted toward poor people, he or she has to help them now in their need as much as possible. If a sinner has damaged his neighbor in his earthly possessions, he must repay him as much as possible. If a sinner has robbed his neighbor of his good name by slandering and defamation, he must now strive, as far as possible, to restore his good name. If this person has corrupted his neighbor, he or she must now strive to prepare him or her to improve his or her thoughts by good example and also by word. All this should not be done because of selfish love but because of love for God and one's neighbor.

This is a worthy fruit of penance. Who brings such fruit has concluded to not sin again and shows that his or her repentance of sins is truthful and holy. That it is good and done for love of God will show when it bears beautiful fruit.

However, consider and recognize, my dear Christian, that this is impossible with a *bad person* "[…] *but for God all things are possible.*" Therefore, do not rely on yourself, but put all your trust entirely in God. When you prepare for confession, ask Him in the name of Jesus to give you strength and grace. Firmly conclude to guard yourself against sin and sinful opportunities and to serve God faithfully. Then do as much as you can. Do not think that God will do everything for you. God tells you: "Help yourself and I will help you. What you can do, do." What you will not be able to do, God will do.

One can see from what has been said here about a heartfelt act of contrition and a firm resolution that empty and unfruitful confessions of Christians are therefore rejected by God. "[H]e *said to the gardener, 'For three years now I have come in search of fruit on this fig tree but have found none. [So] cut it down. Why should it exhaust the soil?'* God our Lord speaks so about the unfertile sinner who does not bear any of the fruit of penance because his repentance of sins is only at the tip of his tongue and his resolution is an empty tree bearing no fruit. But God's representative who takes care of His vineyard asks for it saying: "*Sir, leave it for this year also, and I shall cultivate the ground around it and fertilize it; it may bear fruit in the future. If not[,] you can cut it down.*"

Think, my dear Christian, if you too are not this barren tree in God's vineyard. Maybe God would go looking for three more years to find the ripe fruit of penance in you, but would not find it. God's substitute, your confessor, is perhaps trying as hard as he can to ignite in your heart a true repentance from sins and a firm resolution to improve yourself in order to produce the prized fruit of penance which God has been seeking in you for so long. However, all is in vain and He cannot help you when you fall again into your old sinful habits and wrongdoings soon after confessing. Think about the words of God your Lord and be afraid "*Therefore every tree that does not produce good fruit will be cut down and thrown into the fire.*"

This is, my dear Christian, how you always prepare for confession. Examine your conscience, thoroughly regret your sins before God and for love of Him, conclude firmly to improve yourself and to avoid sinning in the future.

After such preparation come with trust before your confessor as did Mary Magdalene when she came before Jesus. Think that you come before Jesus as well. Forget about the person sitting in the confessional and think only of Jesus whose substitute the confessor is. Come to confession with trust and fear. Come with trust because God evidently shows you through the Sacrament of Penance that He does not want the death of a sinner, but wants your repentance and eternal life. Come with fear because confession has to remind you of God's judgement at which Jesus, whose substitute is the confessor, will judge you harshly for your all unrepentant sins.

If you have to wait long to attend confession, wait patiently and with decency. Do not waste your time while you are waiting, but read, pray or think about Christian truths.

When confessing, tell your sins humbly, faithfully and quickly. A sinner has to *humble* oneself if he or she wants the forgiveness of sins not only before God but also before his or her confessor. Nothing else defeats God's heart as quickly as humility. Wish and strive that your confessor would know you well. Do not pretend before him to be better than you are before God. The more you will truly want to be recognized as a sinner, the more you will be forgiven of sins. Remember the humble sinner from the temple who realized that he was a great sinner and how he went out of the temple forgiven of his sins.

Beware, however, that out of love and humility you do not tell too much at confession, but only tell *faithfully and justly* everything that is on your conscience not more and not less. Tell your confessor thoroughly about all those circumstances that make your sin bigger or smaller. You do not have to talk about other circumstances. Tell as many sins as possible. You are not obliged to talk about everyday weaknesses. This is also almost impossible. However, if you were undisciplined and committed a bigger sin, it is your duty to say how many sins you have.

Never hide a big sin at confession, my dear Christian. Strange is the blindness of a person who keeps a big sin hidden from his confessor. Why does such a person go to confession at all? It would be much better not to come. Such action makes this person an even bigger sinner because he or she has one more grave sin in addition to all of their other sins, namely sacrilege. My dear Christian, beware that this misery never happens to you. If you do this, remember that you lie to the Holy Spirit because the apostles and all those inferior to God received the Holy Spirit from Jesus. Who lies to them, lies to the Holy Spirit. Holy Scripture describes a horrific example of Ananias and his wife Sapphira who sold a piece of property. They brought the money to the apostle Peter and said it was all they received. However, this was a lie because they kept some money for themselves. Both were punished with quick death. Saint Peter said that they did not lie to a person but to the Holy Spirit. Do not say that you do not lie if you conceal a sin in confession but are merely quiet about it. It is true that you do not lie with *words* if you keep quiet, but with your *action* because you pretend to be better than you are before your confessor. Beware of God! If He does not punish you immediately as He did with Ananias and Sapphira, you will not escape His punishment if you will not truly repent.

If you were so unfortunate, my dear Christian, that you kept a sin for yourself at a confession, think whether you completed all your duties as a Christian. Whoever does not tell a mortal sin in confession, has to repent truly because such a person committed a sacrilege. Such person must think in his or her heart *"For I am a man of unclean lips* [...]." and must tell the confessor at how many confessions he or she concealed this sin. This person also needs to tell whether he or she received some other blessed sacrament while having this sin and has to repeat all unworthy confessions.

Strive, my dear Christian, to tell you confessor all your sins *clearly*. Speak in a way that only he will hear you and nobody else. Tell your sins directly and do not twist your words, so that your confessor will soon be able to recognize the state of your soul. If you choose words with a hidden meaning and do not speak clearly, you are in danger of misleading your confessor and making your confession incomplete. Wish that your confessor would know you as God knows you. Furthermore, always use decent and honorable words as is appropriate before God's substitute.

Do not talk about irrelevant things, but explain *shortly* what you have found while examining your conscience. Do not talk about irrelevant circumstances when confessing because you are wasting the time of your confessor and of the people who are waiting in line for confession. Time is worth more than worldly goods. Do not talk about people while confessing if it is not necessary. It is not right at all to talk about your neighbor and to name him or her. It is only appropriate if confession could otherwise not be made completely.

After completing confession, humbly listen to the words of your spiritual father and receive them as if they would be given to you by Jesus himself. Listen to your confessor as Maria listened to Jesus. She forgot about everything timely and worldly, and abandoned it. She only listened to Jesus' words. In the same way, when your confessor speaks to you during confession, forget all your worldly tasks, all your problems and inconveniences and

listen with the full presence of your soul to the teachings of salvation of God's substitute. These teachings
are predominately more salvific and worth more than
sermons, as a preacher speaks to all his listeners and
cannot tell everyone separately what would be necessary.
When you are confessing, my dear Christian, your confessor recognizes the special needs of your soul and his
teaching is tailored to you. You will hear many things in
these teachings that cannot be explained so precisely and
clearly from a pulpit.

Furthermore, it is true that preachers received a special grace from Jesus Christ to give redeeming lessons to
sinners. A priest cannot truly be Jesus' substitute and act
like Him when he is not in a confessional because

1. Jesus came down from heaven "[…] *not to do my
own will but the will of the one who sent me.*" A confessor
does not come into a confessional because of his own
will or because of himself, but because of God, to fulfill His holy will because He wants to deliver forgiveness of sins to sinners and grant grace through the holy
Sacrament of Penance.

2. Jesus says "*Those who are healthy do not need a physician,
but the sick do.*" Jesus is truly our most benevolent and
merciful doctor. He healed our souls and saved them
from death. Similarly, a good and faithful confessor
is truly a healer of souls. A sinner has a sick soul; his
soul is wounded and sometimes its wounds are hidden.
However, a sinner opens up to his confessor and shows
him his or her most secret wounds, to which a confessor
applies healing medicine, i.e., the teachings of salvation
that heal the soul of a sinner with God's help.

3. Jesus preferred to teach sinners and said clearly:
"*I have not come to call the righteous to repentance but sinners.*"
Although His pretentious and ruthless enemies blamed
Him for always walking and eating with sinners, He did
not get distracted from His love for sinners because He

loved them and sought them out only to draw them to repentance. Doesn't a confessor do the same? Whenever you see him in a confessional surrounded by repentant sinners waiting to be forgiven for their sins and awaiting teachings of salvation, think of Jesus who shows sinners the way to penance and steers them toward it. And recall how Jesus forgave sins to all those sinners who repented and said to them: *"Courage, child, your sins are forgiven."* *"Look, you are well; do not sin any more, so that nothing worse may happen to you."* A confessor, who is His real substitute, does the same.

4. Jesus told us a beautiful parable about the lost son and his merciful father. Who is this merciful father? It is Jesus, our Lord and God, our giving Savior about whom the prophets said that *"[A] bruised reed he will not break"*, i.e., that even though a sinner deserves to be crushed and rejected, He will show mercy to this sinner if he truly repents and turns back to God. And to give confidence to the sinner to find his way back to God, he told us this beautiful parable. In the holy Sacrament of Penance, Jesus is the merciful and kind Father who receives His lost son so kindly when he returns to Him. He put confessors in His place, gave them power and recommended they accept kindly and bring back to Him the repentant sinners who want to return to God.

A confessor is then truly Jesus' substitute and his teaching is Jesus' teaching. Then, my dear Christian, listen to him faithfully and with a grateful heart, and take care not to act against him. The more you recognize that he is Jesus' substitute, the more you are obliged to preserve and complete his teaching of salvation. Your punishment before Jesus will be severe if you do not follow the teachings of a person whom you see in Jesus' place.

If a confessor gives you absolution after completing the teaching, receive it with a grateful and penitent heart. Think that Jesus is saying to you *"Courage, child, your sins are forgiven.*" Resolute firmly to abstain carefully from sin and sinful opportunities and ask God to give you grace and help.

If you do not receive absolution, do not grumble against your confessor, but accept humbly that you are not worth it. Do not follow those who want to get absolution from a confessor with force and argue with him if he declines their request. This is indecent and sinful. Trust that your confessor understands better what you deserve.

After receiving spiritual instructions, you will be given a penance. Listen carefully to what your confessor instructs you to do and receive everything humbly. If you do not understand, ask him. Do your penance faithfully and without delay. You do well when you do more than your confessor has told you to do because the penance given by your confessor is mostly inadequate compared to your sins. In this matter as in every other, you must act based on wisdom and obedience if you want to remain on the right path. If you want to do some special penitential works, consult your confessor and submit yourself completely to his will. If you do some penitential works based on your own will and not on your confessor's, your penance is in vain. God does not appreciate your penance. He would appreciate your obedience more than all your self-willed penance. Some hardheaded Christians are cheating themselves in this very heavily. They sometimes do severe penance without permission or even against the will of their confessor and think that they gained great merit before God. However, God rejects all this because He wants obedience. He prefers obedience more than any offerings and all penitential works. Why was the penance Jesus made for us sinners on the Cross so pleasing to His Father? St. Paul says that because Jesus was obedient to His Father till His death, even till His death on the cross. Make no mistake, my dear Christian, but surrender completely in your penitential works to the will of your confessor. One single Lord's Prayer that you pray at the will of your confessor as a penance is worth more before God (due to humble obedience) than harsh fasting and other penitential works without or even against the will of God's substitute.

The general works of penance are: prayer, fasting and almsgiving as is written in the Holy Scripture: *"Prayer with fasting is good. Almsgiving with righteousness is better than wealth with wickedness."* About these three good works the Holy Scriptures teaches that they are penitential works. It says about *prayer* that *"[T]he prayer of the lowly pierces the clouds [...]."* The person with a humble heart and in the spirit of penance asks God for the forgiveness of his sins, as King David did, is especially pleasing to God. This person will gain what he or she desires, i.e., the forgiveness of sins.

The Ninevites who saved themselves from damnation with true penance, give an example of *fasting.* Besides conversion and improvement, their penance consisted of fasting. St. Basil says that if the Ninevites had not fasted strictly, they would not have escaped being killed. The most beautiful example of penitential fasting was given to us by Jesus. He fasted in the desert for forty days so strictly that He did not eat anything, not because of His sins, as He did not have even a small one, but because of ours, which the Lamb of God took upon Himself.

The Holy Scripture describes how through *giving to the poor* or almsgiving God chooses to forgive sins and shows mercy to all those who are merciful to their neighbor. The book of Tobit states: *"Almsgiving is a worthy offering in the sight of the Most High for all who practice it."* It states further: *"for almsgiving saves from death, and purges all sin. Those who give alms will enjoy a full life."*

That mercy with the poor is a good penitential work for the forgiveness of sins when it derives from the spirit of penance can be seen from the advice prophet Daniel gave to King Nebuchadnezzar when he said: *"Therefore, O king, may my advice be acceptable to you; atone for your sins by good deeds, and for your misdeeds by kindness to the poor; then your contentment will be long lasting."*

It is evident that prayer, fasting and gifts to the poor are truly penitential works if the sinner does them in the spirit of penance. Along with penitential works, patience in difficulties and afflictions is a good penance as well. God announced to our first parents who sinned in Paradise that they will suffer greatly in this world because of the sin they committed. We can see that all difficulties of our earthly life are given to us as penance. For as long as the first people lived in innocence, without sin, they did not suffer. When they became sinners, they experienced suffering. If we all who are sinners would think thoroughly about this, we would accept and suffer the difficulties of this life differently. If we do not think through and do not take this to our heart, we will only suffer and nothing will help us reach salvation.

This truth would have to be thought through thoroughly, especially by the people of a low, poor class. They have a lasting opportunity with their willing endurance of their troubles to do good penance for their sins. Their life is full of troubles and suffering. Constant hard work, all difficulties and inconveniences due to the weather – now heat, then cold. Predominately bad and poor food, poor clothes, many pains and illnesses and many other difficulties and pains. This is their life on this earth. The saddest thing on top of this is that all this suffering is mostly lost for eternity and without any merit because it is not accepted and endured in the spirit of penance, but with impatience and with a multiplication of sins. What God gives these people out of His eternally good purpose for penance and to gain absolution from their sins, they turn to their damnation with a multiplication of their sins, i.e., with impatience, anger and curse. Therefore, they suffer here and will suffer eternally there if they do not convert.

Do not think, my dear Christian, that you do not have to repent because Jesus Christ did enough by His Heavenly Father and gained forgiveness for all our sins and that His merit is immeasurably bigger than the sins of the people of all times. It is true as well that a person alone cannot erase one single sin from him or herself with penance and rectify the divine justice that was ruined by sin. All this is true as the holy faith teaches us. Besides, it teaches us that we are obliged to do penitential works because without them we cannot become *partakers* of Jesus' merits and His infinitely sufficient penance for us. It is true, my dear Christian, that the merit of Jesus' penitential suffering is always infinitely great; however, it will not help *you* if you do not do your part as He himself tells you according to the teachings and commandments of His holy Church. What is truly left is that you will finally gain eternal salvation not through your penance but through the eternal merit of Jesus Christ. But you have gained His merit through your penance.

In order to see and understand this better, think the following parable through carefully. If a king would invite a poor prisoner who is incarcerated because of a large debt with no property to pay of his debt, "Ask me and I will pay off your entire debt," and if this poor prisoner would not ask his generous king, out of negligence or presumptuousness, he would always remain angry because he would never be able to pay off his debt, even though his king has enough money to pay his debt off and even more than that. However, nothing will help this person because he does not want to fulfill the king's will. However, if he would ask his king, his king would pay his debt and he would be saved from his sorrow. This person would then be able to recognize that he was saved by the goodness of the king. But at the same time, he would be able to recognize that if he would not have done as the king told him, he would never have been saved. The same can be applied to the sinner. If he or she does not do at least the amount of penance given to him or her by God through the mouth of confessors and spiritual teachers, he or she will not be saved, even though Jesus' merit is eternally great. It does not count for *him* because he does not want to gain it.

My dear Christian, let me recommend *a long confession* to you here. If you have never done it, do it and prepare as well as possible for it. It is recommended to do such a confession several times in your life, especially if a Christian is planning to change his or her status. A long confession *is necessary:*

for all those who are so miserable and blind that they keep quiet about a sin for a long time and meanwhile make confessions that are worth nothing;

for all those who have been living in some sinful habits for a long time, namely in drunkenness, impurity, injustice, hate etc. If they want to really convert and reconcile with God, they need a long confession to correct previous confessions made without any fruit of penance because they returned to the same sins to which they had previously confessed.

XII

A FREQUENT HOLY COMMUNION AND AS WORTHY AS POSSIBLE

Jesus says: "I am the living bread that came down from heaven; whoever eats this bread will live forever."

Jesus, our merciful Savior, gave us by His infinite mercy the blessed Sacrament of Penance through which He forgives us our sins and cleanses our souls. However, this was not enough for His incomprehensible love. He gave us another Sacrament in which the soul reaches completion after being cleansed through the Sacrament of Penance, and bonds with the soul tightly, so that He remains in the soul and the soul in Him. In this Most Blessed Sacrament, Jesus' love displays itself the most.

His love is *infinite*. Therefore, it completes the soul, unites with it, gives it the sign of eternal salvation, lives in it, and becomes the soul of our souls, and so, that unification with our souls begins in this world and continues into Eternity, which will be its outmost happiness, our unspoken joy.

It is *immeasurable*. Therefore, it was not enough for Him to give us all the other Sacraments, through which He gives us his holy graces in all circumstances of our life from birth to death. However, this was not enough to His love because it knows no measure. Therefore, He gives not only His graces in this Most Blessed Sacrament, but He gives Himself.

It is *almighty*. The almightiness of Jesus can be seen and recognized in all of the Sacraments. There is no other Sacrament though, in which his love is shown as mightily as it is displayed in the Most Blessed Sacrament in which He himself lives. Only the almighty love was able to make Him move to the humbly image of bread, to dwell among us and to remain among us, even though we know so little about His exceedingly wonderful love and we give so little in return.

It is *incomprehensible*. Who will ever be able to understand this incomprehensible Sacrament of Jesus' love? It is not only impossible for us who are weak creatures, but also for the angels who always pray to Him in the Blessed Sacrament. They can only wonder, but cannot understand, how their and our Lord and God was able to go so far in His love for people. And even in the happy Infinity when we will not see Him through mysterious images, but face to face, His immeasurable love to us will be an eternal and continuously new astonishment.

The soul finds its most beautiful and most effective aid in this Blessed Sacrament. If you want, my dear Christian, to gain eternal salvation, and you certainly want this, strive to receive Holy Communion frequently and as worthily as possible. Whoever neglects this Blessed Sacrament, shows that he or she does not possess a true and burning desire to be redeemed. Jesus tells us that if we do not eat His flesh and drink His blood, i.e., if we do not receive Holy Communion, there will be no life in us, i.e., eternal life in heaven. And He states further that *"Whoever eats my flesh and drinks my blood has eternal life, and I will raise him on the last day."*

According to the words explained this way and such loving promises of our merciful Jesus, it is truly impossible not to develop a true and burning desire to be redeemed, and to neglect this Most Blessed Sacrament through which Jesus wants to bestow holy salvation upon us.

Then, my dear Christian, lovingly receive Him often, and as worthily as possible. In this way, you will recognize more thoroughly how this Most Blessed Sacrament is an abundant source of graces and aids. Jesus speaks to us in this Sacrament: "*I am the bread of life; whoever comes to me will never hunger, and whoever believes in me will never thirst.*" Therefore, visit Him often and lovingly, and your soul will not starve: "*filled with the fruit of righteousness that comes through Jesus Christ for the glory and praise of God.*"

Whatever your soul needs, ask Jesus in Holy Communion. He will give you everything according to His holy will. As God once said to wise King Salomon: "[…] *Whatever you ask I shall give you.*" So does Jesus in the Blessed Sacrament tell your soul.

Think sometimes, my dear Christian, *who Jesus is* whom you receive in the Holy Communion. You will get to know more and more about how unspeakably He loves you. In this way you will love Him more and more, and will never be afraid of anything more in this world than of sin which insults your Jesus.

1. Jesus is *your Lord and your God*. The eternal God is Jesus, God's Son, eternal Son of eternal Father. Through His infinite mercy he became man, equal to us in all things but sin. Sin, this terrible wickedness, drew man away from even approaching God, let alone from being one with Him. Then God – oh, this incomprehensible mercy! God approached man, became one with him, took into His eternal and divine nature broken human nature and became fully human, although He did not cease to be God. Jesus especially lets us know this in the Most Blessed Sacrament. Here, angels, archangels and all holy men pray to Him. Here, a man receives Him and becomes fully one with Him; a sign that a man has

reconciled with God and that he is ready there to the delight of his God to be eternally united with Him.

2. Jesus is your *redeemer*. He saved your life. Not only your earthly life, as sometimes a person saves another person's life, but He saved your eternal life. Without Him, it would be completely impossible to gain eternal, heavenly life. Without Him, the immortality of your soul would become your greatest and infinite misery. In this Most Blessed Sacrament, Jesus gives you to eat from His living bread of heaven in order to preserve the life He saved for you.

3. Jesus is your *father*. He is that benevolent father who receives His lost son with heartfelt goodness when he returns back to Him. Think, my dear Christian, how many times you were accepted by Him in the Sacrament of Penance, although you deserved so many times to be cast away from His face because of your unfaithfulness and ingratitude. And after being received kindly and embraced by Him, as a sign of a heartfelt reconciliation and forgiveness, He leads you to His table and offers you infinitely better food than the father offered to his converted son in the Holy Scripture.

4. Jesus is your *brother*. He declares to you in the Holy Scripture "*I am going to my Father and your Father, to my God and your God.*" He further says that the person who will fulfill the will of His Father, will be His brother and His sister. Therefore, if you truly want, if you truly strive to fulfil God's will, then Jesus is always your brother. And he wants to unite with you in the Blessed Sacrament in order to show you His infinite love more and to share His graces more abundantly.

5. Jesus is your *friend*. He said to His apostles that if they do what He commands them to do, they will be His friends. He says the same to you. He has pledged His word to you, and if you live according to His holy teachings, He will be your friend. He is such a faithful friend

that He even called Judas His friend at the moment he came to betray Him. How much more will He recognize you as His friend when you will come to Him without betraying Him to His enemies, but accepting Him in your heart with love.

6. Jesus is your *teacher*. He is your "only and good teacher." All that is worthy to be known, you were taught by Jesus. Only He has the words of eternal life. Only He revealed the truths that are eternally valuable to be known. All the rest that you know is empty; it is nothing. Saint Paul, who was such a knowledgeable man, realized that all he knew is nothing compared to the supreme knowledge that he received from Jesus. Jesus teaches you all the beautiful virtues in the Blessed Sacrament. Listen faithfully with the ears of your soul and with a clean and peaceful heart to how He teaches you to surrender yourself in all things to the will of the Heavenly Father. Be meek and humble from your heart. Be obedient and patient, pure, and decent, faithful and pious in the service of God. Be full of firm faith and live by it. Be full of holy trust and reject all worldly. Be full of heartfelt love for God and because of God to all people. He accomplished all these works and He teaches you to do the same if you contemplate Him in the Blessed Sacrament in the right way. You will be happy if you sit at His feet with Mary and listen to Him.

7. Jesus is your *soul's healer*. In the holy Sacrament of Penance, He heals your soul from all of its wounds and ailments. In Holy Communion, He gives your soul the best tools to ward off future sins, which are a sickness of a soul. The Council of Trent states that *"the most holy Eucharist is a medicine that cleanses us from our daily offenses and protects us from mortal sin."* As when He lived on this earth, Jesus opened the eyes of the blind, unstopped the ears of the deaf and caused the muted tongue to shout for joy, so does He do to your soul if you receive

Him in this holy Sacrament often, with joy and as worthily as possible. He lets the soul see and realize His infinite beauty and kindness and becomes one with it, so that the soul cannot depart from Him any longer; all worldly joy becomes nauseating and all worldly beauty seems unpleasant.

He allows the soul to hear and understand the inner voice of His love with which He invites the soul to Himself, leads it to the desert of its heart and speaks there kindly about what He wants the soul to accomplish and to contribute with actions, leaving the soul less and less susceptible to worldly temptations. He lets the soul talk to the Lord, its God. He gives it the grace of inner prayer through which the soul talks to Him as if it were looking at Him from face to face.

8. Jesus is your *spiritual shepherd.* He is the good shepherd who gave His life for you, His beloved sheep. Moreover, He prepared an infinitely good pasture for the soul in His holy teachings that you hear always through preaching, and in His grace, which He is always giving you. However, this was not enough of His love for you. He gives Himself in the Blessed Sacrament and feeds you with the living bread that came from heaven to keep you in the eternal life because whoever eats from this bread will live forever. This is the good shepherd because he feeds His beloved sheep with the heavenly bread of the pasture which is His Holy Body.

9. Jesus is *the bridegroom of your soul.* A good bridegroom loves his bride, is faithful to her, nurtures her, takes care of her, is patient and kind to her, and looks for ways to make her happy as much as He can. From this, learn what a good bridegroom Jesus is to your soul. His love for your soul is infinite when the soul is in God's grace. You will never be able to completely know and understand His love for you, neither in this life nor in eternity. Eternity will not be long enough to think about this love.

He is always and firmly faithful to you. It is your soul that is often unfaithful. However, He does not abandon it immediately, but takes it in His grace when the soul returns to Him with love, and regrets its infidelity. He cares benevolently for the soul and feeds it with *"the miraculous bread"* that keeps it beautiful and healthy if the soul strives to receive Him with humility and gratitude. He patiently endures its weaknesses and He warns the soul and teaches it. For the soul to become stronger, He gives it to eat *"the bread of the strong"*. *"He got up, ate, and drank; then strengthened by that food, he walked forty days and forty nights to the mountain of God, Horeb."* The soul that is Jesus' bride is happy, it is happy in His love. It suffers greatly on this earth because it does not look its beloved Jesus directly, face to face, because it is always surrounded by temptations and in great danger of offending and losing Him. The soul wants to achieve the state in which there will be no more temptation, where it will be completely impossible to commit the slightest sin. These wishes and this hope console the soul when it is facing troubles, confirm it in good, and rekindle its burning desire to be united with Jesus in the Blessed Sacrament where it will be united with Him eternally.

10. Jesus is *the way and the truth and the life*. He is that narrow way that leads to heaven that is sometimes difficult, thorny and steep. It is short if you think about it in a right way because the longest life here on earth is nothing compared to eternity. That one is long which is without an end. Because there will be trouble on this way, it will be good if you walk faithfully with Jesus who will be always next to you. When you will get tired, He will kindly say to you: *"Come to me, all you who labor and are burdened, and I will give you rest."* In the Blessed Sacrament, He gives you the nutritious dish that helps you walk day and night, continuously, on the way that is Himself. He is the eternal truth that talks in the Holy Scriptures. He

has the words of eternal life. His words are eternal and will never pass away. *"Heaven and earth will pass away, but my words will not pass away.* His words are true, and happy are those who listen to them, hold to them and act according to them in all things. He is life and it is only He who gives life: *"through him was life, and this life was the light of human race."* He does not only give earthly life, but the eternal as well. He is the living bread and *"whoever eats this bread will live forever."* See then, my dear Christian, what Jesus is to you. Think often who Jesus is and how fortunate you are to receive Him, as worthily as possible, in the Blessed Sacrament. If you do not want to accept Him often, you are not being mindful of who He is. If you would think thoroughly and realize who Jesus is, you would wish from all your heart to receive Him often and would strive to live in a way that would allow you to approach His table often and to receive Him always as worthily as possible.

How often one should receive Holy Communion cannot be answered because this needs to be decided on a case-by-case basis. It would be appropriate if all Christians would strive to receive Holy Communion at least once a month; some even more often.

My dear Christian, try to be among those who often receive Holy Communion. However, do nothing without permission from your good and caring confessor. If you want to come even closer to Jesus, and if you feel that Holy Communion makes you more faithful in the fulfilling of your duties and more zealous in your love for God and for your neighbor, tell this to your confessor and ask him to allow you to approach the table of the Lord often. After that, completely submit to his will.

One can never receive Holy Communion too often if the person received it in honor of God and for the salvation of his or her soul, because this is the real reason why Jesus gave us the Blessed Sacrament. The First

Christians, who were almost all saints, "[…] *devoted them-selves to meeting together in the temple area and to breaking bread in their homes. They ate their meals with exultation and sincerity of heart.*" This is Holy Communion. Saint Ambrose says that you should live in a way that you could receive Holy Communion every day. It is desirable that the daily bread of the soul would be received every day.

Receiving Holy Communion does *often* not save you *per se*, but does produce a worthy will in you. If you do not strive to live in such a way that you are always pre-pared to approach the Lord's table as worthily as possi-ble, frequent Holy Communion will be your ruin. If you truly strive to live faithfully according to Jesus' teachings and examples, to love God above all and your neighbor for God's and for your sake, there will be nothing else that would confirm you in goodness and keep you as will receiving Holy Communion frequently, as Jesus will truly remain in you and you in Him. You will live, but not you, Christ will live in you.

Fear no worldly misfortune more, my dear Christian, than being *unworthy of receiving Holy Communion*. If a per-son knows that he or she has a mortal sin and did not confess it, or if a person confessed, but was not absolved from the sin, yet comes to God's table and receives Holy Communion, this person received it unworthily. This is a terrible sin, a sacrilege, the sin of Judas Iscariot of whom Jesus said he "*is a devil.*" It has been said that when he re-ceived the Most Holy Body of Christ from Jesus' hands at the last supper "*Satan entered him.*"

How horrible this serious sin is can be seen from the words of St. Paul: "*Therefore whoever eats the bread or drinks the cup of the Lord* [i.e., receives Holy Communion] *unwor-thily will have to answer for the body and blood of the Lord.*", i.e., will commit an equal sin committed by those Jews and non-believers who nailed Christ's body to the cross and shed His blood. As this same holy apostle says someplace else that great sinners "[…] *are recrucifying the Son of God for themselves.*" He says further: "*For anyone who eats and drinks* [i.e., who receives Holy Communion] *without discerning the body, eats and drinks judgement on himself.*"

The most holy Body of Christ, which is the most wonderful food and the most effective medicine for our soul is the most horrible poison, condemning to eternal damnation those who receive it unworthily. This wonderful mystery of Jesus' love that He gave our souls as a pledge of eternal salvation and eternal unification with Him, becomes to such a one, the source of endless suffering through removal from God. This living bread that came to us from heaven to take us to Him into heaven becomes condemnation to eternal death for Him, or much more, eternal life in suffering. This heavenly manna that comes from heaven to save us from the power of the wicked enemy and to confirm us in the holy and salvific worship, becomes condemnation for him to the eternal slavery under the evil Satan who was responsible for Christ's apostle to receive Holy Communion unworthily, and who leads all those who receive it unworthily into a horrible sin.

Oh, how horrible these things are! Oh, my dear Christian! I recommend to you once more: do not fear a bigger misfortune in this world than the *unworthy Communion.*

If you were so unfortunate and have received Holy Communion in a mortal sin, although you knew that you had a mortal sin, think whether you truly regretted this horrible sin, have thoroughly confessed and have faithfully done all that your confessor recommended to you. If you do not remember very well that you have done all this, do not hesitate to confess it thoroughly at the first possible occasion and say clearly that you hate your sin with all your heart and repent. Ask God in Jesus' name to forgive you the sin and conclude firmly to never commit it again. Ask your confessor to give you a special penance for this sin. If it is necessary, make a long confession, as faithfully and completely as possible.

In order to avoid receiving Holy Communion unworthily in the future, think often about what was just said about this horrible sin. Further, think about these words of the apostle Paul: *"A person should examine himself, and so eat the bread and drink the cup."* He says further that before you receive Holy Communion, you must prepare thoroughly for Confession, question your conscience exhaustively and explain all this precisely to your confessor. If you receive absolution from your sin and permission to receive Holy Communion, then receive this Blessed Sacrament.

Think well, my dear Christian, further on what St. Paul says. Next to questioning your conscience and having confessed, you have to think thoroughly about *the state of your soul in general.* Think then, whether you did not turn away from a sin on an occasion in which you could if you really wanted; if you are a good friend to all people; if you speak friendly to all when you have the opportunity; if you did not damage the people near you in any way and if you have returned everything; if you have already corrected your possible indecencies as much as possible; if you have a true and transcendent wish to love God more and to do everything that is pleasing to Him and to dismiss what is offensive to Him out of love for Him.

If you ask yourself in this way and learn, and if your conscience does not contradict you in anything important, come humbly to the table of God and trust firmly that you will not receive Holy Communion unworthily.

Books of the holy teachers of the Church show some horrible examples how God punished those Christians who approached His table unworthily.

To exemplify, writes Saint Cyprian, there was a Christian woman in mortal sin who attended God's table and received the Blessed Sacrament. However, shortly after that she started feeling as if someone were strangling her, her whole body was shaking and she fell dead to the ground. St. Cyprian says further that God sometimes punishes sacrilege already in this world so as to scare Christians and make them more conscious.

It is this same holy teacher who wrote that there was a Christian woman who wanted to receive Holy Communion, although she was in mortal sin. When she tried to approach God's holy table, fire burst towards her and forced her to move back. She was lucky if she realized that this fire symbolized the eternal fire of hell that she deserved because of her horrible sin.

Our most horrible example is the first unworthy Holy Communion ever taken in this world. Who can remember without horror Judas's reception of Holy Communion and the punishment upon him. He, who was full of evil thoughts, sat down for the last supper and accepted the Eucharist from the hands of the benevolent Savior without any realization of His eternal goodness; therefore, instead of God's grace, the living Satan entered his heart after receiving the Eucharist. As soon as he received Him, he stood up and went to sell Jesus to His enemies.

And then, this unlucky human gave up on his salvation and finished his life in a horrible way.

Think about the fruit of the first Holy Communion received unworthily, i.e., a disciple and friend of Jesus got obsessed by Satan. God's Son is sold to the Jews. The apostle of Christ despairs and is damned forever.

Think now, my dear Christian, how you have to prepare to receive Holy Communion in order to receive it as worthily as possible. The best preparation to receive Holy Communion is to live a holy life as a Christian. Whoever lives a saintly life is always united with Jesus in a heartfelt love. When such a person receives Him in the Blessed Sacrament, he or she unites even more closely with Him.

Furthermore, always prepare separately with great zeal when you are allowed to approach Lord's Table. After you have cleansed your conscience of sin in the holy Sacrament of Penance, ask God cordially, especially in the evening at Evening Prayer (Vespers) before receiving Holy Communion, and at the morning prayer on that day you would like to receive Holy Communion, to give you grace to receive Him humbly and to His liking so that this Blessed Sacrament would not be a source of your damnation, but for the eternal salvation of your soul. Think a lot about this happiness and the grace of accepting the living God and think how impossible it would be to prepare a worthy and likeable dwelling for Him by your own strength. When King David built a temple for the Lord so that He would have an earthly dwelling, he realized, how little he could do to prepare a worthy residence. Although God did not choose David to build Him a house, God was pleased by his good thoughts. So will your thoughts be likeable to Him as you prepare Him a pleasant dwelling in your heart if they will be united with wholehearted and humble requests and with true effort.

Here are some recommendations for how to prepare for receiving Holy Communion.

1. *Humble* yourself before the Lord, your God, as much as you can and realize that you are completely unworthy on your own to receive Him. Think who God is and who you are; think about His immeasurable and infinite greatness and holiness, and then think how poor, weak and wicked you are. The humbler you are before God, the more He will prefer to come to you and become one with you, because God likes to look after the poor and the humble; He comes close to them and draws them to Himself. However, all those presumptuous, haughty, and

wise (based on the wisdom of the world) He leaves to their own wisdom, which is foolishness before God, and He turns away from them.

2. Pray to Jesus in the Most Blessed Sacrament in which you will soon unite with Him. If you have time, it would be good for you to pray to Jesus every day in this incomprehensible mystery. Pray to Him with all your heart especially when you prepare to receive Him. Ask Him with trust and in His name (because He said *"If you ask anything of me in my name, I will do it."*) to forgive you everything that you have done so far against His holy will.

3. Reignite a true *faith* in your heart as you would see Jesus in the Blessed Sacrament. Believe even more firmly as you would if you would see Him with your earthly eyes because eyes deceive us often, but God's love never does. Do not look at Jesus here with your bodily eyes, but with the eyes of your soul. If you only look with your bodily eyes, you only see outward images that are of little value. By looking with the eyes of your soul, you will see Him at the seat of mercy, surrounded by God's angels who pray to Him in this unimaginable mystery of His love to people.

4. Rekindle a firm and invincible *trust* in Jesus in the Blessed Sacrament. Here He is truly at the seat of mercy that St. Paul speaks about, saying: *"So let us confidently approach the throne of grace to receive mercy and to find grace for timely help."* Think, my dear Christian, who Jesus is in the most Blessed Sacrament (as was already mentioned) and reflect what He gives you here, and your heart will be filled with great trust toward Him. He gives you the biggest gift here, namely Himself. Trust then that He will not decline giving you smaller gifts after he just gave you the biggest gift, to His honor and to bring your soul in salvation.

5. Awaken a heartfelt and burning *love* for Him. Love is especially necessary for receiving Holy Communion as worthily as possible. If you would be capable of loving Jesus as much as He loves you, you would accept Him completely worthy. However, it is not possible for you; therefore, your value will grow toward perfection with your growing love.

Love is that wedding garment your soul needs to put on when it comes before its Heavenly Groom and wants to be liked. Jesus' love for us manifests itself in all Sacraments because out of love, He shares us graces through them. However, there is no Sacrament where this would be more clearly and beautifully shown as through the Blessed Sacrament. This truly is the Sacrament of His love for us. Therefore, prepare, my dear Christian, to receive this Blessed Sacrament with special love. However, this love should not only be displayed in words and feelings, but must be shown in actions, in faithful fulfillment of all your duties, commandments and teachings that Jesus gives you. It must be shown in avoiding sin because it offends Jesus, and especially in love for your neighbor because it is Jesus whom you will see in the person of your neighbor. If your heart is filled with such love for Jesus, He will love to get into your heart and remain there.

6. When you are preparing to receive Holy Communion, remember always that Jesus gave us this Blessed Sacrament *as a remembrance of His suffering and His death*. We learn this from His own words at the Last Supper: "[…] *do this in memory of me*". The same can be seen in the words of St. Paul: "*For as often as you eat this bread and drink this cup, you proclaim the death of the Lord until he comes*." Remember then that your merciful Savior took willingly His suffering upon Himself and concluded it with His death on the cross soon after the Last Supper at which He administered this Blessed Sacrament to His

Holy Church. Be sincerely grateful to Him for His unimaginable love and ask Him to make you a part of His endless merit.

You are happy, my dear Christian, when you receive Holy Communion well prepared. For this great fortune and grace thank Jesus through Holy Communion. Here is some advice for your gratitude as was previously given for the preparation.

1. Be *amazed* at the eternal and unimaginable love of your Jesus. Then, thank Him from all your heart that he did not look upon your sins, your unfaithfulness, and unthankfulness, but on the needs of your soul. He came to make your soul happy and to rejuvenate it with the Living Bread which gives eternal heavenly life to all those who receive it with love and gratitude. Be amazed with cordial gratitude that your Lord and God comes to visit you, poor thing. St. Elizabeth said in her amazement: *"And how does this happen to me, that the mother of my Lord should come to me?"* On the contrary, the Lord Himself comes to visit you, the eternal, almighty God. Then say with humble amazement: Where does this good fortune come from that my God comes to me? And then realize that this fortune comes from His infinite love alone and not from your worthiness.

2. Because you believe and acknowledge that God Himself comes to you through the Blessed Sacrament, *pray* to Him as angels pray to Him in this incomprehensible mystery. If you are so blessed that you are allowed to approach the holy table and receive Holy Communion, you can justly say with St. Paul that Jesus lives in you. Remember how happy you are and do not waste such a pleasant opportunity to pray to Jesus, completely submit to Him and ask Him to bestow you with plenty of His graces. Jesus is always and everywhere present because He is your God. However, He is especially present when He completely gives Himself to you in Holy

Communion. As He completely gives Himself to you, so should you give yourself all to Him. Give Him all your heart and do not split it between Him and other things. Give Him your entire soul so that only He will be the Master of your soul – your most inner soul. Give Him all your thoughts and your wishes so that all your thoughts will face only Him and His Holy Law and that you will never wish for anything else but to fulfill His holy will always and everywhere. Ask Him in this happy hour to give you all that you need for your soul and body. Ask Him for virtues, especially for those you need the most. Ask Him especially for meekness and humility because He especially recommends these two to learn from Him. Ask Him for obedience to God and to people as He was obedient to God and to people, obedient until His death, even until His death on the cross. Ask him for holy patience so that you will willingly carry your cross after Him for the rest of your life and will come by the way of the cross to His kingdom. Ask Him to give you His holy blessing and tell Him with a loving heart which He likes "[…] *to bring a blessing upon yourselves this day.*"

3. Besides asking Jesus to grant you grace to obtain beautiful Christian virtues and to live in them, resolve firmly that you will *use* His graces *faithfully*. Do not think that you will be able to acquire all virtues with mere prayer. Prayer is truly necessary to acquire virtues as without prayer, nobody gained true Christian virtues. However, prayer is not enough. Next to prayer, there has to be a true and permanent effort to fulfill God's will in all things. Not everybody who says "Master, Master," will be redeemed, but only the one who will live according to God's will. Resolve firmly, my dear Christian, in the happy hour after your Holy Communion that you will always faithfully fulfill God's will in all your Christian duties. Remember then your venial sins and weaknesses and resolve firmly to avoid them for now on even more

carefully. In addition, ask Jesus to give you grace so that you will truly improve yourself. After receiving Holy Communion, do not forget immediately what promises you made to Jesus when He was in you at the happy hour of the Holy Communion.

Ask Jesus in this happy hour to strengthen you in your *faith*. He gave us the holy faith and all that we know about God, and He revealed to us all eternal truths. Ask Him to give you a heartfelt faith that will manifest itself in your life so that you will learn from it *"the righteousness of God from faith to faith."*

Ask Him to strengthen your *trust* so that all your trust will be in Him, in His marvelous love, in His eternal merit, in His holy name: *"There is no salvation through anyone else, nor is there any other name under heaven given to the human race by which we are to be saved."*

Ask Him to fill your heart with *love*. He is love, and all holy love only comes from Him. He is the groom of your soul when it is in God's grace. Ask Him to multiply your love for your neighbor, which He cherishes so much that He regards all good done to our neighbor as if it were done for Him.

Pray to Jesus after receiving Holy Communion, my dear Christian, for everything you need for your body and soul and pray for all those for whom you are obliged to pray. Trust that your requests and prayers which you make in that happy hour when Jesus lives in you will be especially answered if they are for the honor of God and the salvation of your soul.

Spend *"the day of Holy Communion"* nicely and as a Christian. *"[…] there shall be a declared holy day for you; no heavy work may be done."*

1. On Sundays, be especially faithful and diligent in the service of God. During the week, come to church as much as your other duties allow you. Do not follow the example of those unfaithful Christians who leave church

soon after receiving Holy Communion. (Only a great force and necessity, or some mighty work of Christian love can justify them). Whoever leaves church soon after Holy Communion unnecessarily, acts as Judas did, when he "[…] *took the morsel and left at once. And it was night.*"

2. Spend your entire day peacefully and quietly. Speak only as much as is necessary and as much as is appropriate. On that day, do not socialize if it is not necessary. It would be even less appropriate if you would enjoy some worldly pleasure. Restrain from unnecessary talking, rejoicing and laughter at home as well. Think that you have unified with Jesus today about whom it is written that he cried, but never that he smiled.

3. If anyone comes to visit you on that day, be especially careful not to slander against the love of God and against the neighbor. Think that today Jesus put Himself on your tongue by his infinite goodness. Therefore, do not whip Him with this tongue. Do not return his incomprehensible love for you in this way. Whoever talks badly about his neighbor, beats Jesus with an even sharper whip than was used by the Jews.

4. Read some good holy books on that day if it is possible for you. When you are praying, you are talking to God. When you read holy books, God is talking to you. St. Paul tells you always "[…] *attend to the reading* […]" as he did once to his spiritual son, Timothy. Reading holy books is especially recommended on the day you receive Holy Communion.

5. It is good and decent that you go and visit Jesus in the Blessed Sacrament on the day when you will also receive Him. If possible, make the visit, and do it with especial love and fervor so that you at least give back a little bit to Jesus for His infinite love for you.

6. Think thoroughly about how you have spent that day during evening prayer. Thank Jesus once again for this great grace He gave you, repeat your good intentions

and promise to live only for Jesus and ask Him to give you grace to keep Him always in your heart with love until you are allowed again to approach His holy table.

XIII.

THE MASS AND VISITS TO THE BLESSED SACRAMENT

"Lord, to whom shall we go? You
have the words of eternal life."

My beloved Christian, when you attend Mass or when you come to visit the Blessed Sacrament, you really come before Jesus, one's Lord and God. If you listen to Him faithfully and let Him speak to your heart, you will clearly hear the words that give eternal life.

Before I continue speaking about the most holy mysteries, I suggest that you think about how holy are our churches in which the holy mysteries are celebrated and preserved.

Every Christian Catholic Church is a House of God and is thus a holy place. *"There they will put the most holy offerings—the grain offerings, the sin offerings and the guilt offerings—for the place is holy.* You should enter this place with holy fear as *"This is none other than the house of God; this is the gate of heaven."* You should attend church with holy thoughts and purposes because *"holiness adorns your house."*

Those who do not respect God's house commit a sin and dishonor God. This is a sin committed by all those who inappropriately look around while in church, who sleep instead of praying or listening to the Word of God, who, with no reason, speak or laugh, and who mostly attend church to look at persons of the opposite sex and vice versa. Speaking with Christ, all those who act in this way deserve to be hit by lightning as they dare to commit dishonor in God's own house.

Everything you see in church shall fill your heart with feelings of holiness and respect.

Holy water shall remind you that whenever attending church, you should clean your heart and soul from all unnecessary and obscene thoughts. In the old days, the Israelites had to cleanse themselves with water prior to performing God's service in the temple, although their cleansing was predominantly an external gesture and their heart remained deaf due to injustices. This is the reason why in the new liturgy Jesus offered to clean our hearts more than our hands if we want to pray to God truly and in spirit. When you sprinkle yourself with holy water, you should remember that the House of God deserves holiness, and therefore drive away all unholy thoughts that do not belong in God's service as well as ask God to cleanse your heart and soul.

The confessional shall remind you that it is the place where God, your benevolent father, approaches you as if you were the lost son wanting to return to Him after fulfilling real penance. It should remind you about God's endless mercy and warn about God's harsh judgment during which God will not call you before Him to forgive your sins, but to condemn you to eternal suffering if you won't truly repent.

The pulpit shall remind you of God's glorious teachings which can be heard from there so many times. How fortunate you are to have the opportunity to hear God's Word so many times. You will be even happier by keeping it always in your heart and living by it because *"Blessed rather are those who hear the Word of God and obey it."* My dear Christian, you are not aware enough how happy and grateful you should be to God when you have the opportunity always to hear the Word of God? Here, I surmise, in this land of millions, are many Christians who, due to lack of priests, rarely hear God's Word, albeit they very much wish to do so. For example, there are many Christians who almost never hear the Word of God when they have to travel to distant places. Oh, how these Christians would be happy if they would have the same opportunity as the one you have. If you do not turn your opportunities more faithfully toward your own salvation, these abandoned Christians will protest against you at God's judgment. Whenever you see the pulpit, you should commit to listen always to God's Word faithfully and to live up to it.

Images of the suffering Jesus shall remind you of His eternal love for a person and your ingratitude toward Him. You should be amazed at His love and regret your own ingratitude. It is sad and indecent when a Christian goes by the image of the crucified or suffering Jesus without any thoughts or feelings. This is exactly why the Holy Christian Church keeps and honors the images of Jesus so that they would awaken holy and loving thoughts and feelings toward God in our heart.

Images of saints shall remind you how these friends of God lived beautifully here on earth. How much they endured out of love for God and how happy they are in heaven where God wiped off their tears and turned their short-lasting sorrow into eternal happiness. You should remember that you have been called to this eternal happiness as well, and that you will certainly receive if you try truly. This is exactly the reason why you come to church: to serve God as saints served Him and to hear that preaching helps you gain eternal happiness.

The altar shall remind you that this is the exact place where Jesus – who offered His life on the cross for the salvation of the world – offers Himself during the Holy Mass to His Heavenly Father. The only distinction is that He does not literally shed His blood here as He did once and for all when He was nailed to a cross.

The tabernacle shall remind you about Jesus' presence as He is always present there in our midst in the Blessed Sacrament. It is this beautiful mystery that makes the church truly a House of God. The smallest and poorest church which houses Jesus in the Most Blessed Sacrament is more eminent than was Salomon's temple which all glittered in gold and housed the Ark of the Covenant containing two stone tablets onto which God, our Lord, wrote His commandments. God, our Lord, is present there as the only source of holiness and justice.

Look, my dear Christian, how many holy things and holy memories are kept in a church. If you misbehave in a church and do not think about where you are, you dishonor God in His own house. However, all those people who behave nicely and appropriately in church are not automatically considered to be pious and good Christians, but all those who behave inappropriately in church are surely bad and unworthy Christians.

You need to behave nicely and decently, especially while attending Mass as it is the most holy and sacred service of the Holy Catholic Church. Here, Jesus offers Himself to His Heavenly Father as He did once on the cross with the difference that back then it was a bloody sacrifice and now it is not. Imagine, my dear Christian, that while attending Mass, you are with the Virgin Mary under the cross on which Jesus offers Himself to God for your own salvation and for the salvation of all people. You should connect your thoughts as much as you can with thoughts that the most holy Virgin Mother had when she offered her beloved Son for the salvation of the world. And you should pray to Him in union with the holy angels who always pray to Him in this unimaginable mystery.

My beloved Christian should think continuously about what kind of offering the Holy Mass is and why Jesus always offers Himself to His Heavenly Father.

1. As Jesus offered Himself on the cross to His Father to *honor Him highly* with His own love and repentance, so does He always offer Himself during Mass for the multiplication and elevation of His Godly honor. The Holy Christian and Catholic Church cannot honor God in any other way better than through the offering of the Holy Mass, as the prophet Malachi prophesied four hundred years before Christ, saying: "*My name will be great among the nations, from where the sun rises to where it sets. In every place incense and pure offerings will be brought to me, because my name will be great among the nations.*"

2. Jesus offered Himself on the cross to God, His Father, for the *forgiveness of sins of the entire world.* This innocent lamb of God took the sins of all people upon Himself, from Adam to the last person to live on this earth. With nails, with which His holy body was nailed to the cross, "*our legal indebtedness*" was nailed and shown as well. This was to prevent our eternal doom. This is why Jesus, while being nailed to the cross, explicitly asked God for His killers too, so that God would forgive them – that they would be with Him in heaven. So does Jesus offer Himself during the Holy Mass to His Heavenly Father for the forgiveness of our sins. Not that His sacrifice on the cross would be defective because "*he entered the Most Holy Place once for all by his own blood, thus obtaining eternal redemption.*" On the contrary, it was the sacrifice on the cross which He keeps repeating during the Holy Mass for the forgiveness of our sins.

3. While on the cross, Jesus acquired for us not only the forgiveness of sins, but also *all other graces* so that without the eternal grace of Jesus' death, people were never able to obtain the smallest grace from God. All that is necessary for our salvation comes from Jesus, and without Him we are nothing but dust. Jesus is "*the sun of righteousness.*" Just as life cannot exist on earth without the sun (because if the sun would seize to exist, all life

would soon come to an end), so is our soul not able to exist without Jesus. If our soul leaves Jesus and moves away from Him, it perishes forever. It is by offering the Holy Mass that Jesus shares His greatest mercies with Christians. The Mass is the lasting and abundant source of all God's graces. The Holy Church cannot perform any other better or mightier prayer, piety or devotion when it wants to obtain mercy from God than to celebrate the Holy Mass. This can be observed in the Church in all great needs. During Mass, the priest asks God for all people in the name of Jesus, who, upon the hands of the priest, offers Himself to the Heavenly Father as He did on the cross for all people.

4. When all was done and fulfilled by Jesus for the salvation of the world, He said loudly and with a happy and grateful heart while being nailed to the holy cross: *"it is finished."* Oh, how grateful to God and unspeakably happy Jesus' heart was when He saw His tremendous suffering with which He saved the whole world from the eternal suffering finished! On the Mount of Olives Jesus asked His Father with His face covered in blood to take His suffering from Him. But this was not God's will. He had to endure suffering. Now, it was finished. Oh, how happy and grateful His heart is now. So does the Holy Mother Catholic Church with its holy happiness celebrate and offer the Holy Mass to the Heavenly Father and thank Him in the name of Jesus for all His graces and good deeds. When God grants some special grace to Christians, the Holy Church cannot thank Him better than with the Holy Mass.

My dear Christian, if you thoroughly think about all this, you will recognize that the Holy Mass is the most prominent, the most holy and the best among all works which are offered by the holy Christian and Catholic Church. Thus, you should be happy when you find an opportunity to attend the Holy Mass. Happy are those who are able to attend this most holy offering every day.

When you attend the Holy Mass, you should pray with the expected piety. Prayer books offer prayers which are recited during Mass. You should pray more with your heart than with your mouth. You should never lose this merciful time of the Holy Mass. When at Mass, you should forget about your current tasks and troubles as well as timely works and only think about what is happening at the very moment. Time at the Holy Mass passes quickly. A priest always goes on with his holy work. If you think about something else during the Holy Mass, you will miss a part of the Mass.

Oh, how many God-given graces will you receive if you pray holy and devoutly during Mass. When you are devoutly attending Mass, you are, so to speak on Mount Calvary under the cross on which Jesus sacrificed Himself to God, His Father. There, you can hear Him pray for His killers. Look, if He asks His Father for His killers, how much more will He ask His Father for you who love Him. Jesus *"is at the right hand of God and is also interceding for us."* This thought should fill your heart with even greater love for Him. Oh, how happy we are whenever we can approach God, the Father, through our worthiness and in the name of Jesus *"because he always lives to intercede for [us]"*. You can see Him there, on the holy cross, lovingly accepting the repentant sinner into His mercy. *"Today you will be with me in paradise"* He is telling the repentant criminal on His right. If your conscience burns during the Holy Mass because of grave sins you have committed, you should not give in to them. You should like to attend Mass. You should imagine being on Mount Calvary below Christ's cross; you should repent and hate your sins from the bottom of your heart. You should decide to truly improve yourself and lift the eyes of your soul and look at Jesus who is nailed to the cross in unspeakable suffering. You should say to Him with true trustworthiness: "*Jesus, remember me when you come into your kingdom.*" Then, you shall remember that He is now in His kingdom where He prepared a place for everyone who has decided to improve in loving God continuously.

You can see Mary Magdalene there, the repentant woman, embracing the cross with her wholehearted and burning love and with an unspoken gratitude toward Jesus who has saved her soul from condemnation and whom "*her many sins have been forgiven—as her great love has shown.*" Trust! You will be forgiven if you start loving Him with a full heart and do so persistently.

My beloved Christian, if you memorize this, you will pray with great trust and transcend love during Mass and will receive many graces from Jesus. While being here on earth, Jesus has always distributed goodness and grace to people. The greatest graces given by Him to people were through the Holy Cross. Thus, He loves to share His grace among people whenever they ask Him. He gives abundantly when people with living faith and firm trust ask Him for grace while He sacrifices Himself on the altar to His Heavenly Father.

My dear Christian, you can see how Christians can become sinners when they inappropriately behave in church, in the House of God, where such holy and un-imaginable mysteries are celebrated. Here, you can find some examples to help you recognize this.

The Holy Bible tells the parable how God became offended when in the Jerusalem Temple, which was not as holy as our churches are, dishonor took place. This Temple housed a lot of silver and gold that the king of Asia desired. He thus sent Heliodorus to Jerusalem to obtain this gold and silver. As Heliodorus presump-tuously entered the Temple to fulfill the task given to him by his king, he found out how sacred this place was and how people offend God by behaving obscenely and sinfully. Two angels approached him and beat him to the extent that he was almost dead when carried out of the temple. If God were not so merciful and patient, how many times would angels, who always pray to Jesus in the Most Blessed Sacrament, come and beat up the obscene and sinful Christians who only enter God's House to dishonor God in His own House. *"If anyone destroys God's temple, God will destroy that person; for God's temple is sacred, and you together are that temple,"* says St. Paul.

The second example shows how offended God was when the Jerusalem Temple was dishonored as can be found in the Holy Scriptures. Jesus was pure meekness and love. But when God's House was dishonored, He showed sharpness. The Holy Gospel tells us that whenever Jesus came to Jerusalem, He always went first to the Temple. *"In the temple courts he found people selling cattle, sheep and doves, and others sitting at tables exchanging money. So, he made a whip out of cords, and drove all from the temple courts, both sheep and cattle; he scattered the coins of the money changers and overturned their tables."* These people were selling in the Temple what Jews needed for offering to God. Nevertheless, Christ was very offended by it.

He is even more offended by a Christian who does behave inappropriately and horribly in church, especially during God's service, and sells his own soul and the souls of others to the evil spirit.

Church texts about St. Ambrose, the bishop of Milan, state that dishonor which was committed against God's house deeply insulted St. Ambrose's heart, and although he was meek, humble and full of love, he treated these people who misbehaved in church in a severe manner. He once saw a fine-looking lady who was very inappropriately and haughtily dressed entering the church. This pierced his heart to the extent that he spoke to her in a fierce manner: "Where are you going?" "To the church," she replied. Then the bishop said to her: "One could say that you are going to a ball or to see a comedy. Go away from here! Cry over your sins, repent them and do not come again into the house of God dishonoring Him so clearly with your sinful haughtiness.

Christians should always attend church, which is a House of God, with holy fear. God has already commanded this to the Israelites, saying: "*Observe my Sabbaths and have reverence for my sanctuary. I am the Lord.*" This refers even more to us as Christians as our churches are more sacred than were the Tabernacle of Israel or Jerusalem's Temple.

The most holy thing there is in our churches is the Blessed Sacrament. Christ, our God, who is the source of all holiness and love, is truly and always present in this unthinkable mystery. He is the beginning and the end of all our faith and devotion. He is our *all* and without Him nothing can be done for our salvation as He states: "*Apart from me you can do nothing. If you do not remain in me, you are like a branch that is thrown away and withers; such branches are picked up, thrown into the fire and burned.*" Only in Him and in His name is all our hope, our salvation: "*Salvation is found in no one else, for there is no other name under heaven given to mankind by which we must be saved.*" This is why Jesus recommended praying in His name. "*Very truly I tell you, my Father will give you whatever you ask in my name. Until now you have not asked for anything in my name. Ask and you will receive, and your joy will be complete.*"

Christians should not only *ask* God the Father in the name of Jesus, but also *thank* Him for everything in His very name as the apostle Paul teaches us: "*And whatever you do, whether in word or deed, do it all in the name of the Lord Jesus, giving thanks to God the Father through him.*" This means in His name.

Jesus can be worshiped best through *Mass* and *Holy Communion*. At the Holy Mass, Christians remember His redeemable suffering and His death for our salvation.

By receiving Holy Communion, Christians become one with Him and receive His eternal merits which He gained through His suffering and death for us.

Beside these two most sacred services, Jesus can be especially worshiped through the visits to the Blessed Sacrament. Christians sometimes go on a long pilgrimage someplace where the Almighty God, through the intercession of His saints, sometimes grants people a special grace. With great troubles they arrive at their chosen place, wasting a lot of time. However, they forget the Blessed Sacrament that is present in their local church as is in all the other churches and is the most excellent *place of graces*. The most sacred, the best and the most loving pilgrimage site is the visit to the Blessed Sacrament. My dear Christian, what I am about to tell you here is aimed toward getting a better insight and a deepening of your faith.

1. Christians sometimes go on a long pilgrimage, spending much time that they could use more wisely for their daily work. Moreover, their soul is in danger while they are on a long pilgrimage, especially for young Christians. This is well known to all confessors. Other Christians who are thinking things through can realize this as a sad experience often shows.

Christians who are able to recognize the place of grace, which is where the Most Sacred Heart of Jesus is, do not have to go far to be on this most sacred pilgrimage place. Every Sunday – if they cannot come more often – they come to this holy place without losing time or facing dangers. And those who love Jesus more than anything, even more than themselves, find their sweetest joy and their greatest trust in Him, and receive more graces through this visitation than being on the longest pilgrimage.

2. Christian texts and other holy books say that the most holy servants of God and the greatest teachers of

the church occasionally wrote against visiting pilgrimage sites and they suggest that Christians remain at home rather than to go on a pilgrimage. It has been stated by Gregory of Nyssa, the great teacher of the Church, that a certain pilgrimage site can be appropriate for one's salvation, but that they are mostly unnecessary and often harmful. And he states further that Christians should rather go out of themselves more and reach out to God than to go on their own to some other geographically distant place. Other church teachers, most holy spiritual shepherds and teachers often advise against pilgrimages.

No holy teacher ever advised against visiting the Blessed Sacrament. On the contrary, there are many writings by the most holy teachers, enlightened by God, who recommend visits to the Blessed Sacrament. From this fountain of all holiness, they captured all their strength and persistence in temptations, all their patience during times of nuisance and suffering. To sum up, they captured all their holiness in great abundance. What spiritual teachers recommend carefully and what holy saints are performing faithfully is certainly more pleasing to God and thus more redeemable than what Christians are often advised against.

3. The reason why Christians go on a pilgrimage is to visit some holy feature or a body of a certain saint and to ask for his or her intercession so that based on this intercession, they might receive a certain mercy from God. All this is right and just and the Holy Mother Catholic Church teaches us that Christians should commend themselves to the petitions of God's saints so that they who are God's friends ask for us, sinners. This is all good.

However, it is much better to visit the *Lord of all saints*, with the abundant trust, in the Blessed Sacrament. Here, no sacred image is glorified and no saint, but the Living God who is really present in the form of bread. It was not a body of some venerable servant of God that rose here but the body of Jesus Christ our Lord who was nailed to the cross for the redemption of all our sins. He rose venerably from the death in an effort that hope is given to every Christian to rise from the death gracefully and to reign eternally with Jesus in His kingdom.

In addition, my Christian, consider that the Holy Bible states that Jesus, our merciful Savior, "[…] *is at the right hand of God and is also interceding for us.*" If you have the right trust in Jesus, your intercessor and defender before His Heavenly Father, if you come and visit Jesus in the Blessed Sacrament, and if you are facing troubles and in need, commend yourself to the Merciful Heart of Jesus, you will certainly gain more mercies than those undertaking the longest pilgrimage

4. Christians who like to go on a pilgrimage think that God's graces are tied to a certain place, that they can be received more abundantly in a certain place compared to some other place. It is true that God delivered great graces to Christians in the early years of the Catholic faith and also several times later at a grave of a certain martyr or some other saint. He did this because of the deep trust they had.

If Christians would come with the same amount of trust before the Blessed Sacrament and would ask Jesus, Jesus would certainly "[…] *do it*" and they would not have to search for graces someplace distant, but could gain them at home.

5. A pilgrimage rarely makes Christians a better person, as more is necessary for a true improvement than just an outward pious deed. There are many Christians who like to go on a pilgrimage and continue to perform outward pieties and penitential works for many years, but have not bettered themselves and still live in their old, sinful manners. All the holy places they visited are of no help for their salvation, but keep them in a dangerously mistaken belief thinking that they are pious

Christians, although they may be worthy of eternal condemnation before God.

It is something completely different to visit Jesus present in the Blessed Sacrament. All those who are diligently visiting Jesus in this unimaginable mystery of eternal love cannot entertain a sinful attitude for very long. If Christians are miserable and commit sin, Jesus shows them this sin when they come before Him and He warns them kindly, with the result that they promise to Jesus not to commit this sin again. Nothing can become a sinful habit if Christians visit Jesus in the Blessed Sacrament and talk to Him there as a friend to a friend. However, if people fall into a sinful habit and do not want to quit it when Jesus kindly warns them, then they are departing from Jesus. A pilgrimage route to the Blessed Sacrament is not the same as other pilgrimage routes. While on other pilgrimage routes, some Christians carry all their evil habits with them and do not leave them behind, and they do not leave pilgrimage routes as well. Some act like this their whole life. Christians would not carry their sinful habits along for a long time. They would have to leave one or the other behind. If they do not want to leave their sinful habits behind, they would have to abandon their visits to the Blessed Sacrament and would never find joy in this piety or devotion. Jesus would turn away from such people, who, on their part, would never experience how sweet the Lord is. Their heart would become restless, they would be distracted and at the end they would get tired of all their piety. St. Paul said to the first Christians and he repeats to us: "*For what do righteousness and wickedness have in common? Or what fellowship can light have with darkness? What harmony is there between Christ and Belial?*" Belial is identified with the evil spirit and wickedness and darkness with those who sin.

6. Christians can recognize from the words of St. Paul that the Blessed Sacrament, in which Christ Himself

truly and eternally lives, is the most excellent and the most holy *place of graces* in which Christians can gain graces greater than at any other pilgrimage site, if they approach it with trust. Jesus is present in this marvelous and most holy mystery only out of love for us. He is our Great Priest who by His own experience knows our weaknesses and troubles. As St. Paul states: *"Let us have confidence and approach God's throne, where there is grace. There we will receive mercy and find grace to help us just when we need it."* God's throne is especially the Blessed Sacrament in which Jesus gives so many graces to faithful Christians. How fortunate are those who see with their soul's eyes Jesus on this throne. Jesus invites all Christians to Him and says kindly: *"Come to me, all you who are weary and burdened, and I will give you rest."* Jesus speaks so especially in the Blessed Sacrament. Happy are those who hear these words with ears of their souls and love to come before Jesus in all their troubles and needs.

Jesus says further: *"All those the Father gives me will come to me, and whoever comes to me I will never drive away."* Jesus says this regarding all Christians who truly convert to Him. He especially talks about those who visit Him in the Blessed Sacrament. He said these words when He first proclaimed that He would offer Himself to us in the Most Blessed Sacrament. He explains that it is the will of His Father that He should not lose any one of those who were given to Him, but to give them eternal life. At which pilgrimage site could this be found in the words of truth?

My dear Christian, you can see in all this that no pilgrimage route can be better, more glorious and pleasing to God than the pilgrimage route to the Eucharistic Presence of Christ. If you really want to join the eternal joy of your Master and eternally look at Jesus in heaven, then you should come with joy and often visit Him in the Most Blessed Sacrament. It is sad to see how this holy duty to Jesus is very badly followed. There are only a few Christians who faithfully visit Jesus in the Blessed Sacrament. Around the thrones of earthly kings are always many servants who serve their kings with great obedience and humility and honor them. Why? So that they receive some small timely goods from them. On the contrary, the throne of grace on which the eternal King of Heaven and Earth is enthroned and ready to give us the greatest and eternal graces, there are only a few of His servants who approach to honor Him, to commend to His mercy and to receive these graces from His hands.

If you my dear Christian, who read this, like to visit Jesus in the Most Blessed Sacrament, you are fortunate. You should always perform this holy duty to Him as well and faithfully as you can. Furthermore, you should guard yourself thoroughly against all sins.

If you have not fulfilled these duties to your generous Jesus until now, I ask and recommend you cordially to start visiting Him regularly in this eternally holy mystery which is the summary of all graces and all love of Jesus.

Oh, how many wonderful graces, how much consolation and strength you will gain if you visit your Heavenly Friend often in the Sacrament of His love. If Christians approach the throne of their Heavenly King and ask for some kindness, they might sometimes withdraw full of dust and as poor and in need as when they arrived, but when they come before the King of Eternal Honor in a humble manner, with trust and love, they will never leave empty from the throne of His mercy. It is true that sometimes Christians do not see or recognize immediately what they have gained, but by remaining loyal in visiting, they will soon notice a multiplication of God's graces and a greater strength to overcome evil temptations, as Jesus promised to invigorate all those who would come before Him. But if Christians who often visits Jesus in the Most Blessed Sacrament would never see anything nor recognize the purpose of these visits, they would nevertheless have to remain faithful in improving this holy duty toward Jesus, protect themselves against sin and trust firmly that Jesus will make them even happier in eternity, even if in this world He does not return immediately what they do out of love for Him.

If Christians who visit Jesus faithfully in the Blessed Sacrament and at the same time carefully avoid sin and think things over, they will never complain of not receiving any graces from Him, because these are exactly the infinitely great graces Christians should always receive restraining from sin as much as possible.

My dear Christian, if you are able and if it is possible, go and visit your Heavenly Friend every day. If you cannot go every day, go and visit Him at least on Sundays and Church holidays. Although you are trying very hard to protect yourself from sinning, many sins are committed during the week. Therefore, it is a right thing to do if you go and visit your benevolent Savior. One humbles himself before Him and asks Him to forgive one's sins committed during the week, and give such person grace so that they could avoid sinful opportunities even more carefully in the following week. People visit their friends in order to continue and preserve their kindness with them. My Christian, so should you repeat your kindness with Jesus in the Most Blessed Sacrament, at least on Sundays, when you have more time for prayer.

When worldly people sadden God in particular ways, like going to a dance, or to other worldly entertainments, or even cause a scandal, you should visit Jesus even more readily if you love Him wholeheartedly. One can read in the lives of the saints that God's loyal friends lived in great distress in God-offending times. In such sad times they worshipped and loved Jesus to a greater extent than people offended Him. You should imitate these friends of God and visit Him in sad times even more often and with greater love. It is to be pitied, indeed, that in times in which this mean world has so many friends and servants serving the world so faithfully, the kindest Jesus would not have good friends who would restore honor and love which secular people take at every opportunity. You should be His friend and should never leave Him, even if others leave. You should remember what Jesus said to His holy apostles and how they responded. When He saw that there were many who had left Him when He spoke to them about the Blessed Sacrament and were not willing to listen to His teachings, He turned to them saying: "*You do not want to leave too, do you?*" Apostle Peter replied to Him wholeheartedly: "*Lord, to whom shall we go? You have the words of eternal life.*" My beloved Christian, you should answer in the same way to our beloved Jesus and should be faithful to Him. You should not go where sinners would draw you but should remain with Jesus to love Him even more if you see that others are insulting Him. You promise Him firmly that you will never abandon Him even if everybody else does. Furthermore, you should remember that St. Peter, this loving apostle, made this promise to Jesus, but then betrayed Him because he trusted himself too much and did not commend himself to Jesus. When you give a heartfelt promise, you should also meekly commend yourself to His holy mercy and help.

If you strive to visit Jesus in the Blessed Sacrament, the evil spirit, who is the enemy of all good, will try to divert you away from this holy and redeemable piety. He will put dangerous temptations into your thoughts, especially at the beginning. For example, that visitations of the Blessed Sacrament are worthless because of your distraction and beside you feel empty and indifferent; without visits to the Blessed Sacrament, you will come to heaven as well; others are not visiting Him either. When such thoughts emerge, my dear Christian, remember that they are from the evil tempter – let that be enough for you. Discard and hate such thoughts from the beginning.

If you are not composed during these visits, you should think about where these distractions come from. If you recognize that you are sometimes consciously not composed, you should humble yourself before Jesus and conclude firmly to avoid such distraction from now on. You shall ask Jesus for help and strive steadily to collect your thoughts. If your distraction is unwilling, you shall humiliate yourself before Jesus and recognize how weak and poor you are and ask Him for the help and grace to be able to pray thoughtfully to Him as His saints pray before this Most Holy Mystery. If you recognize that your distraction is a result of your worldly life, because you are often in a worldly company, decide to leave this dangerous company, and not Jesus' company. You will have to leave one or the other. If you do not want to leave the worldly, it will have to be Jesus' company. If you reconsider either by faith or by intellect, you will be able to recognize that it is infinitely better to leave the worldly company which is terribly dangerous than to leave Jesus' which is so redeemable

Think about where your emptiness comes from as well. The Almighty God sometimes allows even holy souls to experience emptiness in their prayer and thoughts, although they are truly full of love for Jesus as we can read in hagiographies. This is an opportunity for the holy souls to lower themselves before Him and to bond even more closely with Him. The more Jesus hides from a soul who loves Him, and acts as if He would like to depart from it, the more does this soul lovingly move closer to Him and asks Him with an unimaginable force of love not to leave. As were those two disciples who went to Emmaus kindly urging that Jesus would remain with them, so does the soul that is loyal and filled with love tell with a holy force: "Remain with me, my

Jesus, do not leave me. It is already getting gloomy. I am more and more in the dark. Remain with me, oh, my Jesus, the eternal sun of righteousness, and enlighten me if this is your holy will. If you want me to remain in emptiness and darkness, then thy will be done. Just grant me the grace to love you dearly here and to look at you eternally in the heavenly light in eternity." You should say this to Jesus in your darkness and emptiness, and then fully submit to His holy will and wise caution. You should conclude firmly to never abandon visiting the Blessed Sacrament.

My dear Christian, consider that darkness and emptiness can sometimes be a just punishment from God for negligence, unfaithfulness and the evil of a sinful soul. If you realize, based on your conscience, that you live in sin or evil through a sinful habit, you should recognize that God turned away from you and you should conclude with a broken and sad heart to abandon sin and a sinful opportunity and reconcile with God through the sacrament of Penance. If you do this faithfully, will Jesus, as did the Biblical Father who accepted His lost son with such goodness, again embrace you with His grace so that you would again be able to pray with a peaceful consciousness and a joyful soul before the Most Blessed Sacrament. However, if you voluntarily remain in sin and in sinful opportunity, you will not visit Jesus any longer because *"For what do righteousness and wickedness have in common? Or what fellowship can light have with darkness? What harmony is there between Christ and Belial?"* Or, you are damned if you prefer to leave Christ and not Belial. The one that is chosen on this earth will be the one whose entire eternity will be shared with.

If the evil spirit distracts you by suggesting that visits to the Blessed Sacrament are not necessary, that you will be redeemed without them, you should consider that such visits are a good tool for salvation and Christians are obliged to do as much as possible for their salvation. If they depart this way out of neglect, laziness or carelessness and do not do what they could for God and for the salvation of their soul, they would experience the same as did the lazy servant who buried his master's money instead of making something good out of it: "*And throw that worthless servant outside, into the darkness, where there will be weeping and gnashing of teeth.*"

It is a dangerous temptation if you want to act as the majority of people act. Jesus did not tell us to take the wide road that is taken by most people, but to take the narrow one on which only a few can navigate. He also did not say that the hordes of indifferent and lazy Christians are on their way to salvation, but He said much more, which is that so many are called but only few are chosen. Jesus says to all saintly and ardent Christians who want to love and follow Him and not the evil world: "*If you belonged to the world, it would love you as its own. As it is, you do not belong to the world, but I have chosen you out of the world. That is why the world hates you.*" If you want to love Jesus, my dear Christian, serve Him and be redeemed, do not be satisfied with what others do for God and for their salvation as the big hordes of Christians do, but strive to join the small number of His faithful and fervent servants and friends so that you will be able to join the company of the few chosen in heaven.

So, my dear Christian, with the help of God, overcome and discard all temptations which the evil spirit instills in your mind in order to distract you from the visits to the Blessed Sacrament and be brave and faithful in fulfilling this holy duty to Jesus. You will most certainly experience a multiplication of God's graces and strength in all good, and when you recognize and experience how abundant the source of God's graces and joys of the soul in this holy duty are, you will never abandon it.

However, my dear Christian, be careful that your joy of visiting Jesus in the Most Blessed Sacrament does not drive you into some injustice or disobedience. God does not want that. If you would neglect the duties of your profession and life in order to visit the Blessed Sacrament, you would not be acting according to Christian rules. You should go and visit whenever there is time and you are able. And if you cannot remain a bit longer before Jesus, you should spend a short, albeit a more cordial and kind moment of visit.

My dear Christian, you should never say that you do not know what to say to Jesus when you visit Him. This is again a temptation – do not listen to it. At the beginning, the following book can be helpful: *Visits to the Most Blessed Sacrament and the Blessed Virgin Mary*. This book was written by St. Alphonsus Liguori. In 1831, the book was translated into our language with some additions to it. You should pray prayers included in the book thoughtfully. When you get more used to the visits, you will be able to thank Jesus with your own words and this will be even better. You should not think that you should talk to Jesus in a high and learned manner. He does not like it. During His life here on earth, He always spoke with a great amount of humility and without any pretense as the most poor and uneducated talk, although He was the eternal wisdom and the source of all knowledge. He recommended this holy simplicity to His apostles and to all Christians, and to show this more explicitly to them, he blessed a child when He sat among them and said: *"Truly I tell you, unless you change and become like little children, you will never enter the kingdom of heaven."* This is especially recommended to us in a prayer. As a child who can barely speak talks to his or her father, so should Christians talk to God in a prayer. You should talk to your Jesus present in the Blessed Sacrament as if He was present before you. Oh, how many things you can ask for! And for how many things you can be thankful to Him! You should think about *who Jesus is* and who *you are*. This will be helpful to you to never remain without words when staying before Him.

Earlier in the book (when we were talking about receiving the Holy Communion on a regular basis) it was explained who Jesus is in the Blessed Sacrament. You should think about this while visiting Him and should ask Him for forgiveness of sins. You should ask for holy graces and the necessary Christian chastity. You should not only ask for yourself, but for others as well, especially for all those for whom you are obliged to pray. You should often pray for the conversion of sinners and non-believers.

My dear Christian, you should strive to love Jesus right from the heart. If you love Him in the right way, you will come to Him easily. You will always find something that you would like to receive from Jesus. If it occurs sometimes that your heart is empty and there is nothing to talk about with Jesus, you should humble yourself before Him and exhale at least shortly: "My Jesus, have mercy on me because I am a big sinner! Remain with me, my Jesus, never leave me! Oh Lord, if you want, you can heal me!"

You should never leave because of emptiness and indifference of your soul, which can be felt while visiting Jesus, but remain before Him with a humble heart; you should remember that God sees and knows why you came, and that He is so pleased having a visitor. If you humbly accept occasional emptiness of your soul and bear it patiently, you will gain great graces, although you might think that you have done nothing good.

XIV.

RESPECT FOR PRIESTS

"Whoever listens to you listens to me.
Whoever rejects you rejects me."

After contemplating the holy things and mysteries that happen and are found in the Church, consider also the status of those to whom God has entrusted these holy things on earth, and reconsider your duties to them.

The clergyman's status is a holy, venerable and salvatory status for Christians. You can realize this, my dear Christian, if you contemplate the duties of this status. Almighty God who is the source of all holiness and all graces, distributes His holy graces to us predominately through the tasks of this status.

1. God, by His grace, *forgives our sins*. This happens through the holy sacraments of baptism and penance, which priests administer according to God's command. When the Jews asked St. Peter after his first sermon what they should do for the salvation of their souls, he answered them: *"Repent and be baptized, every one of you, in the name of Jesus Christ for the forgiveness of your sins."* And Jesus said to His apostles and all priests: *"Receive the holy Spirit. Whose sins you forgive are forgiven them, and whose sins you retain are retained."* How holy and salvific is this status to which God gave the power to forgive sins! With this, He makes him a partaker of His omnipotence. Only Almighty God and those to whom He chooses to give this power can forgive sins.

2. God gives us the strength and grace *to protect ourselves from future sin*. This grace is obtained through prayer and the worthy reception of the holy sacraments, especially Holy Communion, which saves us (as the holy Church teaches) from everyday sins and *protects* us from mortal sin. However, the benevolent God distributes this grace to Christians primarily through the duties of the priesthood. Priests teach Christians to pray properly, i.e., in spirit and in truth, not just with the mouth, and they always pray for the faithful, especially at the Holy Mass. At this sacred Offering, through the words of the priest, Jesus becomes present in the form of bread and remains with us in this mysterious form to give Himself to Christians to be received by them and to preserve their souls in His grace for eternal life. How venerable is the status to which such incomprehensible mysteries are entrusted!

3. God himself has given people the knowledge of heavenly mysteries and eternal truths. He is our true teacher as St. Paul says: "*In times past, God spoke in partial and various ways to our ancestors through the prophets; in these last days, he spoke to us through a son* [...]." Jesus, the Son of God, God and man, revealed everything to us and announced everything that we need for eternal salvation. But since He did not want to stay on earth longer and teach, He handed over the preaching of eternal truths to His priests. Therefore, only priests have the power and the right to preach those holy and Christian truths, which enlighten our minds, teach and confirm us in faith, give us hope to find pure and incomprehensible joy in eternity, and fill our hearts with holy love for the benevolent God. Jesus put the priests in His place because He said to the holy apostles and to all the priests in particular: "[...] *As the Father has sent me, so I send you*." "*Whoever listens to you listens to me. Whoever rejects you rejects me*." How prominent the position of the priests before

God must be if Jesus wants their words to be given the same honor as His own!

That priests are God's substitutes on earth is evident from other words of the Holy Scripture. St. Paul says for example: "*So we are ambassadors for Christ, as if God were appealing through us. We implore you on behalf of Christ, be reconciled to God.*" Remember also what was said when frequent and good confession was discussed, that the *confessors* are truly *the substitutes of Jesus*. It is further written in the Holy Scripture to *bow* our *head* before someone of a higher status, and before a priest, we have to *humble our soul.*

In the same way, Church teachers write that priests are the true substitutes of God. St. Chrysostom says for example: "Priests are the very special possession of God. They are His servants and His substitutes."

Jesus Christ is the high and the true Shepherd of his flock. He is the first Teacher, Consecrator, and the Bishop of our souls. He is the eternal Priest. He makes the priests partakers of His eternal priesthood; He gives them the authority to feed His sheep for eternal life, with the words of eternal life and with the heavenly bread that gives eternal life. Through this authority, they chase away the evil spirit, forgive sins, and perform the holiest sacrifice to God. Jesus himself appears to them submissively and comes by their words to them on the altar and dwells in the incorruptible mystery of the most holy Body of Christ.

Consider as well, my dear Christian, the great and holy *duties* you have toward the priests whom the almighty, eternal God has placed in His place in this world.

1. You can realize that the first duty to such a holy and venerable status must be *the special honor* that you must show to the priest: "*Honor God and respect the priest; give him his portion as you have been commanded.*" St. Paul says

that priests, especially those who preach and teach, are worthy of double honor.

One can read in the stories of ancient times that even nonbelievers, who did not know the true God, revered their priests highly. We read, for example, that Persians honored their priests so much that their king had to be a priest, otherwise they would not recognize him as a king. The Egyptians had such honor and trust in their priests that they did not want anyone else but a priest to judge their greatest trials and problems, and they immediately subjected themselves to this judgment. The Romans held the priesthood in such honor that they did not allow just anyone to become a priest, but only such men were admitted to this status who had previously enjoyed some high-level status or performed some venerable service. Since the nonbelievers so highly honored their priests, who were the servants of the evil spirit (*"what they sacrifice, [they sacrifice] to demons, not to God"*), how much more should Christians honor their priests who are not only servants but substitutes of the true and living God. However, there are many among Christians who have little respect and reverence for priests. They unjustly speak ill of them and despise them, and their smallest imperfections are proclaimed and exaggerated as great sins. What they do with the best of intentions and according to their duty, is many times turned against them and interpreted wickedly.

Priests are people, like others, therefore there are many priests who do not live according to the sanctity of their status. Among the twelve apostles whom Jesus chose, there was one who was a *"devil"*. Woe to such a priest! God will judge him severely and punish him severely in eternity if he does not truly repent. However, even such a priest, my Christian, you are obliged to respect. Not because of him, even less because of his action, but because of his status, and because of God's law to fulfill His commandments. Do not despise him at all, do not talk about his sins if it is not really necessary, but conceal them and defend them as much as you can justly. Jesus gave you a beautiful example of this. He knew his betrayer well and He was well aware of his evil intentions, yet He never said anything bad about him, but always respected him like all His other apostles. He always had him in His company, and when He sent them to preach and gave them power to make miracles, while He himself was still teaching, He made no distinction between this apostle and the other apostles. At the Last Supper, He did not want to say out loud and clearly who would be His betrayer, and He gave him the most holy Eucharist just as He did to all the others. On the Mount of Olives, when this unfortunate apostle came to betray Jesus to His enemies, Jesus, as a sign of His love and honor for His apostles, called him His *friend*. St. Ambrose says that Jesus did all this to show how highly honorable is the status of the priest of Christ.

It is true that priests are also people like others; however, they are exalted above all others because of their status as God's substitutes. A priest should live a decent and holy life. And yet, even if he were as unworthy as Judas, he is still a better substitute as long as he remains in his status and in true faith, and one must respect him according to the example of Jesus and for God's sake. Despising spiritual shepherds leads a person into licentiousness and into the greatest sins. Such person does not respect the Christian faith and everything that is holy. For the most part, only presumptuous, vain and sinful people despise priests and the priesthood. God punishes such people who despise His substitutes mostly by leaving them to their arrogance and blindness and allowing through His horrible and holy justice that they die without the holy sacraments and without the help of those whom they despised in their life.

2. The second principal duty of a devout Christian toward priests is *obedience*. (This duty has been discussed earlier in this book when Christian obedience in general was discussed.)

3. Since the spiritual blessings which these substitutes of God share are so great, your *gratitude* for them must be great, my dear Christian. St. Chrysostom says to the Christians who are ungrateful to the priests: "Ungrateful Christians! Is this the way you thank your priests for all their great gifts? Are not your sins forgiven through the works of priests and you are reconciled with God again? Are not the priests offering the most holy sacrifice for you? Are not the priests those who offer the most holy Body and Blood of Christ to you? Do not priests teach you eternal truths? Do not priests break the bread of God's word to your children? Do they not preach the kingdom of God to you? Do they not pray for you to come to God's kingdom?"

It is true, however, that the spiritual blessings that priests share with us come from God, and therefore Christians must, first of all, be grateful to God for them. But God still wants us to show gratitude to the priests for them. After all, *temporal* and *physical* blessings, which our parents and other benefactors give us, are actually God's blessings because all good things come from God, yet God commands us to be grateful to them. How much more should we be grateful to the priests who give us *eternal blessings*. Therefore, be grateful from the heart, my dear Christian, to your spiritual shepherds and teachers, and show them at every opportunity your gratitude in word and in deed. Pray for them that God would grant them the grace to always fulfill their sacred duties faithfully, to the honor of God and for the eternal salvation of the souls entrusted to them, that they would find themselves with the Good Shepherd in eternity.

Faithfully fulfill these Christian duties to all priests, especially to those whom God's providence has given you to teach you and lead you along the path of penance and Christian virtues towards Heaven. You need their help the entire time of your life; you will especially need it on your deathbed. Beware of everything that they forbid and do what they recommend to you. Believe everything that they teach you in God's justice and throw away what they tell you, and you will be happy already in this world and in eternity.

Here you will now find some examples, my dear Christian, from which you will understand even more how highly God's substitutes should be revered on earth and how God is offended when someone sins against His servants and substitutes.

Moses was the holiest servant of God and His substitute among the Israelites with whom God spoke face-to-face as a friend speaks to his friend, and he faithfully preached God's word and will to the Israelites. It happened that Aaron and Miriam (his brother and sister) grumbled against him, saying: "*Was God only speaking to Moses? Was God not speaking to us as well?* Moses, who was the meekest man on earth, listened to their evil talk with willing patience and said nothing. God, who wanted to honor His servant and substitute, called them to come to Him and sharply rebuked them for their foolishness and presumptuousness. As a punishment Miriam became all leprous, i.e., all white as snow for seven days. If Moses had not asked for her, she might not have survived.

Another example can be found in the Holy Scriptures, from which it is evident that sometimes already in this world (and certainly in the next) God punishes presumptuous people who do not respect priests and are not obedient to them. King Uzziah was good and God-fearing in the beginning. Later on, however, his luck and royal highness made him arrogant, so that he left the

Lord, his God, and arrogantly wanted to enjoy priestly honor. He went to the temple and wanted to make an offering on the altar of incense. God commanded priests alone to do this, and strictly forbade all others. When the high priest Azariah saw this, he rebelled against the king and said to him: *"It is not for you, Uzziah, to burn incense to the Lord, but for the priests [...]."* Then the king, who was holding a censer for burning the incense, became angry and scolded the priests, but at that moment leprosy broke out on his forehead. When the priests saw how God struck him, they quickly rushed him out of the temple, and he himself rushed out, all terrified, because he felt the hand of God striking him, and he remained leprous until death.

If God does not always show already in this world how grieved He is when disobedience and dishonor are shown to His substitutes, He will punish the despisers of the priests all the more surely in eternity, as the priesthood in our Christian times is more sacred than it once was among the Israelites.

In the stories of the people of Israel we read the example of the nonbeliever king Alexander the Great, how highly he worshipped the high priest in Jerusalem. This king, after having destroyed many other cities, progressed with his army towards Jerusalem with the intention of destroying this city and killing all Jewish priests. When the high priest Jaddua learned of this, he humbled himself before God with his priests and all the people and begged Him to protect them in this great danger. Then he put on his priestly robes and went with his priests to meet King Alexander. When the royal soldiers saw them from afar, they thought that Alexander would order them all to be killed right away. But when the high priest came near, the king took such a stand that he threw himself on the ground before him and prayed to God whose priest and substitute Jaddua was. Then he showed himself benevolent to the Israelites and allowed them everything that Jaddua asked of him for them.

Since a nonbeliever honored God's substitute so highly, how will secular Christians defend before God the contempt with which they often treat Christian priests who are even more God's substitutes and therefore even more worthy of honor than the Jewish priests were?

Emperor Constantine the Great, who was the first Christian emperor, held priests in high esteem. He never allowed anyone to speak ill of the priests in front of him. And he said many times that when he would see a priest sinning, he would cover him with his imperial cloak to hide him from the people. With this, he wanted to make known how great a duty and how necessary it is for Christians to hold the priestly office in honor, because by dishonoring this holy office, a lot of bad things and sometimes even false religion come. That is why it is written in the Scripture: "*Strike the shepherd that the sheep may be scattered* [...]."

Even the emperor Theodosius the Great always showed honor to God's substitutes. This emperor was a devout Christian, but once he greatly sinned against God because he ordered the murder of many people in the city of Thessalonica who had rebelled against him. There were many innocents among these people. When he came to Milan, he wanted to go to church, but St. Ambrose, who was the bishop of this church, stopped him and did not allow him to enter the church. The emperor was surprised and told the bishop that King David committed great sins, however they were forgiven. St. Ambrose replied to this: "*Since you imitated David in error, imitate him also in penance*," and Theodosius, although he was a mighty emperor, humbly submitted to the penance imposed on him by God's substitute Ambrose, and after he had completed it, he was absolved and was allowed to go to church.

If we consider this great example, we must be amazed when we see poor people who are quite grieved when the priest warns them because of their sins. When a priest does this, he fulfills the duty of love to God, to his neighbor and the duty of his status. Woe to the Christian who does not accept with humility and in a spirit of penance the admonitions of the spiritual shepherd. If one answers him or opposes him, one opposes God, and adds a terrible weight on one's conscience for the day of judgement.

Beware, my dear Christian, that you never fall into this sin. Listen to the voice of your spiritual shepherd and God's substitute as the voice of God. If he warns you, he does his duty. Listen to him humbly and in a spirit of penance, and be obedient to him. In this way you too will do your duty. Do not dwell on his own faults and imperfections. Not even on his birth, if he is of noble or of poor parents. Not even on his personality or on any other external circumstances, but remember the status he maintains now and his high standing because Jesus Christ put him in this place. Remember the authority that God gave him, his holy tasks and the great mysteries that God entrusted to him, and think that you see Jesus Christ in front of you in the person of his substitute.

XV.

BEWARE OF EVIL

*"Do not be conquered by evil but
conquer evil with good."*

After contemplating the fine Christian virtues and duties, my dear Christian, you will find here good advice about what you should avoid and what you should do to become a *righteous Christian*.

The Christian truth says: *The way to overcome evil is to do good.*

I. Beware of evil speaking.

All those who want to live a Christian life marked by tranquility and enjoy eternal peace in eternity have to avoid evil speaking. The Apostle Peter states: "*Whoever would love life and see good days must keep the tongue from evil and the lips from speaking deceit* [...]."

There is no better way to commit sin more easily and more often than through evil speaking. In the Holy Scripture it is written: "*In the mouth of the fool is a rod for pride, but the lips of the wise preserve them.*" and St. James says: "*If anyone does not fall short in speech, he is a perfect man,* [...]." Jesus teaches us: "*By your words you will be acquitted, and by your words you will be condemned.*" These words from the Holy Scripture that are the eternal truth should awaken a firm resolution in our hearts to guard carefully against all evil speaking. To more firmly conclude and faithfully keep what was just said, my dear Christian, consider the following teachings.

1. Never use any obscene or indecent language. St. Paul teaches us that *"any impurity or greed must not even be mentioned among [us]."* Impure words and poems awaken impure thoughts and evil desires in our heart. They are extremely dangerous, especially to young people, and they stain the soul of those who use them as well as of all those who like to listen to them. Whoever has the habit of using such language and claims not to mean anything bad, shows that their mind is dimmed, their spirit thwarted, their conscience is numbed and their heart is deaf.

However, you should not only avoid overtly obscene language, but also such euphemistic talk that can have negative consequences in that it tempts others to think about something obscene. Such talk can sometimes be more dangerous than overtly obscene language because, like a venomous snake, it is more dangerous when hidden in grass than if it is visible lying on the path.

Carefully beware of sinful words that are used by worldly people who do not love God and use such words when they are angry. Beware of curse words. Christians should not know such words because a Christian should be aware that God is omnipresent and always hears us.

Here is another suggestion. If you have a habit of invoking God's or Jesus' name unnecessarily, strive to abstain from this habit. God's name is so holy that God forbade others from even saying His name openly if not necessary. Invoke it always with respect and humility and never in laughter, astonishment or unnecessarily, for as the Lord says: *"You shall not invoke the name of the Lord, your God, in vain. For the Lord will not leave unpunished anyone who invokes his name in vain."*

2. Do not speak hastily and unwisely. You should not only avoid evil and indecent language, my dear Christian, but guard yourself from speaking unwisely. Do not imitate those who only want to speak *themselves* when they are among people. The Holy Scripture says: "*Do you see someone hasty in speech? There is more hope for a fool!*" Therefore, do not speak a lot, but rather listen: "*let your words be few.*" Favor silence. However, your silence has to be wise and humble. It has to derive from your love of God and not from some hidden pride, fear or great sadness.

Never answer a question before another person has finished asking the question because "*[W]hoever answers before listening, theirs is folly and shame.*" It is rude to interrupt someone who is speaking: "*interrupt no one in the midst of speaking.*" Never speak nor judge about something that you do not know or understand well. Never fight over something that does not concern you or that you do not care about. If you determine that God is offended because of what was being said, do not participate in this, but go away if you can. "*Do not dispute about what is not your concern; in the quarrels of the arrogant do not take part.*"

3. *Never spread gossip about your neighbor.* To *spread gossip* means to tell others about your neighbor's bad qualities. The one who knows that what is being said about one's neighbor is false, but spreads such false statements anyway, is guilty of *slander.*

All those who speak about a sinful act of their neighbor that is already *known*, commit a sin against the love of the neighbor. However, an even greater sin is committed when someone talks about those sins of their neighbor that are true but are *not known*. Great shame and damage might be caused to such a person. The gossiper has a debt before God to repay as much as possible for all the damage he has done to his neighbor. *Slander* is an even greater sin. Consider more thoroughly, my dear Christian, how ugly these sins are in order to guard more carefully against them.

Consider first *how and when* somebody commits the sin of gossip. Those who unnecessarily discuss the sins of their neighbor commit this sin. It is sinful when someone continues malicious talking by explaining and revealing certain unknown circumstances; when someone makes fun of how his or her neighbor acts or behaves; when someone explains and interprets the purposes of his or her neighbor in a bad way not knowing why this neighbor acts in a certain way; all efforts to diminish or degrade the good works of a neighbor are done with malicious intent. Guard yourself from all these, my dear Christian: "*Dishonest mouth put away from you.*"

The sin of gossiping is sometimes committed through *silence*. Let me point out that if someone would rightfully praise a person you know well in front of you and you would remain silent, your action would suggest that this person is not worthy to be praised because you know something bad about him or her. You would commit an even greater sin if you would say: If I really wanted to talk, I could say something else negative about this person, but I do not want to do so. If you would say so, you would actually not be reporting anything negative about this person, however, you would be gossiping maliciously. Whoever would hear you speak in this way, might think that this person is worse than he truly is.

Someone who is gossiping about someone and at the same time showing *mercy* to this same person might think that he loves this person. On the contrary, he is already acting heavily against love. This sometimes happens to devout souls as well and it is thus all the more dangerous. If a person gets accustomed to gossiping, his or her piety is empty before God because the Holy Scripture says: "*If anyone thinks he is religious and does not bridle his tongue but deceives his heart, his religion is vain.*" Therefore, guard yourself from such gossiping, my dear Christian. Here is an example for better understanding. You would be guilty of gossiping if you knew who committed a certain sin and reported this to someone as follows: Have you heard what has happened? How sad this is! These are such good people. This is such a clever girl. This is such a faithful servant. Who would have thought! Oh, how sorry I am for him! Pray for him! And after saying these words of Christian mercy, you would repeat what sin your neighbor committed. This is ugly, evil, and hypocritical gossiping. It is similar to a situation in which a person would hold a sharp knife in one hand and in the other a healing medicine, and when approaching someone would first cut this person deeply and then quickly apply medicine to the wound. Wouldn't it be much better not to cut this person in the first place and avoid the need for the medicine? St. Francis of Sales said that such gossiping is like a poisoned arrow dipped in oil to pierce even deeper.

Be careful, my dear Christian, and always beware when you are in company not to say or do anything that would work against the good name or the honor of your neighbor. A single word, a ridicule or shaking one's head may cause somebody to think or believe something bad about his or her neighbor. These evil thoughts would not exist if you would guard yourself more closely.

Think about the *source* of gossip as well. Some are doing it out of evil, envy or hatred. Their goal is to harm their neighbor. Others gossip out of habit and foolishness without harboring evil intentions because they like to tell whatever they know. Those who gossip with evil intentions commit an even greater sin than those who gossip out of foolishness and without evil intentions. However, even these people are sinning. Gossiping is always a sin.

However, if someone with *really true intentions* talks to the one who is *responsible* for this person about certain sins of his neighbor truthfully, with wisdom and caution, this is not gossiping, but performing the good work of Christian love while fulfilling one's duty at the same time. This might help this neighbor to gain eternal salvation by stopping their damaging or perverse behavior. If someone would remain silent in such circumstances and not speak up, this person would not be acting appropriately. It is better to disclose the evil acts of a certain person to his or her superior than to allow damage or injustice or perversion to happen to others. The justice we owe to our neighbor comes before love. Even more, justice is the first duty of love to our neighbor.

Consider also, my dear Christian, how *ugly* and *shameful* is the *sin* of gossiping. To understand this more deeply, think about how many good virtues this sin opposes.

Gossip stands in opposition to *justice*. Justice opposes injuring one's neighbor. However, with gossip, first you cause damage to those who listen to you because you enable them to participate in your sin, and, secondly, you cause damage and sometimes even great damage to the person you are gossiping about because you diminish or completely take away his or her honesty and good name, especially when you are reporting the sinful actions of your neighbor that are known to you alone. You can cause exceptional damage to this person, even greater than if you were to commit theft against them because "[*A*] *good name is more desirable than great riches* [...]." You can recognize from this that gossiping is contrary to justice and sometimes causes even graver injustice than theft. Theft is more easily repaired that a good name that has been ruined.

Gossiping is also opposite to the most beautiful and most necessary virtue, namely *the Christian love of neighbor*. This virtue dictates that one love their neighbor as themself and to refrain from doing to another what one would not want to be done to them. Recognize, my dear Christian, that you are working against Christian love if you are gossiping about your neighbor. Remember how every word directed against you hurts. Perhaps you are using many words against your neighbor without thinking and realizing what you are doing. If you choose to talk negatively about your neighbor, you do not love this person as a Christian should: "[F]or *whoever does not love their brother and sister, whom they have seen, cannot love God, whom they have not seen.*"

Gossiping contradicts *Christian wisdom*. A gossiper is truly acting unreasonably when he does not hold his tongue, because he is not honoring and respecting the good name of his neighbor, but is hitting this or that person with it. The words of a gossiper are like poisonous arrows that are recklessly thrown around. Woe to such a foolish tongue. "*I tell you, on the day of judgment people will render an account for every careless word they speak.*" How will it be possible for a gossiper to render an account before God over so many *foolish* and *sinful* words?

Gossip contradicts *humility*. A humble person lowers oneself, raises another person and regards this person as being better than oneself. A gossiper, on the contrary, despises and humiliates his or her neighbor and prefers to talk about this person's vices and bad qualities. The more the gossiper humiliates his or her neighbor, the more empowered he or she feels. The gossiper is presumptuous and blind so that when this person is spreading gossip, he or she believes that they are less wicked than the person they are gossiping about. The gossiper does not acknowledge his or her own big sins and equally bad habits.

Woe to you, gossiper, you presumptuous and blind person! How can you forget about how you really are? Open your soul's eyes and take a look at how ugly you are! Why are you not listening to your conscience that understands and reports back to you what you are truly like? Unfortunately, you do not want to listen nor do you believe what it is telling you. You have to realize that when you denigrate another person by gossiping, you denigrate yourself more than the other person. Are you, who enjoys talking about the sins of your neighbor, without sin before God? Consider that Jesus is speaking to you when He addressed the Jews who denounced the woman as a sinner: *"Let the one among you who is without sin be the first to throw a stone at her."*

It might be that you are an even greater sinner before God than are those you are gossiping about and are able to see only sins of your neighbor and not your sins because you are being blindsided by your own foolish pride.

Consider *how great a sin* gossip is. It is sometimes a venial and sometimes a mortal sin. The graver and more hidden the sin, the greater is the sin of the gossiper who reports it to others. The more it is done with an evil intent, the greater is the gossiper's sin. On the contrary, if someone speaks ill of a neighbor but without evil intent, the smaller the sin of the gossiper, unlike that of the one who gossips with evil intent, or out of envy, or hatred etc. The more someone is obliged to honor and love the person that he or she is spreading gossip about, the bigger is the sin before God. For example, a person who is gossiping about priests, rulers and the next of kin is a greater sinner than someone who is gossiping about some other person, and yet this behavior is very common among people. Oh, how many sins are committed in this way and how rare are those who are truly willing to recognize their sins and convert! Beware of gossip, my dear Christian, and fear God, your Lord because priests are His surrogates, and according to His providence and law, earthly rulers are above us, and from Him comes all power they have. There is a specific commandment according to which every person shall honor and love one's own parents and provide for one's own relatives more than for other people in all things, that is, in preserving their honor and good name. *"And whoever does not provide for relatives and especially family members has denied the faith and is worse than an unbeliever."*

An even greater sin than gossip is *slander*, i.e., when someone utters something negative about another, knowing that this is not true. This is truly a large and serious sin. If gossiping is contrary to the many beautiful virtues (namely *justice*, *love*, *wisdom*, and *humility*), how much more contrary to them is slander, which completely banishes virtue from a Christian's heart. How horribly evil and black is the soul and how completely depleted of love the heart of a person must be who dares to claim that a neighbor has committed sins and acts of wickedness that they have not! This person's tongue *"is like the venom of a snake, like that of a serpent stopping its ears."* This sin is so big that the king's prophet calls for God's justice so that such sinners get what they deserve while still in this world: *"on their tongue are subtle lies. Declare them guilty, God; make them fall by their own devices."*

Think further, how *common* the sin of slander is. The sad truth is that almost every person, more or less, is caught up with this sin. It is truly sad to see that Christians who should truly love their neighbors are so quick to denigrate them and deprive them of some of the pride and good name, *"which is worth more than great riches"* and to hit them more heavily and harmfully with a tongue than with a stick. How many times a Christian makes himself unworthy of the name Christian through this sinful habit of denying and throwing away the sign by which Jesus said that we will be recognized as Christians: *"This is how all will know that you are my disciples, if you have love for one another."*

Gossiping is common among some people, that is, among those who are *in dispute*. How evil they mostly speak against each other! They believe that they do not sin, especially when they know that justice is on their side. However, they err, my dear Christian. Consider that the person who is doing you some injustice is still your neighbor whom you are obliged to love according to Jesus' commandment, namely to love as you love *yourself*, more than your possessions because you do not love all your possessions as you love yourself. If your conscience tells you that someone is doing you wrong, you are allowed to seek justice under the law. However, you are not allowed to hate and spread gossip about the neighbor who does you wrong. If you act in this way, you will do more harm to yourself before God than your neighbor does to you.

Gossip is common among people who are *jealous*. A jealous person rarely reveals this sin and they hide it from themselves as well as others. Someone who is jealous is an enemy and an evildoer to one's neighbor, however, this person means and says that he or she does not hate nor do harm to the neighbor. But is gossiping not a greater evil than any other work of evil? Someone who snaps with the tongue strikes harder than with a sword. Wounds inflicted by a gossiping tongue are more difficult to heal than bodily wounds. A gossiper, and especially a slanderer, steals more from the neighbor than the biggest thief because "*a good name is more desirable than great riches.*"

Friends are usually *gossiping* among themselves. Secular friends usually tell everything to one another, especially about somebody close. This is an evil and sinful habit. Beware of such kindness, my dear Christian. Love your friends. Love God even more. Love your friends only in God. Those who truly love their friends and love them in God, do not want to do any harm but only something good to them, and they only want to rescue their friends and do not want to place them in danger. The one who gossips with a friend is putting this friend in danger of sinning because their cooperative listener commits sin.

If this person continues to spread gossip, he or she commits an even greater sin.

Gossiping is commonly taking place among people who like *secular visiting*, i.e., who like to go around and visit other people in their homes and like it when others visit them in the same manner. Oh, how much beautiful and much precious time is lost through such unnecessary visits and how many sinful words are spoken! On such occasions, one's neighbors are predominately discussed, i.e., how they are, how they live, what they have done etc. Certain circumstances about one's neighbor are especially suitable to be discussed while someone is visiting, especially when someone decides to change a certain status, gets a job or helps oneself in a certain situation. Is this the case, everyone feels entitled to report something about this person and it often happens that a lot of harm can be caused to one's neighbor by such evil conversation. Therefore, protect and guard yourself, my dear Christian, from all unnecessary secular visits because they are dangerous. Never seek nor love danger as you might get lost in it. Only one type of visit is strongly recommended to you, that is, the visits to the Blessed Sacrament. There you come before Jesus who is your best friend. He speaks only holy words to you, the words of eternal life. Listen to Him faithfully and humbly and ask Him: "*Teach me to do your will, for you are my God.*"

Consider at this point *what you should do* if you were *to spread gossip* about your neighbor and take away, or at least diminish his good name. Because gossiping is a sin against justice, it is not enough to confess to it, but you have to right the wrong if you have caused some injustice to your neighbor by gossiping. Under these circumstances, it is your duty to speak good about your neighbor, especially to those who have heard you gossiping. You should also make it known that you are sorry about speaking in this way about your neighbor.

If you were so foolish and sinful and have been *slandering* your neighbor, i.e., if you have talked about your neighbor's sins and wickedness while knowing that your neighbor did not commit them, it is your duty to tell the people who heard you slandering that what you have told them is not true. You must also strive to make known to all who heard your slander and learned from it that what you said was not true. Do not say that if you do this, you will lose the good name you have among people. Even if you lose your own good name, it is your duty to restore the good name of the neighbor you have wrongfully taken away. This is a definite responsibility as is the responsibility to return stolen goods despite the chance that you might face poverty. As a thief does not gain forgiveness for his sins unless he repays what was stolen, so is the slanderer's sin not forgiven until he reestablishes honesty and restores his neighbor's good name as much as is possible.

The *wicked judgement of a neighbor* is sinful in addition to gossiping and slander and is often the beginning of evil gossiping. Never judge your neighbor immediately. Think about what is written regarding this in the Holy Scripture. Jesus says: "*Stop judging, that you may not be judged. For as you judge, so will you be judged,* [...]." Jesus says further: "*I do not judge anyone.*" And you, poor sinner, dare to judge your neighbor before God even if you might be a bigger sinner. "*Therefore, you are without excuse, every one of you who passes judgment. For by the standard by which you judge another you condemn yourself, since you, the judge, do the very same things.*" And if you have not done what your neighbor did, or what you think your neighbor did, you have possibly committed a lot of other things that are even more sinful before God. Therefore, do not judge anyone, my dear Christian, and do not think anything bad about your neighbor because you cannot see into your neighbor's heart. You do not know why and with what purpose your neighbor has done a certain thing. Whoever judges his or her neighbor fairly harshly based on what can be seen from the outside and thinks or says something sinful about the neighbor, has no true love for this neighbor because St. Paul clearly states that love *"does not rejoice over wrongdoing* [...]."

Beware of evil judgement and all evil thoughts about a neighbor when an injustice or damage happens to you. When you hear that there is a negative rumor about you spreading around unjustly and you do not know who started this gossip, and when your goods or property have been damaged but you do not know who did so, do not accuse anybody, never blame anyone and do not believe immediately what someone tells you about your neighbor on these occasions, but remember that God is our only judge. Remember His cautiousness that sometimes allows someone to experience an inconvenience or harm in order to have the opportunity to show his love for God, or for his neighbor, or to get to know oneself better. Beware of sin more than of any other damage and loss because one single sin causes greater damage and a bigger misfortune than a loss of all worldly goods. Surrender to God's will with a humble heart and remember: *"We know that all things work for good for those who love God,"* especially inconveniences and troubles of this world. St. Paul praises especially those Christians who *"joyfully accepted the confiscation of* [*their*] *property, knowing that* [*they*] *had a better and lasting possession."*

Keep away from occasions, my dear Christian, in which damage or an accident might occur, keep away from all superstition and empty faith. Remember all teachings you hear in church or read about in good holy books. Reject everything that is contrary to these teachings. If someone defends such empty faiths and superstitions in front of you, bear witness to the Christian truth and justice; give grace to God who is the only God of all things and who at His infinite cautiousness, incomprehensible wisdom, and love always acts and allows what is in His honor and for the salvation of souls. Humbly submit and act according to His benevolent intentions and His holy will.

Consider as well, my dear Christian, how you should act when you *hear gossiping*. Never prefer listening to the gossiper. Do not *"fall victim to one [tongue] lying in ambush."* If you can, stop and warn this person. If you cannot do this, refuse to listen and go away so that you will not have to hear him or her. If this is not possible, show a sad face signaling that you do not approve of such a talk. The Holy Bible states that "[*T*]*he north wind brings rain, and a backbiting tongue, angry looks.*" Remember God and ask Him to give you the grace to never feel drawn to gossip. Remember also what St. Bernard says: "The gossiper has the evil spirit *on the tongue*. The person who likes listening to gossips has it *in the ears*." Ignore and forget what you have heard about your neighbor and do not tell anything to anyone. "*Let anything you hear die with you; never fear, it will not make you burst!*" If you hear something bad about your neighbor, never believe it immediately. This is written in the Holy Bible: "*Whoever trusts others too quickly has a shallow mind, and those who sin wrong themselves.*" Do not even believe such gossip that is known and spread everywhere because people are generally prone to this sin and prefer to listen, believe and spread information so that quickly the evil somebody says again his neighbor is known. Oh, how sinful and distorted a human heart is! Whenever someone hears *something good* about his or her neighbor, this person does not believe it immediately and thinks and says that it might be done with some bad intention. When this person hears something *evil*, he or she believes it immediately and believes much more than what was said. That is all the more sad because it can be seen often that even such Christians who like to pray, regularly attend church and often receive the Sacraments are caught up in this! Beware, my dear Christian, of this evil habit. Do not believe the evil you hear against your neighbor, especially if you do not have any *authority* over your neighbor.

Consider finally, my dear Christian, how you would act should somebody *spread gossip about you*. If you hear that somebody is spreading something evil about you, do not get angry and do not believe everything immediately. Maybe the rumor spread about you was not as bad as you are told. Experience teaches us that people who like spreading gossip, tend to talk about things slightly differently and sometimes completely differently than what was said at the beginning. Do not immediately say something bad about the person who spread the gossip against you because St. Paul says to us: "*Do not repay anyone evil for evil.*"

Afterwards look into the mirror of your conscience and consider carefully if you really are what they say you are. If you recognize that you really are what they say, tell yourself with a humble heart: what is happening to me is right. I deserve this and much more. Do not make excuses and do not cover your old sins with new ones (by lying), but be silent and in a spirit of penance bear what you deserve.

If you find that you are not guilty of what is being said about you or that you are not as guilty as much as you were accused of being after questioning your conscience, accept this cross with humility and patience as if it came from God's hands. Consider whether you have not contributed initiating the gossip by acting uncarefully, albeit without any malice. If you realize you really have provided this opportunity, humble yourself before God and trust that your benevolent God will not count this as a sin if you will now willingly endure gossiping because you did not act with evil intent. Conclude firmly that you will be more careful in the future and will more thoroughly protect yourself against evil tongues.

If you recognize, however, that you are not to blame for gossip and slander that rose against you, cover yourself in the cloth of your innocence and a clear conscience and let the storm of evil tongues roar for as much and as long as they want. Remember your Jesus who was more slandered than you and consider how He endured everything with incredible patience and humility. Trust in God. If it is His holy will, i.e., if it is to His honor and for your salvation, He will sooner or later reveal that you are innocent. If He does not make it known in this world, He will make it known at the Last Judgement before His angels and all people, if, following the example of His beloved Son, you will willingly and steadfastly suffer the injustice done to you.

4. Do not argue and do not say any offensive word to anyone. If someone is habitually arguing and being angry with a neighbor, this person is lacking a true Christian spirit and is not a true Child of God because God is called *"God of peace"*. Jesus says: *"Blessed are the peacemakers, for they will be called children of God."*

Arguing is a serious thing and it causes a lot of problems in the world. It often tears apart the link of kindness, turns away the hearts of brothers, banishes peace from one's heart, fills one's heart with hatred and evil thoughts and makes entire families unhappy. Arguing is like a dangerous fire that can catch fire easily and is hard to put out. Many times, one can witness how great misfortunes, inconveniences and problems emerge from fighting or are the result of some evil and unwisely used words during a quarrel.

Arguing is in strong opposition to the Christian spirit that is love. It is contrary to reason as well. If you consider it a little, my dear Christian, you would recognize how unwise it is to argue. About what do people mostly argue about? Sometimes because of one single word, other times because of some small injustice or damage which is a lesser misfortune than a venial sin. How unwise and unchristian it is to drive *peace* away for such small things that Jesus addresses all Christians, with the words *"Peace be with you."* Love, *"that is, the bond of perfection"* and *"the fulfillment of the law"* is wounded by arguing and *"[…] your brother is being hurt […] for whom Christ died."*

To make you realize even more how sinful it is when a Christian fights and gets angry, consider that it is a Christian's duty to act according to Jesus' example. Jesus says to us all: *"[…] learn from me, for I am meek and humble of heart."* This "Good Teacher" showed exceeding meekness and patience during His entire life. Despite being surrounded by enemies and persecutors, He never argued with them and never used rude and offensive words against them. *"When he was insulted, he returned no insult; when he suffered, he did not threaten."* Following Jesus' example, a good and faithful Christian is patient with his neighbor and returns polite words for harsh ones as St. Paul tells us: *"Bless those who persecute [you], bless and do not curse them. […] Do not repay anyone evil for evil […]. If possible, on your part, live at peace with all."*

Consider, my dear Christian, what is a person like when he or she is angry. Is he or she a person? A Christian? Is this person not more similar to a wild beast without any sense? The Christian law is a law based on love and peace. An angry person, however, tears and bites one's neighbor with sharp, offensive words that dig into the neighbor's flesh more deeply than would the teeth of a wild beast dug into his corpse.

Therefore, beware of anger and arguing and strive to maintain a permanent peace with your neighbor. *"Turn from evil and do good; seek peace and pursue it."*

I recommend especially two tools that will help you to protect yourself from arguing easily. The first and the most effective tool is *prayer*. If you know that you have the tendency to fight and argue, ask Jesus continuously to give you the grace to imitate Him in His heartily meekness. The second tool is learning with God's help to *be quiet* when you feel that your heart is offended and wounded by a foolish or wicked word of your neighbor. Quickly think of God and always be silent out of love for Him. However, if you have to talk, talk only kindly and benevolently even though the evil tempter is trying hardly to lead you into using evil and sinful words. *"A mild answer turns back wrath, but a harsh word stirs up anger."*

Insulting words include *blaming* and *scolding*, both of which you should avoid, my dear Christian. Blaming is threefold. *Firstly*, when someone reproaches his or her neighbor for some physical imperfection, i.e., if this neighbor is in some way impaired, i.e., in mobility, speech or physically, or if the neighbor is blamed for something that represents dishonor to his or her parents or lineage. This kind of blaming sometimes greatly offends or wounds the heart of a neighbor. Those who do this show that they are not very intelligent and have even less Christian love. *Secondly*, when somebody blames his or her neighbor for the good deeds he or she has bestowed upon their neighbor. Such blaming deprives good works of all merit before God and these good works are done in vain. *"Say no harsh words to him nor distress him by making demands." Thirdly*, when somebody blames the neighbor for sins. This is sometimes good and sometimes vile. If somebody, especially a person who has authority over his neighbor, desires in Christian love and wisdom that this neighbor would become truly better, and shows this neighbor the sins he or she has committed, this person does a good thing. And if this neighbor gets upset by being told about own sins, that neighbor alone sins. However, if someone is angry and blames a neighbor for his or her evil works without the wisdom and intention to help this neighbor become a better person, this is evil, especially when there are other people around. Such unchristian blaming sometimes causes great hatred and other sins, especially if a neighbor is accused of sins about which others did not know until then.

Guard yourself, my dear Christian, from all this blaming. Remember that God *"who is love"* and who hates everything that is contrary to love, hears you. Whenever somebody blames you for something, however, remain silent and bear it willingly following Jesus' example, and you will obtain merit before God.

Moreover, insulting includes *mockery*, i.e., the habit of mocking and ridiculing one's neighbor at every opportunity. Whoever has this bad habit, does not have many friends, because ridiculing offends everyone. The more insulting and frequent the ridicule is, the bigger the sin. It is a particularly great sin when someone mocks or blames his or her parents, superiors and even spiritual shepherds. It is a terrible sin that equals sacrilege to mock sacred things, commandments and services of the Church or even the Sacred Mysteries of Faith. *"Make no mistake: God is not mocked* [...].*"*

My dear Christian, if you were so unlucky as to have offended your neighbor with your evil words and have lost his or her kindness, it is your obligation to repent from your sin and be reconciled with your neighbor. And do not claim that you do not have anything against this person and that, if this person has something against you, he or she should come to you and be the first to offer a word of reconciliation. Remember that Jesus teaches us: *"Therefore, if you bring your gift to the altar, and there recall that your brother has anything against you, leave your gift there at the altar, go first and be reconciled with your brother, and then come and offer your gift."* Your prayer and all your service to God is not pleasing to God if your neighbor has something against you and you do not strive to reconcile with him, especially if you alone are guilty by saying the offensive word that earned your neighbor's anger. However, if you truly strive to reconcile with your neighbor and your neighbor does not want to listen to you, you have fulfilled your duty before God. It is nevertheless your duty to pray for that neighbor and to strive for reconciliation with that neighbor later on.

I recommend to you further, beware of viciously *communicating* gossip, i.e., carrying news speedily from one house to another or telling a neighbor about something bad that one hears against him. A lot of evil is committed in this manner, a lot of hatred and anger is involved, and many times peace is driven away. This sinful habit can often be observed by women who live in a constant state of sin in this way. St. Paul says that they experience "[…] *condemnation* […]. *And furthermore, they learn to be idlers, going about from house to house, and not only idlers but gossips and busybodies as well, talking about things that ought not to be mentioned.*" How God dislikes a person who takes away peace and unity from people by such transmission of gossip is testified by the Holy Spirit in the Holy Scripture: "*There are six things the Lord hates, yes, seven are an abomination to him.*" And this seventh is "[…] *the one who sows discord among kindred.*" The Holy Bible states further: "*Cursed be gossips and the double-tongued,* [the one who takes gossip from one house to another] *for they destroy the peace of many.*" Pope Gregory I states: "By saying that those who work for peace (all those who love peace and preserve it among others) will be named the *children of God*; Jesus Christ lets us know that those who take away peace are the *children of Satan.*"

Beware, my dear Christian, of this ugly and harmful sin. Beware of people who have this sinful habit. Do not listen to them, do not believe them and let them know that such talking annoys you. Remember that the tongue speaking before you against your neighbor will soon speak against you when you will not hear it. The *"double-tongued is truly cursed"* before God and before people! Such a person should never be your special friend and could never be a faithful friend. *"Dishonest mouth put away from you, deceitful lips put far from you."*

5. *Never lie.* A lie is always a sin because it is contrary to the truth and because it is against the conscience of the one who utters it. It is true that a lie is not always a mortal sin if it is small. However, habitual lying, even if it is a small lie, is a terribly wicked, sinful and destructive habit. This habit opens a door to many other sins and to wickedness.

A liar speaks contrary to what he thinks is dishonest and not straightforward. Such a person is mostly unfaithful in promises and unjust in own intentions. A liar has no love an no fear of the Lord his God who knows and hears everything. The one who develops a habit of lying is ready for any sin, especially for theft, fraud, gossip, slander and finally for perjury.

Oh, how ugly a liar is before God! The Holy Bible states that among the six things God hates is a *"a lying tongue"*. It says further: *"Lying lips are an abomination to the Lord* [...];" *"whoever utters lies will perish."* *"[A] lying mouth destroys the soul."*

A lie comes from the evil spirit. He brought the lie from hell to earth and has led countless inhabitants of this earth into hell. The evil spirit led our first parents into sin with lies and its lies caused the damnation of the whole world. Jesus says that the evil spirit *"[...] is a liar and the father of lies."* St. Ambrose says that all those who lie are its children. St. Augustine writes that as the truth comes from God, so does a lie come from the evil spirit.

Beware then, my dear Christian, of such sin that is so ugly and disagreeable to God and harmful to the soul. Beware of all lies, small or big and be always and everywhere just and truthful. God is the truth and whoever remains in the truth, remains in God. Whoever departs from truth, departs from God and becomes miserable.

Conclude firmly and repeat this conclusion several times: I would rather die than lie, and consider this fine example. St. Augustine writes about the holy bishop Firm who firmly concluded that he would rather suffer everything and even die than to speak against Christian love or to lie. It happened that a man they were looking for to kill, ran to the bishop and asked the bishop to hide him. The bishop felt sympathy for this man and he hid him. Then came the servants of the Roman emperor who were looking for this man. They asked the bishop where the man was. Bishop Firm answered: "I cannot give you an answer because I cannot lie and I also cannot tell you where he is." The emperor's servants were not satisfied and began pushing him, treating him badly and wagging that they would kill him if he would not tell them the location of the man they were seeking. The bishop replied to them: "I would rather suffer everything or die than to lie or to speak against the love of a neighbor." When these people saw his steadfastness, they brought him before the emperor and told him everything. The emperor marveled at the holy steadfastness of this bishop and he let him go. He told his servants to leave the man alone for whom the bishop showed so much love.

II. Beware of the seduction of the evil spirit.

My dear Christian, here are many teachings in regards to the sins committed with the *tongue* because these are the most common.

Now, consider the *source* of sins, i.e., the *temptations* that emerge from our own distorted nature, from bad habits and opportunities that we come across everywhere, and from the evil spirit who is our perpetual enemy and tempter. Or, in fact, all these three temptations are combined into one temptation, they are contained in the *temptation of the evil spirit*. All the weakness and evil of our *nature*, which the evil spirit incites and uses to lead us into sin, derives from the temptation of the evil spirit who tempted our first parents into sin. In the same way, in all the *bad examples* and *evil opportunities* that the world gives us, there is the evil spirit, whose helpers are everywhere, bringing people under its power.

Then, everything is based on the fact, my dear Christian, that you become well acquainted with the evil seduction of our enemy and that you know well how to protect yourself from him. I will teach you how to do it.

"Be sober and vigilant. Your opponent the devil is prowling around like a roaring lion looking for [someone] to devour. Resist him, steadfast in faith [...]" This is how St. Peter, the most important apostle, warns all Christians. The evil spirit *"was a murderer from the beginning* [...]" Through its temptations and confusion, the evil spirit wants to push all people into eternal misery. The evil spirit came to tempt and seduce the first two people who lived on earth and they were indeed seduced by it and made unspeakably miserable. In the same way, the evil spirit wants to prepare every person in the world for sin and eternal damnation and there are only a few who withstand the evil spirit as firmly as they should.

There is no place unknown to the evil spirit, no status too venerable, and no degree of sanctity too high. It is *"[r]oaming the earth and patrolling it."* The evil spirit does not only find the worldly man in the midst of his vain and sinful joy, but also the solitary hermit practicing severe penance in his silent, remote and distant forest. It even found Jesus Christ, the eternal Holiness, in the quiet desert by the most holy work of prayer and fasting.

Do not be surprised, my dear Christian, if the evil spirit finds you, disturbs you and temps you not only in your worldly duties among people, but also during prayer and at the most holy activities before God. Do not think that you will be able to avoid it. The evil spirit will find you everywhere; it will walk around you and will seek to devour your soul. Therefore, never dare to think that you will never be tempted. In spite of this, strive to get to know well how dangerous temptations of the evil spirit are and learn how you can withstand and defeat them.

The evil tempter is a liar and the father of the lie. He is full of tricks and hypocrisies and does not show himself in his wickedness and unknown ugliness because everyone would be afraid of him. He comes with cunning, lying words. He does not come as a fatal enemy, but as a good friend. This is evident in the case of Jesus' temptations where the evil tempter always spoke kindly and benevolently. He wanted Jesus to satisfy his hunger after his austere fasting. The evil tempter wanted to honor Jesus and give Him the opportunity to be carried on the hands of angels. He wanted to give Jesus great wealth, royal honor and power. The tempter even spoke with the words from the Holy Bible. St. Paul says: *"And no wonder, for even Satan masquerades as an angel of light."*

Listen, my dear Christian and be on guard. Do not rely on your own good works as you may have until now, not even on your Christian virtues in which you may have lived faithfully until now, but be always alert, or the enemy will come soon as a thief and will take everything from you or at least cause great damage. Remember those workers who worked diligently, were sowing good seed in the field and fulfilled their duty faithfully, but then fell asleep and did not guard the field. While everyone was asleep, the enemy came and did great harm to the field.

My dear Christian, in order for you to more easily guard against evil and dangerous temptations and distractions of a permanent enemy, thoroughly consider lessons you can find here.

When someone is a known liar, no one believes that person anymore. But there is no liar more known than the evil spirit, because Jesus, the Eternal Truth, tells us clearly that the evil spirit is a liar, the patriarch and the source of all lies. Therefore, do *not believe* anything the evil spirit *suggests*, my dear Christian, but quickly remind yourself that when you have evil thoughts and temptations, they come from the evil spirit, the spirit of lies and fraud. Ignore them immediately. Do not listen nor talk to the evil spirit, but promptly discard and hate everything it puts in your mind. If you argue and talk to the evil spirit, you place yourself in great danger of potentially believing the evil spirit at the end because it is full of tricks and nice, sweet and pleasant words that are terribly dangerous, deceitful and poisonous. Eve, our first mother, did not believe the evil tempter immediately and did not want to do what he told her right away. If she had left then, she would not have sinned. But then she continued to talk to the evil spirit and finally believed its deceitful words and sinned.

May this example always be before your eyes when you are tempted, my dear Christian. If you hear a seducer who wants to lead you into a sin, remember that he is a servant of the evil spirit. This spirit of lies has its servants everywhere to help it lure people into sin and eternal damnation. What a man does by his servant, he does himself. When the seducer speaks to you and wants to seduce you into a sin, it is as if Satan himself were speaking to you. Do not believe him and do not speak to him, but drop everything and go away.

Consider, my dear Christian *how* the evil spirit, this knowledgeable tempter, leads a person into a sin. If you get to know this well, you will more easily guard against the dangerous seductions of the evil enemy.

Firstly, it strives to hide the *magnitude, the ugliness, and the wickedness of sin.* A sin is in itself and in the sight of God so ugly and terrible, and it is such a great wickedness that when a person recognizes it properly, he fears it and hates it from the heart. The evil spirit knows this very well and therefore tries to deceive a person so that this person would not see the sin as it is in itself. If the evil spirit is able to accomplish this, then it will lead a person into it. Remember this, my dear Christian, when you are facing temptations and do not believe the evil seducer when he offers you this evil thought: *This is not such a big sin; this is not a mortal sin.* Be on guard, my dear Christian, as it might truly be a mortal sin that you are planning to commit. Especially in life you were called to live or your circumstances; however, the evil spirit is blinding you that you do not see how big it is. If you are so unlucky as to commit a sin, your eyes will open and you will realize with a sad heart how ugly and big your sin is. Similarly, the seducer tricked our first parents into sinning. Afterwards their eyes opened and they saw all the wickedness and horror of their sin. Although it is not exactly a mortal sin that you intend to commit, conclude firmly to not commit even a small sin *on purpose*, because you will put yourself in danger potentially to commit a grave sin.

Since the evil spirit is a constant seducer and liar, it lies again in a different way after the sin is committed. Before the sin is committed, the evil spirit tries to *diminish* it so that a person does not realize all its wickedness and ugliness and commits it more easily. When the sin is already committed, the evil spirit tries to *magnify* it and shows it as even more wicked and terrible than it really is, so that the sinner will despair of God's grace and say with the miserable Cain: "*My punishment is too great to bear.*" Again, this temptation is very dangerous and there are many of them through which the evil spirit gains power with this.

Recognize this, my dear Christian, and keep on guard again. Do not believe at all in these evil thoughts the enemy is sharing with you. Beware of sin more than you would guard against a venomous snake because a snake can take away only your temporary, earthly life, but a sin takes away your eternal, heavenly life. Beware of sin as much as possible – not only of mortal one, but of venial sin as well. However, if you are so foolish and unfortunate as to commit a sin, do not despair and do not enlarge your sinfulness with the terrible sin against the Holy Spirit, by despairing against God's grace, but trust in the merciful God, trust in Jesus' merits and remember the words of the loving apostle St. John: *"My children, I am writing this to you so that you may not commit sin. But if anyone does sin, we have an Advocate with the Father, Jesus Christ the righteous one."* Trust, my dear Christian. Hate your sin, regret it, abandon it, do penance and God will forgive you everything because He does not want the death of a sinner but his conversion and life. Trust in the immeasurable merit of Jesus because one single drop of His holy blood would suffice for the salvation of the entire world. Trust in the most holy blood of Jesus because *"There is no salvation through anyone else, nor is there any other name under heaven given to the human race by which we are to be saved."* Believe so and do so, and you will be forgiven. Trust Jesus, who tells you that your sin will be forgiven if you bear the worthy fruit of penance, more than the evil spirit who says: "Your sin will never be forgiven."

Secondly, the evil tempter strives to make a sin appear *really sweet and pleasant* and thus awakens a great desire in the heart of a person to commit this sin. In the case of certain sins, the evil tempter is trying even harder and he leads many people into sin. A sin is like a sweet poison with a pleasant taste. What follows are pain and death. So does a sin truly have its pleasantness and happiness; however, it is soon followed by suffering and sometimes by eternal suffering. Consider thoroughly, my dear Christian, and do not be fooled. Consider how short-lived, poor and uncertain is the joy that the unfortunate person experiences in his or her sin. Even if someone spent *the entire span of his or her life on this earth* happy and joyful in his or her sin, this joy would last for only an extremely short time because this joy would only last in this world; in the next world, this person would only suffer. And what is the longest human life compared to eternity! However, this is an error, too. A sinner can never live in this world in eternal joy. This person's conscience is always secretly reminding and stinging him. A sin is like a thorn in one's conscience. In the midst of a worldly joy this person has no joy or a peaceful heart because *"There is no peace for the wicked, says the Lord."*

Before the sin is committed, everything seems different to a person than it really is, due to the deception of the evil spirit. Therefore, let your own experience and that of other people teach you that sin is poison. And poison is poison, no matter how sweet it is.

Thirdly, the tempter is trying to awaken the thought in one's heart that it is *too difficult or impossible to restrain from this or that sin.* This is a terribly dangerous temptation and whoever believes in it soon gets so weak that they cannot withstand the sin any longer and think that it is futile to defend oneself against it, because this sin cannot be contained and one cannot restrain from it. Do not ever think so, my dear Christian. Remember what Jesus replied when in sadness His disciples said they wanted to despair of the possibility of salvation: *"Who then can be saved?"* Then Jesus said these comforting words to them: *"For human beings this is impossible, but for God all things are possible."* If a person only counts on oneself, this person will truly recognize and feel the incapability of withstanding sin in temptation. And this is exactly what the evil seducer strives to do, i.e., to take away a person's trust in God, so that the person would only trust in himself and fail. Do not listen to the evil tempter, my dear Christian, do not trust your weak strength and your fickle will. Believe Jesus because He says that it is impossible for a human to save himself. With God's help, however, it is possible to everyone. Consider what the benevolent Jesus says further: "[…] *without me you can do nothing.*" As He said to St. Paul so does He say to every Christian: "*My grace is sufficient for you* […]" And as St. Paul then said is what every Christian should say and think in his heart: "*I have the strength for everything through him who empowers me.*"

Then, my Christian, do not believe the evil tempter but the eternal God. The infinitely good and wise God does not command us to do anything impossible. And if He commands us something, He also gives us the required help and grace to fulfill His command. If a person truly strives to love God and only serve Him, then God's grace does everything "*For God is the one who, for his good purpose, works in you both to desire and to work.*"

Trust firmly in God's help and grace in all temptations. Never say nor think that a temptation is too big and that it is impossible to overcome it. If you would say so, you would contradict what is written in the Holy Bible: "*God is faithful and will not let you be tried beyond your strength; but with the trial he will also provide a way out, so that you may be able to bear it.*" Do not be afraid of the evil tempter as he has to be afraid of you, because you are stronger than he is since the *almighty God* is helping you. Do not be afraid of him, but "*Resist the devil, and he will flee from you.*"

Fourthly, the evil spirit is trying to tempt a person into a sin with the following thought: *If I do this, I will confess and will receive forgiveness.* This temptation is again terribly dangerous and through it the evil tempter destroys many souls. Consider, my dear Christian, how vile and unthankful it is to think and act in this way. If you would know that you would die right after committing a sin, you would not do it, but because it is your hope to gain forgiveness from the benevolent God, you do it. Consider how you act! You are talking with action and not with words when you are saying: *God is good to me, that is why I want to be mean to Him. Because He forgives me, I will insult Him on purpose*! Oh, wickedness! Oh, ingratitude! My dear Christian, consider that if you act like that, you live in the most terrible of sins, which are called the sins against the Holy Spirit, because whoever rudely commits a sin against God's grace and remains unrepentant, lives in these sins. Be afraid of the Lord, your God and always beware of such great evil and ingratitude toward Him!

Temptation in itself is not a sin nor is it only an opportunity to sin, but it is also an opportunity to do good, to earn great merit from God if a person overcomes it steadfastly and holds on to God even more firmly while the evil spirit is trying to separate this person from God. It is therefore written in the Holy Bible: "*Blessed is the man who perseveres in temptation, for when he has been proved he will receive the crown of life that he promised to those who love him.*" Strive, my dear Christian, that in temptation you will never have a happy liking over an evil thought and that you will never submit to what the tempter puts in your mind. It is through successfully facing temptations that you will gain the most merit for eternal life.

Consider also *what to do when you are confronted with temptation*. I especially recommend the four tools that will help you overcome temptation.

1. When you sense temptation *think of God's presence immediately*. God sees me. He hears me. This is a very useful and salvatory thought in temptations. It gives great strength to the soul to restrain from sin. Good examples of this can be found in the Holy Scripture. By thinking this way, the holy young man Joseph of Egypt

overcame a very dangerous temptation and avoided a great sin. The holy woman Suzanna gained strength with this thought and resolved to die rather than to sin.

2. Remember the Word of God that you heard in sermons or read in holy books. This is how Jesus teaches us by His example. For every temptation with which the evil spirit wanted to lead Jesus into sin, Jesus responded with a word from the Bible. There is nothing the evil tempter is more afraid of than the Word of the Lord, because it is the eternal truth and a witness to what a big liar he is. It is appropriate to say the holy name of Jesus in the moment of temptation and to make a sign of the cross because this is what the evil spirit is terribly afraid of as well.

3. Remember the four last things. It is written that "*In whatever you do, remember your last days, and you will never sin.*" Remembering this while experiencing temptation helps to overcome it. Remembering *death* should remind you how quickly everything passes on this earth – how short and deceitful is the joy that a sinner finds in his sin. You will recognize this best on your deathbed. The memory of *the Last Judgement* should remind you that your future judge sees you everywhere and that you will be judged harshly because you dare to do in front of Him what you would not dare to do in front of people. The memory of *hell* should remind you that someone with just a little sense can predict and recognize that this is an infinite stupidity and wickedness if a person is willing to put himself or herself in danger of burning there eternally for the sake of the short-lived joy the sin brings. You put yourself in this danger as soon as you consent to the mortal sin and commit it. The remembrance of *Heaven* should remind you that all the suffering of this time, all self-restraint, and all troubles you are facing in overcoming your temptations are nothing compared to the future honor God will prepare for you in Heaven if you will love him steadily and guard against sin out of love for Him and only serve Him.

4. A good and general tool for overcoming all temptations is *prayer*. Ask God daily to protect you with His grace in the temptations with which you are surrounded all the time and everywhere, and which you cannot overcome steadfastly out of your own power. So does Jesus, our "Good Shephard", in His infinitely beautiful and holy prayer teach us to always ask our Heavenly Father: *"Do not lead us into temptation"*, i.e., guard us that we do not fall into temptation. If You allow us to fall into it, give us the grace and strength to overcome it. If your prayerful desire not be to lead into temptation is sincere in spirit and in truth, you should not lead yourself unnecessarily into temptation, i.e., into a dangerous opportunity. By doing so, you would be tempting God and your action would contradict your prayer. These are the basic tools to overcome temptations. If you use them faithfully, you will be able to overcome all *common* temptations. If you are facing some *specific* temptations, talk to your confessor and be faithfully obedient to him. With the help of God, you will be able to overcome everything and the Lord our God will give you the crown of eternal life.

XVI.

DO GOOD

"The one who fears the Lord will do good."

If you want to be righteous before God, my dear Christian, it is not enough to protect yourself from evil, but you have to strive to do as much good as possible, that is, to fulfill God's will with His grace and help in all things thoroughly out of love for Him. A person who *fears* God will do good. However, the one who *loves* God will do better and live even more perfectly because the one who truly loves God obeys all His commandments.

Strive, my dear Christian, out of love for God, to live well, to fulfill all your Christian duties faithfully, and to unify your will in all things always and everywhere with His holy will. To make it easier for you to do this, you will find here, in addition to the teachings that have been given so far in this book, some *special teachings* for the special circumstances of life.

1. Begin each day with God

"I am the Alpha and the Omega, the first and the last, the beginning and the end." Let God be the beginning and the end of all your days. Give God the first thoughts of your heart every day. If you give those thoughts to this world, or worse, to the evil spirit, you will be terribly ungrateful and miserable. God wants your heart but the evil spirit wants it, too. St. John Climacus says that whoever has the *first thoughts of the heart* will also be the master of the heart for the whole day. Therefore, start each day with

prayer and end it with prayer. (Further teaching about this can be found in the *Guide or Rule of a Christian Life* in the appendix of this book.)

My dear Christian, if you want to love God properly and serve Him faithfully, it is not enough to pray only in the morning and in the evening because Jesus tells us that we must always pray and never stop. Then, even during the day, raise your thoughts and your heart to God repeatedly and often remember His presence, or rather, never forget it. Develop the habit of saying a short prayer when you hear the clock strike. If you want to live a Christian life to the fullest, get used to living according to some rule. The teachers of the pious spiritual life recommend this option and say *that whoever lives according to a rule, lives for God, and has a lot of merit even in everyday tasks, but those who do not live according to a rule have less merit.*

To make it easier for you to carry out what is recommended to you here, my dear Christian, you will find in the appendix of this book the *Guide or Rule of the Christian Life*, which, according to the teachings of enlightened spiritual teachers, is laid out in a way that you will be able to carry it out in action with the help of God, if you really try.

2. Always be decent regarding your clothing

Since it is recommended here (and even more precisely in the *Rule*) that you begin and end each day with God, it is also important to *dress decently* in the morning and to *undress decently* in the evening. This gives me the opportunity to offer you some good advice and recommendation regarding *clothing*.

Consider, my dear Christian, that we have clothes predominately because we are sinners. The Bible teaches us that our first parents were without any clothes from the beginning because they were completely innocent, as are little children. However, after they sinned, their nature became inclined to evil and then they needed clothing. Since we all sinned after our first parents, we need clothes as well. If you will consider with your mind and faith, my dear Christian, you will humble yourself much more for the sake of your clothing than you will exalt yourself because nothing convinces us like clothing *that we are sinners from the beginning.*

When you are dressing and undressing, beware of all sinful looks, and especially of all indecency, because God sees you. Beware of all indecency in front of your family members. Do not let anyone see you until you are properly dressed.

Do not dress in a particular way, and do not follow the ways of the world too much. St. Paul tells us: "*I urge you therefore, brothers, by the mercies of God, to offer your bodies as a living sacrifice, holy and pleasing to God, your spiritual worship. Do not conform yourselves to this age* [...]"

When you get dressed, do not look too much in the mirror, but only as much as is necessary to dress decently. A mirror offers a dangerous opportunity for many conceited, worldly, vain and impure thoughts.

It can never be recommended enough particularly to young people, and especially to girls, that they should beware of all haughtiness or ostentation regarding their clothing. My dear Christian who is reading this, beware of this sin! Arrogance and conceit in general, may reveal itself however it wants; it is the first capital sin, the first sin of Satan! Just as humility is a special virtue among all the virtues, and the Lord's favorite, haughtiness and vanity are the most obnoxious to Him among all the sins.

May you be always dressed in clean, smart and decent clothes and never in worldly and haughty ones. Oh, think, my Christian, if you are haughty in your dress, why do you dress so haughtily and worldly? Whom do you want to please? Certainly not God. You know that well because "*The Lord is on high, but cares for the lowly,*" and not the wise, intelligent, and humble Christians, because they carefully avert their eyes from all worldly vanity and always ask God: *"Avert my eyes from what is worthless; by your way give me life."* Whom do you want to please? Only Satan, that father of all arrogance and those who are mimicking him and "[…] *are allied with him."* Oh, wickedness! Oh, ingratitude and blindness! Saint Paul says: *"Am I now currying favor with human beings or God? Or am I seeking to please people? If I were still trying to please people, I would not be a slave to Christ."*

Consider, this chosen apostle says that a person who seeks to please people in general is no longer a servant of Christ. Whose servant then is the one who wants to please the evil spirit and the people who imitate him? Do not say at all that your conscience does not reproach you for the sake of your dress because you have no bad intention in this matter. Even if it were true that you have no evil intention, your action is still evil and despicable. You err if you think you have no evil intention when you dress haughtily. If you listen to the teachings of preachers and confessors, you must know that secular and haughty clothing is strictly forbidden for Christians. If you nevertheless dress haughtily and ostentatiously, how can you say that you have absolutely no evil intention and therefore no sin? Or perhaps you say that you know very well that haughty clothing is sinful, and then you say that *your* clothing is not haughty. Beware, my dear Christian, perhaps the evil spirit blinds you so that you do not see all the wickedness and the extent of your sin. If priests and other intelligent and pious people tell you that you are dressing too haughtily, listen to them and believe them more than the evil tempter who wants to deceive and destroy you. However, if you do not listen to them and do as they teach you, how will you be able to say and think that you are without sin?

Someone who dresses haughtily not only sins himself, but also leads others into sin. How many indecent and wicked glances and how many sinful and impure thoughts does a haughtily dressed woman awaken in the hearts of young men! St. Bernard says *"that a girl or woman, who is indecently and haughtily dressed, is an instrument used by Satan to destroy souls."* Oh, infinitely unhappy woman who puts herself like a tool in Satan's hands for the destruction of immortal souls!

Beware, therefore, a Christian woman, that the evil Satan does not deceive you! Fear the Lord your God and His dreadful judgment! Remember that the benevolent God has given you a guardian from Heaven, a holy angel, who always reminds and warns you in order to protect you from the tempter who wants to destroy you. It is written in the Bible that God did not want Moses' burial place to be known to the Israelites, because otherwise they would have taken his body to worship him as an idol. The evil spirit wanted this body to become known to the Israelites so that they would pray to him. However, the angel of God opposed him and did not allow it. Look, Christian woman, in the same way the evil spirit wants you to show your haughty and ostentatious body to people, so that through this they could pray to the idol of impurity. But the angel of God, who is your faithful guardian and who is full of zeal and love for God and for you, wants to turn you away from all haughtiness, so *"that your life is hidden with Christ in God,"* and that in the humility of your heart you would serve only God. Oh! Listen rather to God and His holy angel than to the evil spirit and his servants.

If you dress haughtily, you want in your heart (even if you hide it with your words) that young men see you and that they like you. Oh! You should be ashamed before God and yourself! A Christian woman must be ashamed when some young man looks at her. The one who dresses haughtily wants and seeks to be looked at. The Blessed Virgin Mary was very frightened when she saw an angel in front of her looking like a young man and did not know where to look. As for you, a worldly and haughty woman, you dress purposefully in such a way that people look at you. Oh, wickedness! Oh, terrible judgment!

A Christian woman who behaves haughtily *is not worthy of being named a Christian*, because she breaks and discards the holy promises she made at baptism. At her baptism she promised to renounce the evil spirit, all its works and all its vanity; however, she takes it all upon herself again. Consider further, oh Christian, that Jesus said that whoever wants to be His disciple, that is, *to be a Christian*, must be humble as a child, must live penitently, must take up his cross and thus follow Him. If a Christian does not do this, he or she will not enter the kingdom of Heaven. All this is well known to you, oh Christian woman. But if you have the habit of dressing haughtily, you are giving up on Jesus and His teaching. Does it mean to be humble when you want to rise above others with your beautiful clothes and be seen before all others? Are these your penitential works; is this your penitential spirit? Do you take up your cross and follow Jesus when you hang haughty clothes over your sinful body and go to show yourself to young men and therefore help Satan to kill their souls? If, despite all this, you still want to go to Heaven, you have to look for another Heaven, not the one Jesus speaks of, and to which He showed us the narrow, steep and thorny path: the path of humility, the path of penance, the path of the cross, and the path of denying oneself.

Arrogance in dressing is more common among women than among men, but it is also found among young men. If then, oh, young man who reads this, you have the habit of dressing haughtily, take to heart the teachings that you find here. In addition, consider what the Holy Spirit says in the Holy Scripture: "*Do not entertain any thoughts about a virgin, lest you be enmeshed in damages for her.*" If you see a woman in haughty clothing, remember God and say with the kingly Prophet: "*Avert my eyes from what is worthless; by your way give me life.*" Do not look at her, so that an unclean spirit does not pass through the door of your eyes into your heart.

Christian mothers have a duty of conscience to protect their children in their youth and further on to prevent them from falling into the sinful habit of dressing haughtily. Woe to the mother who allows her daughter to pursue worldly vanities, through which she is becoming more and more accustomed to haughtiness. Instead of protecting the soul of her child and sparing it to God, she gives it over to the evil spirit, to this spirit of pride, which, with its haughtiness and conceit, has made itself and an infinite number of people eternally miserable. However, sevenfold woe to that mother who herself loves worldly vanity and arrogance and seduces her children into Satan's sin by her own example!

3. Enjoy working and work hard

Do not fear or avoid work, my beloved Christian, but fear laziness, for laziness is the beginning of sin. The Holy Scripture says: "*for idleness teaches much mischief.*" St. Bernard writes: "*Laziness is the gathering place of dangerous thoughts. Laziness breeds impurity, kills all chastity, kills the soul. Laziness is the grave of a living man and the receptacle of all sins.*"

It is sad to see that this shameful sin and even more, the source of these sins can be found everywhere, with every state in life and in every age. In order to protect more effectively against sinful laziness, consider the following:

1. It is God's will that every man should work diligently according to his or her state in life. We read in the Bible about the first man that the Lord God "[…] *settled him in the garden of Eden, to cultivate and care for it.*" Even then, when man was still innocent and without sin, God commanded him to work. But he commanded him to work even more harshly when he became a sinner. At that moment, God told him aforehand that he would only gain what he needs to survive by much work and in the sweat of his face. Whoever does not want to work acts against the will of God, against the will of his Lord, although he or she knows it well, and will be severely punished, for as Jesus says: "*That servant who knew his master's will but did not make preparations not act in accord with his will shall be beaten severely.*" He states further that he ordered to "[…] *throw this useless servant into the darkness outside, where there will be wailing and grinding of teeth.*" Whoever is lazy and does not want to work according to his status is not worthy before God to live on earth. We recognize this from the Word of God, as it is written: "[…] *if anyone was unwilling to work, neither should that one eat.*" If somebody does not deserve to eat, he is not worth to live since food preserves life. Be therefore diligent and industrious, my dear Christian, to fulfill God's will and live according to the law He has given us all. Consider the words of God that you find here and also consider that God will only judge us according to His holy Word and law and not according to the ways and customs of the world, i.e., of the worldly people.

2. *Work is assigned to us as a way of penance.* We are obliged faithfully and willingly to perform the penance that the confessor imposes on us during confession, even more the penance that the Lord God Himself imposes on us. God's penance is work and all the difficulties related to work. It is true that God commanded a man to work when he was not yet a sinner, but then there was no talk of any problems. The work back then was pleasant and was performed without any problems. However, when a

man sinned, God commanded him harshly to work and he combined the problems associated with work. And these difficulties, which are more or less present in every work, are given to the man who is a sinner as a penance. Whoever then avoids work because of problems that come with the work, refuses to perform penance that God has imposed on him or her. Consider this well, my dear Christian, and never avoid work because of difficulties, but willingly and humbly suffer them in the spirit of penance that God imposed on you thinking that if man were not a sinner, he would have nothing to suffer in this world.

All people are obliged to work before God, each according to his own state in life, especially young people, each according to his or her own strength. This duty of young people can be recognized:

1. If a young person gets used to laziness and grows up with it, it will not be easy for him or her to become diligent and hardworking. Moreover, if a young person spends his or her youth in laziness, this person will develop many bad habits, which he or she cannot leave easily because the proverb says: *"Train the young in the way they should go; even when old, they will not swerve from it."*

2. If a young person wastes the time of his youth, he or she suffers great damage. Youth is the best time to learn. It is the time when it is the easiest to acquire knowledge and to learn some kind of work or handcraft. Whoever loses the time of his or her youth through laziness will feel this loss for a large part of his or her life. Consider, oh young person, if you live in laziness in your youth, how sorry you will be when you grow up and find yourself without knowledge and without the good work habits that you should have acquired in your youth. Think about the horrible judgment of God before which you too will be called one day. There you will have to give God an answer regarding your whole life,

but first regarding your youth. If you spend your youth in laziness, oh, how will you be able to justify yourself before God! God will show you all the damage you did to your soul in your youth by wasting the time of your youth: your evil habits, your ignorance, all the waste of your graces. Consider also how many are in hell and are eternally suffering only because they wasted the time of their youth being lazy, or through unnecessary, vain pursuits, with which they gained nothing more than through obvious laziness.

Young people should think carefully about this and should be diligent and hard-working already in their youth. They should strive to spend the time of their youth, with God's help, well and according to God's will.

But since young people are for the most part unwise, reckless and careless, their parents and all those who have young people in their care, are obliged before God to strive as much as possible for their children to spend their youth diligently and well.

It is recommended to Christians of every state in life, of every age, to each according to his or her circumstances and according to God's will and providence, to work diligently. Be therefore always diligent and industrious, my dear Christian, and never waste time, which is so precious and infinitely valuable. Always have a good job that suits your status. The evil spirit quickly joins a lazy man who is without work. On the contrary, the evil spirit is extremely frightened of a hard-working man who is always engaged in decent work, especially when this person follows God's will and sanctifies his or her work in the memory of God's presence. St. Hieronymus writes: "Always live in such a way that Satan will never find you idle. Do not hate your work because of its difficulties, but love it because it is commanded of you by God and because it helps you to be saved. Offer it to God in the morning, and when you start work, ask the Lord to bless it and to give you the grace to complete it in His honor." This is what this teacher of the Church writes, and from his words take these lessons:

1. Be diligent in your work and love to work. Do not just work when you are forced to, but always love to work. Do not be like an evil servant who works only when someone is standing behind him with a stick, but like a good child who works for his father with joy and love.

2. Before you start working in the morning, say your prayer and commend yourself to God for the whole day. Offer Him the work that you intend to do that day. Entwine the difficulties of your work with the difficulties of the benevolent Jesus, who had a difficult, poor, working life in this world without much rest, because He worked throughout day and thought and spent the whole night in prayer out of obedience and love for His Heavenly father and out of infinite mercy to us.

3. During the day, sanctify your work with the perpetual memory of God's presence. Begin all work in the name of God. It is a good Christian custom to make the sign of the Holy Cross before starting any work. The first Christians already had this habit as the holy teacher Hieronymus testifies. Again, offer each work separately to God and never forget that while you are working, God is watching you as you work, and that He sees not only the outward part of your work, like a man, but also all the thoughts and purposes of your heart.

4. In every work, remember the judgment of God and strive to do it as if you knew that after the completion of work you will be able to stand before God's judgment throne and give an answer for your work.

If you always act like this, my dear Christian, even your ordinary daily chores will be good works before God and you will not approach Him empty-handed when He calls you to the Last Judgment, because *your works will go with you.*

4. Enjoy reading good, holy books

A person is happy and has great spiritual wealth as well as a good means of salvation if he or she knows to read and faithfully takes advantage of this beautiful opportunity. One who likes to read holy books learns more and more about the duties of his or her own state in life. This person understands more and more about the teachings of his or her spiritual shepherds. This person gets to know the infinitely loving God more and more and loves Him more and more, because Church teachers say that only those who really know God can truly love Him. And just as the love for God is *awakened* in one's heart especially by reading good, holy books, so it is also *multiplied* and *preserved* through this. Love is like fire. Fire becomes smaller and eventually goes out if new wood is not constantly added to it. The same is true for the love of God if it is not always guarded by holy teachings and contemplation of the eternal truths. It is true, however, that the one who listens faithfully to the teachings of spiritual teachers, and preserves and reflects upon them, and lives by them, will be able to preserve the fire of God's love in his heart and will be saved *as Jesus testifies*. There are many saints in Heaven who could not read. This is all true. However, it is very good to know how to read as those who can read and who read holy books have a much more beautiful and abundant opportunity to hear the word of God and ponder the truths of salvation.

Many souls convert to God by reading good, holy books. This happened many times in the past and still happens many times today. St. Augustine, for example, who has been rejecting God's grace from the beginning, completely and firmly converted to God after reading holy books. He himself testifies that an unfamiliar voice (which was the voice of God's grace) commanded him to pick up the holy books that were lying on the ground and read them. We read that St. Seraphim converted to God by reading the Gospels. According to the teachings of the Gospels, he gave all his possessions to the poor and kept only a little of the poor clothing for himself. When someone addressed him regarding his poverty, he showed the Holy Scripture and said: "Behold, this has made me poor."

Enjoy reading good, holy books, and you will discover what a good tool reading is for salvation. For your reading to be pleasing to God and to serve for your soul's salvation, strive to complement these teachings with action.

1. Just like any work or task you perform, *start* your reading *with God* and ask Him to give you the grace to read in his honor and for the salvation of your soul. A good Christian habit is to make the sign of the cross before you start reading. While reading, never forget the presence of God who looks at you with admiration when you read.

2. Always read with *good intention*, i.e., not just to pass time or out of curiosity, but only for the honor of God and the salvation of your soul. To become better and better, to love God and neighbor more and more, to learn more and more about your Christian duties so as to fulfill them faithfully, to acquire beautiful Christian virtues, etc. These should be your permanent wishes when reading and thus reading will really help you merit your salvation.

3. Read *respectfully.* Your behavior while you are reading should be respectful as well. Remember that when you pray sincerely, you are talking to God. When you read good, holy books, *God* speaks to you. Jesus says to all preachers and teachers of his holy faith: "*Whoever listens to you, listens to me.*" Holy books, especially in our language, are almost always written by spiritual teachers. When they preach and teach, they proclaim God's word with their voices. In books, they announce it in writing.

When a faithful Christian reads a holy book written by a spiritual shepherd, God is really talking to him.

4. Read *slowly* and *with consideration*. It is better to read only a little and to reflect upon it well in order to understand it than to read a lot and in the end, retain nothing. If a person wants to preserve one's health and strength, he or she should not eat too hastily nor consume too much at once. The same is true of holy reading, food for the soul. Therefore, read as much at once as you can. Try to keep in your memory and in your heart what God told you when you read the holy books. When you read, the Lord sowed the good seed of His word in your heart. May He also give you His grace so that this good seed may also find good soil in your heart and bear an abundant fruit of holiness in it!

5. Read *frequently*. Read every day if you can. Do not be careless in this matter, my dear Christian. Those who do not like to read soon find an excuse for not being able to read, yet they waste a lot of time every day in idle talk or laziness. Happy is he who likes to read holy books, that is, he who likes to listen to God who speaks through holy books. That is why Saint Paul, in the person of his beloved Timothy, recommended to every Christian who knows how to read: "*attend to the reading*." If you really cannot read every day, at least read as often as you can, especially on Sundays and on the holy days of obligation.

6. *Do not read certain good books only once, but read them several times*. If you read with a good intention (and always do this), you will realize that when you read good and instructive books a second or third time, you understand more and more and retain the beautiful life-giving teachings that are included in them.

5. Have only good Christian friends

Friends lead a person either to good or to bad, according to the way they are. Some friends and companions are truly guardian angels who faithfully protect a person, especially a young Christian who is on the dangerous paths of this world, and guide him, like the angel Raphael led young Tobiah along the path of Christian chastity with friendly admonitions, with good Christian advice, and by their beautiful example. However, some friends are helpers and servants of the evil spirit whom the enemy of our salvation uses to get many souls under his control and to destroy them eternally. Consider before God, my dear Christian, what your friends and companions are like and then listen to the voice of your conscience, because it is God's voice.

Kindness and *love for one's neighbor* are two things. We are commanded to love all people without distinction. However, we cannot and must not live with all people in kindness.

Kindness is sometimes good and holy, sometimes vain and dangerous, and sometimes sinful. This can be recognized after reflecting over a friend's life and asking why one loves that friend. When someone loves a person because he or she is a good Christian, because he or she serves God faithfully, shows beautiful Christian virtues in his or her life and because he or she strives to bring one's friends to the path of Christian chastity and walk along it with them, this is good and Christian. But when someone loves a person only because he or she is of pleasant appearance, pleasant in company and in his or her behavior, or because he or she is of a distinguished status, then this is a vain and often dangerous kindness that lends an opportunity to worldliness and sin. When someone loves a person and associates with him or her because this person is free in life, because he or she lives according to the ways and customs of this world and does not listen to spiritual shepherds and teachers, because this person lives in worldly joy and according to the inclination of a distorted nature, this is sinful kindness. Evaluate your kindness according to this and you will soon know how God views it.

Throw away all sinful, vain and even dangerous kindness, because it is the kindness of this world. Saint James says: "*Do you not know that to be a lover of the world means enmity with God? Therefore, whoever wants to be a lover of the world makes himself an enemy of God.*" Find good Christian friends and live with them in holy kindness. Such kindness will help you greatly in your salvation.

For your kindness to be Christian and holy, it must be rooted in good intentions.

1. Your kindness must *come from the love of God and Christian virtues*, that is, you must choose your friend for the sake of God, whom he or she faithfully serves, and love him or her for the sake of the beautiful virtues that show through in his or her actions and behavior. Never entertain kindness with worldly people who seek forbidden worldly joy, dancing, drinking, gaming, impurities, or who have the habit of cursing and speaking obscenely, lying, etc. If your friends and comrades are like that, you will soon become like that too. "*Walk with the wise and you become wise, but the companion of fools fares* badly."

2. Your kindness must lead *to a Christian life*, that is, you must love your friend because you hope that his or her good example will lead you on the path of Christian virtue and keep you on it; your friend will be the guardian of your soul by kindly admonishing you and offering you sound teaching. Let those not be your friends who do not conduct their lives according to Christian truths and the teachings of the holy faith and who only seek your kindness for some temporary gain. Their kindness is unworthy of the Christian name and can become dangerous to you. In addition, do not continue in friendship with a person who does not admonish you when you do something wrong. A good Christian friend loves his or her friend for God's sake, loves him or her in God,

and loves his or her soul more than all of his or her possessions. Accordingly, this Christian friend kindly admonishes his or her friend when this friend is observed making a mistake or committing a sin. Pope St. Gregory says: "He is my best friend who warns me when I sin."

3. Your kindness must always be conducted *according to the teachings of the holy faith*, that is, to elevate virtues, to be confirmed in the Christian life and for eternal salvation. You must seek this in your kindness and remove everything that stands in the way. If one of your friends wants you to do or consent to something that is against God's will, reject it and do not consent, because you must love God more than all your friends. Realize that this person is not a good Christian friend and that you must not continue to seek his or her special kindness if he does not improve. Beware of that sinful weakness that sometimes causes a person to do something out of love for one's friend that is against God's law. Such a person loves his or her friend more than God and is unhappy. Jesus says: "*Whoever loves father and mother more than me is not worthy of me* [...]." Then the one who loves his or her *friend* more than Him is even less worthy of Jesus because we are obliged to love our parents more than our friends.

My dear Christian, may your kindness be Christian and holy according to God's will. Do not strive to have *many* friends, but strive to have friends that are *good*. It is better to have one good Christian friend than a whole bunch of worldly ones. The Holy Scripture writes about a good and faithful friend: "*Faithful friends are a sturdy shelter; whoever finds one finds a treasure. Faithful friends are beyond price, no amount can balance their worth. Faithful friends are life-saving medicine;* (They preserve the soul of a friend for eternity.) *those who fear God will find them.*"

When you realize that you have a good Christian friend, never leave such a friend. Even if he or she hurts you sometimes, bear with this friend and forgive him or her, just as He forgives you. A person who refuses to put up with his or her friend will never have a good friend.

6. Strive to please only God

My dear Christian, this world is dangerous and is the enemy of eternal salvation. Therefore, beware of it and do not act according to its customs and laws, but only according to God's law and only strive to please God. The world is full of dangers, especially for young people who do not know it yet. It is full of temptation and seduction. This cannot be different because Jesus teaches us that "*the ruler of the world*" is the evil spirit who is the enemy of all good things, a liar and a deceiver from the beginning and "[…] *as the head of a city, so the inhabitants.*"

Always keep the eternal truths and teachings that our loving Jesus revealed to us before the eyes of your soul. The world does not want to recognize them and has its own teachings and customs. But the righteous God will not judge us according to the customs of the world, but according to his holy law. Here you will find some of those eternal truths of God's law which the world refuses to know. But you, my Christian, accept them with joy and live your life according to them and you will be eternally fortunate.

1. Fortunate is the one who truly loves God and his or her neighbor for God's sake. A worldly person does not understand it and does not believe it, nor does he or she ever feel it in their heart. If a worldly person had heartily believed in this fundamental Christian truth, he or she would not have hung their heart on worldly pleasure. A worldly person loves the world and its joy more than God. And that is precisely why he or she is secular and not pious. Although this person claims to love God more than anything else, he or she is lying and there is no truth in him or her as the worldly life testifies against him or her. If a worldly person does something good to their neighbor, this person is not doing it out of love for God, but actually out of love for themselves. And you, my dear Christian, if you want to be godly and not worldly, strive to recognize properly and to feel in your heart what a great happiness and grace the love for God is. Strive to show this in your life, because whoever lives according to God's law truly loves God. Always recognize Jesus in the person of your neighbor and you will be truly happy.

2. *God's grace is worth more than all wealth, and sin is the greatest misery.* The world has never believed in these truths. This can be seen from the actions of worldly people because they are ready to commit sin, even a great mortal sin, and lose grace, in order to gain a temporary thing or avoid certain loss. If people would firmly believe that the grace of God is more valuable than all temporal things, they would rather lose everything than sin. Between two misfortunes a person always chooses the one that he or she thinks is smaller. But you, my dear Christian, be firmly convinced and believe with all your heart that sin is a greater misfortune than all temporal losses, all abominations and everything that is called *misfortune* in this world. Because all temporal misfortunes, if we receive them in the Christian spirit without sin, are rather graces than misfortunes. Sin, however, is always a misfortune because it deprives the soul of God's grace and makes it eternally miserable if the soul gets separated in sin from this world. And who could think of a greater misfortune than that! One should guard against a voluntary venial sin more than all worldly fortune. Even though a small sin does not take all of God's grace away from the soul, it diminishes it, and this is already a great loss and a misfortune. Whoever is not afraid of small sins will soon commit big ones. Believe all this firmly, live according to this faith and you will be righteous, because *"The one who is righteous by faith will live."*

3. *God's will should be the main authority regarding all your actions.* This truth, which is so necessary for salvation,

is in direct opposition to the customs and habits of the world. A secular person wants to live only according to his own will and only when he or she cannot do otherwise is he or she willing to submit to the will of others and to the will of God, but only out of love for him- or herself. Voluntary denial and the suppression of one's own will is unknown to this person. This is terribly dangerous for salvation. If you want to be saved, my dear Christian, do not be like that, but strive to act in all things according to the most holy will of God, even if it seems so difficult for you and even if the world mocks you and despises you. Consider the beautiful words of *"the good Teacher"* and always act on them: *"Not everyone who says to me, 'Lord, Lord,' will enter the kingdom of heaven, but only the one who does the will of my Father in heaven."*

4. Happy is the one who has something to suffer. This sacred Christian truth seems ridiculous and stupid to a secular person, because the spirit of penance is unknown to them and therefore they do not realize what a beautiful opportunity for salvation a life of willing penitential suffering can be. But you, my dear Christian, following the example of God's friends, understand the value in suffering and realize that you are fortunate when you have something to suffer, e.g., contempt, persecution, poverty, disease, etc. If you are not yet confirmed enough in the holy love of God to desire and seek suffering, as the saints did, at least do not fear it and do not fight against when in His Providence, God allows it. Recognize the good purpose that God has when He allows us to experience trouble and suffering as an opportunity to do penance for our sins and gain eternal life in Heaven. Just as Christ had to suffer and entered into His kingdom in this way, so does a Christian most certainly come into the heavenly Kingdom if he or she has something to suffer and suffers willingly. God never bestows such great favors on His friends as when He sends them something to suffer. This is when His love for them is best shown. *"Welcome is his mercy in time of distress as rain clouds in time of drought."*

5. *The middle status is better than riches.* This is a certain Christian truth, which we know from Jesus' words and from His actions. In all this, a worldly person craves for nothing more than for wealth. How many difficulties does he or she suffer, how many dangers does he or she face, how much of the world does he or she travel through in order to gain wealth! Often it does not seem like too great a price to pay when someone places their soul on the line and runs the risk of eternal destruction in order to acquire earthly wealth. How many worldly souls does the evil spirit get under his power with those deceitful words with which he tried to seduce even Jesus: *"All these I shall give to you, if you will prostrate yourself and worship me."* How many there are for whom Mammon (wealth) is their idol, to whom they pray much more faithfully than to the Lord, their God! Never, my Christian, never ever be so blind. Firmly believe what Jesus said and what He always demonstrated in his actions and you will realize that the middle status, i.e., *"give me neither poverty nor riches; provide me only with the food I need,"* is the best ground for salvation. *"Indeed, religion with contentment is a great gain."* Consider, my dear Christian, that you brought nothing into this world but sin from which the merciful God saved you. And you certainly do not take anything out of this world, except your works, good or bad, by which God will judge you. If you have food and clothing, be content because *"Those who want to be rich are falling into temptation and into a trap and into many foolish and harmful desires, which plunge them into ruin and destruction."*

6. *A Christian must only want to please God.* Even the Christian truth does not appeal to the worldly person. To be honored by people (by *worldly* people) is more valuable to this person and he or she wants and seeks it more

than all Christian virtues. Oh, seductive, worldly honor! How many Christian souls fall into this trap of the evil spirit! The perpetual liar and seducer gives his worldly servants the idea that Christian virtues are ridiculous and despised, that people only mock them, and that whoever lives godly is despised, mocked, and without honor. Therefore, the worldly person is ashamed to live according to God's and the Church's commandments, to know Jesus Christ and take his yoke upon himself. For this person, honor means to live according to the customs and laws of the world and to be like other worldly people, or even more worldly and wicked than others because the worldly person places his or her honor in defeating his comrades in wickedness, in worldliness and in contempt of the holy Christian truths! Oh, the lamentable blindness when a Christian seeks his or her honor in what is his or her greatest shame. And that he or she is ashamed of what is his only honor! Oh, my Christian! God save you from this blindness! Never strive to please people, but only God. *Anyone who wants to please people is not a servant of Christ.* Think about how worldly people, who are ashamed of Christ and His salvific truths and deny Him in their actions, will be ashamed of Christ at the Last Judgment, when Christ will throw them away with shame as He says: "*Everyone who acknowledges me before others I will acknowledge before my heavenly Father. But whoever denies me before others, I will deny before my heavenly Father.*" Never think: What will people say if I do something or if I omit doing it? Rather think: What will God say, my future judge? Let this be your greatest honor: *to be God's servant.* This is how the saints thought and spoke, and they always acted accordingly. And now they are in incomprehensible and eternal glory in Heaven. They reign with Christ and are crowned with "*the crown of life*". Secular people, however, who were ashamed of Christ, and who sought all their honor only in the worldly life, live in the greatest and eternal shame in the next world, because they are slaves of the most evil, the most despicable, and the ugliest spirit!

7. *It is good to always contemplate the last four things.* This is a certain truth because the Holy Spirit who speaks in the Holy Scripture teaches us this: "*In whatever you do, remember your last days, and you will never sin.*" Does any thought seem more unpleasant to a worldly person than precisely this contemplation? This person carefully avoids everything that reminds him or her of *death* and says that this thought makes a person too sad, that it is only good for monks and hermits, etc. Even less does this person remember *the Last Judgment* because if he reflected and contemplated it, he would not live in injustice, in hatred, or in sinful worldly joy without all good and penitent works in which case he will stand empty-handed before the judgment seat. This person also knocks the memory of eternity out of his head as much as he can. The threat of an *unhappy* eternity makes this person sad as his conscience sometimes pinches even the worldliest person and declares him of being worthy of hell. If a person would listen to his own conscience and think about the unhappiness of eternity, he might improve, however, the ruin of a worldly person is precisely that he does not dismiss anything from his mind as quickly as the memory of hell. Moreover, the idea of a *happy* eternity makes him or her sad as well because this person knows how unworthy of heaven he or she is and that makes him or her sad. However, this sadness does not aid his salvation because he is only interested in dismissing the memory of heaven out of his head because he realizes the great loss and damage he is doing to himself by living a sinful life. My dear Christian, do not avoid contemplating this, but according to the teaching of the Holy Scripture, contemplate about your last things in all your works and you will be happy. You will fear and guard against sin more

and more, you will despise this world and its deceitful joy more and more, you will die to yourself and the world and you will "*face death* [every day]", you will judge yourself harshly and you would not be under judgement by God, and after this temporary, poor life here, you will get a fortunate, heavenly life and eternal peace.

All these are eternal and salvific truths which God's servants gladly receive from the mouth of the eternal God Who is the truth itself. The wicked world despises them and has always despised them. Do not listen to the world, my dear Christian, and do not want to please it, but only strive to please God, and only according to His holy will and law direct all your thoughts and words, your actions and omissions to Him and you will be truly and eternally happy.

Honor and eternal glory be
to the triune, one and only God,
who by virtues leads us
to the happiness of eternal peace!

AFTERWORD

I.
PRAYER FOR THE CONVERSION OF UNBELIEVERS

My dear Christian, you can show your love for your neighbor through deeds and through *prayer* as well. Pray every day for all those for whom you are obliged to pray before God and in accordance with your conscience. This is the duty of all Christians. "[…] *pray for one another, that you may be healed.*"

I ask you to pray often, especially for the *conversion of unbelievers.* Oh, my Christian! Believe me that they are worthy of all mercy! I always see here how unhappy they are because they do not know God, because they continue to live in their horrible sins and do not walk the path of salvation, which leads to God, to eternal life.

Stubborn unbelievers, i.e., those to whom the light of faith and the grace of God is offered, but they refuse to accept it, are especially in need of mercy. There are many of them here in this wild land, into which God's providence has sent me to spread the Gospel. It is true what the apostle of unbelievers, St. Paul, writes: "*But not everyone has heeded the good news; for Isaiah says, 'Lord, who has believed what was heard from us?'*"

I especially ask you to pray for them, so that God may grant them the grace of conversion by His great grace, by the infinite merit of Jesus Christ, and by the prayers of the holy disciples and missionaries. All endeavors of missionaries are in vain without this grace.

"So it depends not upon a person's will or exertion, but upon God, who shows mercy."

I have written this Litany for you, my dear Christian, so that you may diligently pray for the conversion of unbelievers, and that you may also pray together with others. Out of love for God and for your neighbor, I ask you to pray it often.

LITANY FOR THE CONVERSION OF UNBELIEVERS

Lord, have mercy on unbelievers.
Christ, have mercy on unbelievers.
Lord, have mercy on unbelievers.
Christ, hear us.
Christ, graciously hear us.
God the Father of Heaven, Almighty God,
God the Son, Redeemer of the world,
God the Holy Ghost,
Holy Trinity, one God,
Jesus, you came into the world for the salvation of all people, ℟. *have mercy on the unbelievers.*
Jesus, you gave grace to the three kings to know you and to pray to you, ℟.
Jesus, good shepherd, you gave your life for your sheep, ℟.
Jesus, you said that you have other sheep that you will lead in your fold, ℟.
Jesus, you asked your Father for all those who will believe in you according to the words ℟.
of the preachers of the holy faith, ℟.
Jesus, you send the preachers of your faith as the Heavenly Father has sent You, ℟.
Jesus, you said to the apostles and to all preachers of faith: Go and teach all nations, ℟.
Jesus, you shed your blood for the salvation of all people, ℟.

Jesus, you said: When I am lifted up from the earth, I will draw everyone to myself, ℟.

Jesus, you rose from the dead so that You may give eternal life to all, ℟.

Holy Mary, ℟. *pray to god for the unbelievers.*

Holy Mother of God, ℟.

Holy Virgin of virgins, ℟.

St. Peter, you welcomed the first unbelievers into the holy Christian church, ℟.

St. Paul, your chosen apostle of the unbelievers, ℟.

St. Andrew, ℟.

St. James, ℟.

St. John, ℟.

St. Thomas, ℟.

St. James, ℟.

St. Philip, ℟.

St. Bartholomew, ℟.

St. Matthew, ℟.

St. Simon, ℟.

St. Thaddeus, ℟.

St. Matthias, ℟.

St. Barnabas, ℟.

St. Luke, ℟.

St. Mark, ℟.

All you holy apostles and evangelists, pray to God for the unbelievers.

All you holy disciples of our Lord, pray to God for the unbelievers.

SS. Cyril and Methodius, who converted many unbelieving Slovenians, pray to God for the unbelievers.

St. Patrick, who taught the unbelieving Irish about the Christian faith, pray to God for the unbelievers.

St. Benedict, who converted many unbelievers on Mount Cassino, pray to God for the unbelievers.

All holy missionaries from the order of St. Benedict, pray to God for the unbelievers.

SS. Rupert and Boniface, who preached the Holy Gospel to the unbelieving Germans, pray to God for the unbelievers.

St. Stephen the Great, who did so much for the conversion of the unbelieving Hungarians, pray to God for the unbelievers.

SS. Dominic and Vincent Ferrer, who preached the Holy Gospel everywhere with a burning zeal, pray to God for the unbelievers.

All holy missionaries from the order of St. Dominic, pray to God for the unbelievers.

St. Francis, the Seraphic Father, who prayed with fervent desire for the conversion of unbelievers, pray to God for the unbelievers.

All holy missionaries of the Seraphic Order, pray to God for the unbelievers.

St. Ignatius of Loyola, who had a burning desire to preach Christ to the unbelieving Turks, pray to God for the unbelievers.

St. Francis Xavier, apostle of India and Japan, pray to God for the unbelievers.

St. Francis Xavier, the most remarkable of all the holy missionaries, pray to God for the unbelievers.

St. Francis Xavier, who won over many hundreds of thousands of Indians for Christ, pray to God for the unbelievers.

All holy missionaries of the Jesuit order, pray to God for the unbelievers.

St. Vincent de Paul, who founded the order of missionary priests, pray to God for the unbelievers.

All the holy martyrs who shed their blood in preaching the holy Christian faith, pray to God for the unbelievers.

Be merciful, spare us, O Lord.

Be merciful, graciously hear us, O Lord.

From Your wrath, ℟. *save the unbelievers, O Lord*
From idolatry, ℟.
From hatred of Christian truth, ℟.
From their sad blindness, ℟.
From all stubbornness, ℟.
From the enslavement of the evil spirit, ℟.
From eternal damnation, ℟.
That you would give them the grace to receive the preachers of the Holy Gospel, ℟. *we ask you, hear us well.*
That you would give them the grace to listen to the teachings of the holy faith, ℟.
That you would give them the grace of true conversion, ℟.
That you would grant them the grace of holy baptism, ℟.
That you would count them among your children, ℟.
That you would receive them into your holy Church, ℟.
That you would grant them grace to completely renounce the evil spirit and all idolatry, ℟.
That you would give grace to all converts to faithfully preserve the holy Christian faith to the end, ℟.
That you would graciously hear us, ℟.
Son of God, ℟.

Lamb of God who takes away the sins of the world, hear us, O Lord.
Lamb of God who takes away the sins of the world, have mercy on us, O God.
Christ, hear us.
Christ, graciously hear us.
Lord, have mercy on the unbelievers.
Christ, have mercy on the unbelievers.
Lord, have mercy on the unbelievers.

Our Father … Hail Mary …

Prayer of St. Francis Xavier

Eternal God, Creator of all things, remember that *You* alone have created the souls of unbelievers, which You have made according to *Your Image*. Behold, O Lord, how to Your dishonor many of them are falling into Hell. Remember, O Lord, Your Son Jesus Christ who so generously shed His blood and suffered for them. Do not permit that Your Son, Our Lord, remains despised by unbelievers, but, with the help of Your Saints and the holy Church, the Bride of Your Son, be comforted. Remember Your mercy, forget their idolatry and infidelity, and make them know Him, Who You have sent, Jesus Christ, Your Son, Our Lord, who is our salvation, our life, and our resurrection, through whom we have been saved and redeemed, and to whom is due glory forever. Amen.

II.
GUIDE OR RULE OF CHRISTIAN LIFE

If you want to live a beautiful Christian life, my dear Christian, it is not enough to know your duties and fulfill them, but it is also important that you do everything in order and at the right time, and that you conduct your life according to some Christian rule. If you do so, you will perform all your Christian duties more completely, more consistently and with greater merit. You will do as St. Paul teaches: *"but everything must be done properly and in order."*

To make it easier for you to complete this in action, you will find here this guide, which is adapted for the people of low and working class. You will be able to fully fulfill it if you really have the will to please God, to serve Him faithfully, and to save your soul with His grace and help.

First of all, consider carefully these words of the benevolent Jesus: *"What profit is there for one to gain the whole world yet lose or forfeit himself?"* St. Ignatius said these words to his friend Francis Xavier repeatedly while he was still living a worldly life. By doing so, Ignatius discouraged Francis especially from loving the world; he revived in Francis' heart the burning desire for eternal life with the help of God's grace and led him to the right path. Following it, Francis gradually attained great sanctity.

Therefore, my dear Christian, you, too, consider carefully this eternal truth and make a firm decision to leave and despise the world and its seductive and evil customs and habits, to walk on the narrow path of Jesus, to love God above all things, and to save your soul. If you really want to accomplish this, and who would not want to reach eternal happiness, read and consider this rule often and follow it faithfully. In this way, you will be certainly saved with God's help.

1.

Believe firmly and steadfastly everything that the Holy Mother Church tells you to believe. Her teaching undoubtedly reflects the word of God. Everything that is holy, pious, salvific, and pleasing to God is built and erected on the foundation of the Christian faith so that what does not come from faith cannot be pleasing to God, as St. Paul teaches: *"But without faith it is impossible to please him [...]."* He states further: *"The one who is righteous by faith will live."* The holy apostle even states: *"for whatever is not from faith is sin."* Here are the following basic Christian truths that you need to believe in firmly.

1. There is one God in three distinct Persons: the Father, the Son, and the Holy Spirit. The Father is God. The Son is God. The Holy Spirit is God. However, all three Persons are one God who is called the Holy Trinity.

2. God the Son is the second Person of the Trinity. The Son of God the Father who equals the Father in all things took our human nature into His eternal and divine nature because He was conceived by the Holy Spirit, born of the Virgin Mary, was crucified and died for our salvation. He rose again from the dead on the third day and ascended into Heaven; He sits at the right hand of God, the Father Almighty; He shall come again to judge the living and the dead, and only because of His infinite atonement of sins, we shall receive grace and salvation from God.

3. The grace of God, which we receive through the merits of Jesus, is so necessary for us that without it we cannot do anything good, pleasing to God and worthy of eternal salvation. "[…] *without me you can do nothing,*" says Jesus, i.e., without His divine help and grace we cannot do anything good.

4. Our soul, created in God's image, is immortal. According to what it earns in this life, it will be either eternally happy in Heaven or eternally miserable in hell. Our body will rise from the death on the Judgment Day; it will be reunited with its soul and remain with it forever happy or unhappy.

5. Jesus Christ, the Son of God, who is our Savior, will also be our Judge. He will judge all people without distinction. He will make the righteous partakers of His heavenly salvation and will condemn the wicked to eternal suffering.

6. Our Lord, Jesus Christ established in His Holy Catholic and Apostolic Church seven holy sacraments for our salvation. These are: Baptism, Eucharist, Confirmation, Reconciliation, Anointing of the sick, Marriage, and Ordination.

7. When we receive Holy Baptism, all inherited sins are forgiven as well as all other sins that a person committed before being baptized, if he is baptized as an

adult. Then we become children of God and members of the holy Church.

8. The Eucharist is the Body and Blood of Jesus Christ under the form of bread and wine. Jesus is both God and man, present under these forms. Jesus is entirely present under the form of bread, and He is entirely present under the form of wine. The most Blessed Sacrament does not contain bread and wine any longer, but only the external forms of bread and wine.

9. The offering of the Holy Mass is exactly the same offering that Jesus Christ, the Son of God, made to His Heavenly Father on the holy cross, with the distinction that Christ does not shed His blood on the altar and does not die, but offers to His Heavenly Father for our redemption and salvation His suffering and His death, which He endured on the cross. He thus makes us partake in His infinite merit.

10. Jesus gave us the holy sacrament of Penance for the forgiveness of sins that we commit after being baptized. Whoever confesses his sins to the priest, these sins are forgiven after making a *good* confession and receiving absolution.

2.

Firmly believe in these and in all other Christian truths taught by the Holy Catholic Church. Because "[…] *faith without works is dead,*" it is not enough just to believe that "*even the demons believe that and tremble;*" you must also live by faith to be righteous before God. Consider further that "*There is need of only one thing* […]." As the greatest of the Apostles commands: "*Therefore, brothers, be all the more eager to make your call and election firm, for, in doing so, you will never stumble.*"

Therefore, my dear Christian, always strive to direct your life, your actions, and omissions toward the truths of the Christian faith, and to live in God. Act faithfully according to this rule and you will live in God.

1. What a faithful Christian should do every day of his life

My dear Christian, if you want to live in God, start every day of your life with God. When you rise in the morning, lift up your heart to God and let the first work of your hands be the sign of the holy cross. Then pronounce the most holy name of Jesus with love and trust, commend yourself to Him and firmly resolve to spend that day pleasing to God. When you get dressed, remember God who is always watching you. Remember also your guardian angel whom you have to respect. Then pray the morning prayer and never abandon it. It is true that a Christian who does not pray the morning prayer faithfully, does not have a true and real desire to spend all his days to please God. If you have to start work early in the morning, it is better to get up a little earlier so that you have time to pray decently before you go to work. A good morning prayer is very important. Through it, the Christian soul finds strength and energy for the whole day. The Scripture says that every morning God sent *manna* from Heaven to the Israelites in the desert. It would suffice for the entire day. God only sent it to them in the morning. Whoever was late to collect it, remained without it that day. Similarly, a good morning prayer is truly the heavenly manna for the soul for the whole day. It is good and right if the entire family prays together in the morning.

Make sure you always perform your morning prayer well. If you pray in a lazy manner and without thought, such prayer counts little or nothing. If you can, get used to meditating at least a little every morning about God's blessings that you always enjoy and about your duties toward Him. Meditate about certain holy Christian truths as well. Such contemplation is immeasurably beneficial for salvation and protects the soul from sin and from sinful habits. It is impossible to meditate heartily on eternal truths every morning and still live in sinful habits. One or the other must be abandoned.

When you pray in the morning, reflect on what your work and tasks will be that day. Foresee the dangerous situations you will get into as much as possible. Firmly conclude that you will avoid all these occasions as much as you can, and carefully guard against sin in those that you cannot avoid. Consider, for example, in what kind of company you will find yourself in today, with whom you will deal with, what places you will go to, etc. Consider what is your *habitual* sin, which you commit most easily and most often, for example, ill-will, anger, cursing, quarreling, gossiping, laziness, envy, lying, injustice, obscene words, etc. Then make a particularly firm resolution to guard against this sin today. At the same time, ask God for His grace and help because without Him you cannot do anything good.

Since it is certain that everything that is not done for the sake of God is lost for Heaven, strive to sanctify all your ordinary daily tasks with a good intention. Conclude in the morning that whatever you will have to do that day, you will do it for the sake of God and according to His holy will. This is how the saints acted who became saintly by performing their daily tasks well. Holiness does not show itself only in great, wonderful works, but in ordinary tasks as well if they are done out of love for God, with a pure heart and the purpose to be pleasing to God only. Whoever acts in this way is truly "faithful in small things" and is pleasing to his Lord. Therefore, whatever you do, be it big or small, always follow this purpose to do everything according to God's will. *"So whether you eat or drink, or whatever you do, do everything for the glory of God."*

This short prayer, which you can find here, will help you a lot. If you really want to live in God and do all your work pleasing to Him, pray it every morning. "O Lord, let *your grace* today be the beginning of all my tasks, that I may do them in Your holy grace. Let *my love for you* be my purpose in all I do. Let *your will* be the only rule of all my action and ceasing. Let *the memory of your presence* be the guardian of all my thoughts, words, and deeds. Let *your divine honor and the salvation of souls* be the goal and the end of all my actions. I ask you for all these graces in the name of Jesus. Amen." Do not say this prayer only with words, but strive to live by it, and you will realize with the incredible joy of your heart that you live in God.

If it is possible for you, my dear Christian, and if it is permitted to you, go every morning to Holy Mass. But if you cannot go every morning, go at least every time you can. This is the holy work of a Christian. Happy is he who does it often and well.

Pray the Angelus every day when the bell rings for it. Do this firstly out of gratitude to the Son of God who became man for you and for all people to save us from eternal damnation. Secondly, commend yourself to the intercession of the most pure Virgin Mary.

Awaken the three virtues of God daily, i.e., faith, hope, and love. Firstly, to obtain great indulgences granted to those who pray for these beautiful virtues every day with a collected spirit, and secondly, because God is especially honored through this prayer. It makes no difference what words you use to awaken these three virtues. If you are unable to say a long prayer, pray for these virtues more often by praying a short prayer. It will be just as good if you only pray with a collected spirit and fervor. Here is an example of a brief prayer.

I believe in You, O Eternal God, Father, Son, and Holy Spirit, who are triune and one in nature. I believe in your only Son, Jesus Christ, our Lord and Savior. I believe all that you, O God, have revealed because you are pure truth, and what the holy Catholic Church teaches, because it is enlightened by your Holy Spirit. Please confirm me and keep me in the holy faith, and give me grace to live by it.

I trust in Your infinite grace, O Lord. In the infinite merit of Jesus Christ and in His most holy name because only in Him is salvation. I hope in You, O my God, in the forgiveness of all my sins. I hope in the grace to protect myself from all future sins, to live and to die in Your holy grace, and to gain eternal life. O my God, make my hope firm.

I love You, O my God, with all my heart and above all because You alone are infinitely worthy of all love, and because You are infinitely benevolent to me and to all things. I also love my neighbor for Your sake as I love myself. Out of love for You, I am wholeheartedly sorry that I have sinned so many times, and I firmly resolve, with the help of Your grace, not to sin again. I am asking You, O my God, make my love more fervent and give me grace to show it in action. I am asking You for all these virtues in the name of Jesus. Amen.

Say a short prayer before and after a meal and remember that all good things, related to body and soul, come from God who is eternal goodness. Remember as well that a man does not live only to eat and drink, but that he only eats and drinks to live and to live *in God.* Therefore, beware of all intemperance in food and drink. Drunkenness is a great mortal sin. Beware and shun the company of those who are accustomed to getting drunk. If it is possible, try to lead your neighbor, whom you see to have this sin, on the right path.

Faithfully perform all the obligatory fasting in a spirit of penance as well as the obligatory abstinence from meat dishes. Do not control whether others fulfill this duty or not. You fulfill it.

Work diligently all day, especially if you are at work, and faithfully fulfill all the duties of your personal state in life in a spirit of penance and out of love for God.

If you can, read at least a little from a good holy book every day. If you have the opportunity, read aloud so that others will also hear the teachings that are in these books. This is considered a good deed before God, and it is highly recommended to you.

As it is a Christian's duty to *begin* the day with God, so it is his duty to *finish* it with God. Therefore, never abandon evening prayer. God commanded Israelites to make two sacrifices to Him every day: one in the morning and one in the evening. With this, He lets us know that it is His holy will for us to start the day with a prayer and to end it with a prayer. It is good for the whole family to pray together if that is possible. Individual prayer is acceptable, too, if it is done well; however, a communal prayer is even better if it is done properly. We learn this from the words of Jesus: *"For where two or three are gathered together in my name, there am I in the midst of them."*

Always question your conscience when you pray in the evening. This has been recommended to us by the holy teachers and by the Holy Scripture as well. *"Before you are judged, examine yourself, and at the time of scrutiny you will have forgiveness."* Ask yourself and think about how you have spent that day. Let this short self-examination that you find here be an example of how you should question your conscience every evening.

How have I been since I last questioned my conscience last night? How did I perform my evening prayer? What kind of thoughts did I have when I went to sleep? When I woke up at night, what were my thoughts? Did I not think, say or do anything wicked that night? Did I make the sign of the cross and think of God immediately when I got up? Was I not lazy when it was time to get up? Did I say my morning prayer with a collected spirit?

Did I go to mass when I could? How did I behave at Holy Mass? Did I work diligently all day and fulfill all my duties? What was my purpose at work? Have I started work in God's name? Did I work with the intention of fulfilling God's will? Have I willingly endured difficulties in my work out of love for God and in the spirit of penance? Have I done my work faithfully all day? Did I shun all worldliness and dangerous revelry? Did I avoid bad company and sinful companions? How did I treat my neighbor today? Was I disrespectful and disobedient to my superiors or unfriendly and unhelpful to my peers? Or ruthless and unfair to those who are inferior to me? Have I willingly endured annoyances and wickedness of my neighbor? If someone has offended me, have I forgiven them immediately with all my heart? Did I get angry and curse? Did I say some other sinful and offensive words? Have I been gossiping about my neighbor and unnecessarily spoken of his transgressions? Have I set a bad example with my sinful speaking? Have I fulfilled my duties to all those I have a duty before God to care for? Did I give them good teachings and examples? Did I enjoy listening to gossip and spread further what I heard against my neighbor? Did I guard against mortal sins, i.e., especially against vanity, stinginess or greediness, impurity, jealousy, intemperance in food and drink, anger, and laziness? Have I not sinned today by *abandoning good works?*

On Sundays and on other holy days of obligation, ask yourself specifically: Have I fulfilled my duties to God today? Did I go to church in the morning and in the afternoon? How did I behave in church during Mass and during the sermon? Has anybody abandoned or poorly performed his duty to God today because of my negligence? Have I done any work today that should not have been done today? Have I not defiled this holy day of the Lord by attending a sinful play, by drinking, by keeping bad company, by speaking obscenely, with worldly revelry?

On fasting days, ask yourself: Did I fast according to the commandment of the Holy Church? Did I not discontinue fasting unnecessarily and without the permission of the spiritual shepherd? If I obtained permission, have I not consented even more to my perverted nature than I am permitted? Did I do any other good work today?

After questioning your conscience, ask God humbly and in the name of Jesus to forgive you, according to His great grace and according to the merits of Jesus, all the sins you have committed that day. If you have been so fortunate that day that your conscience does not reproach you, humble yourself before God and recognize that God knows you better than you know yourself. He sees many impurities and imperfections in you that you do not see. Remember what St. Paul said and repeat with him: *"I am not conscious of anything against me, but I do not thereby stand acquitted; the one who judges me is the Lord."* However, if you were so unfortunate and terribly foolish that you have committed a mortal sin, O my Christian, then recognize the danger you are in. How many times does it happen that a person goes to bed healthy, falls asleep and does not wake up in this world but in eternity. If this person fell asleep having a mortal sin, he would wake up before the angry Judge who would condemn him to hell. This is exactly what could happen to you if you were so unfortunate as to fall asleep in mortal sin. Therefore, regret your sin from the bottom of your heart and hate it. Ask God sincerely to forgive you and make a firm resolve, confess the sin without delay and improve. Then do some penance for this sin and trust that the merciful God will give you time to confess and repent.

After completing the evening prayer, undress decently. Remember that God watches you. Think of the angel of God who is the guardian of your soul and your body.

When you lie down in bed, remember that the bed is an image of the grave, as sleep is an image of death. Remember Jesus dying on the cross and say with him: *"Father, into your hands I commend my spirit."* Reflect on God and all that is of God, and see that you fall asleep in these thoughts.

On this occasion, I advise you that if you have children, do not allow boys and girls to sleep together, even if they are still small. Do not put in danger the souls for which you will have to give an answer at the Last Judgment. It is also not right if parents let their children sleep with them. If these children are still small, there is a danger that they could suffocate, as it often happens. If they are already older, there are even greater dangers.

2. What a faithful Christian should do every week

On Sundays and on holy days of obligation, faithfully attend the regular divine service in your local church. Only sickness or some other major obstacle may deter you from this. Whenever you can, attend God's service in the morning and in the afternoon. Listen to God's word faithfully, with gratitude, and with a heartfelt wish to always live by it. *"Rather, blessed are those who hear the word of God and observe it."* The one who *"[…] is not a hearer who forgets but a doer who acts."*

Sunday is the Lord's Day and a day of prayer. Because God commands to sanctify it, strive to spend that day as holy as possible. Therefore, pray as much as you can and read as much as you can.

If you cannot go regularly, then visit the most Blessed Sacrament at least on Sundays, and follow the teachings you find in books where this visit is discussed.

Furthermore, sanctify this day with holy peace and rest because it is the day of the Lord's rest. Avoid unnecessary work. Do not socialize, but stay away from it as much as possible, especially on Sundays. Abstain especially from noise and worldly rejoicing, dancing and other worldly pleasures.

Continue to sanctify this day with good deeds as much as you can, e.g., give to a poor person according to your wealth; instruct an ignorant Christian in faith; read something to this person from sacred books; visit a patient and tell him or read to him something with Christian content, etc.

My dear Christian, get used to questioning your conscience on Sundays, and reflect carefully about how you have spent the past week. Then humble yourself before God and ask Him to forgive you for your sins. Make a firm resolve with God's grace and help to protect yourself from sin more carefully next week and to serve God more faithfully.

It is also a good Christian habit to meditate on Christ's suffering every Friday. If you can, go to church and meditate in front of the image of the crucified Jesus about what He suffered for you in order to obtain for you-eternal salvation. Or, if you can, do the Stations of the Cross with a collected spirit and a humble heart. At the same time, repent of your sins, ask Jesus to forgive them according to His infinite merit, and to give you grace to love and serve Him only. If you cannot go to church, reflect on the suffering of Christ while you are working. On that day endure the difficulties of your private life and work especially patiently. Thus, you will act according to the example of the saints.

3. What a faithful Christian should do every month

Go to confession at least once every month, my dear Christian. However, it is much better for salvation to go more often (as was said previously in this book). Prepare for each confession as carefully and faithfully as if you knew it was your last confession, so that you could die afterwards and stand before your Judge.

I recommend that you receive the Eucharist at least once a month, although it is desirable to receive it much more often because it is the daily bread for our soul. In order to be able to receive this most holy sacrament as worthily as possible, strive to love God and your neighbor properly and live a proper Christian life. Before receiving the holy Eucharist, prepare well with a humble and good confession and a heartfelt prayer.

Spend the day before receiving the holy Eucharist quietly as much as you can. Think of Jesus and repeatedly invite Him lovingly to come with His many graces into your heart. Spend the day on which you receive the Eucharist in a holy way and do some good work if you can. After receiving the Eucharist, let your Christian conduct and your fervor in love for God and your neighbor show that you recognize the great grace you have received and that Jesus truly lives in you.

Every *first* Sunday of the month, read this guide and think about how you fulfill it. Make a firm decision to fulfill it completely in action. I recommend to you, my dear Christian, that you do this faithfully. You want to be saved! Trust me. According to my conscience and my own experience, I tell you before God that it is an immensely good tool for walking on the path of salvation and a faithful addition to a Christian guide or rule. Once you start reading this guide and living by it, never abandon it without a proper reason. Fear the Lord your God who will judge you not only for your *deeds*, but also for your *omissions*. Consider what my Jesus says: *"No one who sets a hand to the plow and looks to what was left behind is fit for the kingdom of God."* This means: Whoever begins a good work and then abandons it without proper reason, does not walk the path of salvation that leads to Heaven.

This very Sunday carefully examine your conscience and reflect on how you lived the past month. The short examination of conscience that you will find in this guide will help you to get to know yourself and to remember your sins. Afterwards sincerely regret them out of love for God, make a firm decision to guard against sin more carefully in the future, and ask God in the name of Jesus to give you strength and grace.

Every *last* Sunday of the month prepare for death although a Christian must be prepared to die every day and every hour as Jesus tells us: *"Therefore, stay awake, for you know neither the day nor the hour."* It is nevertheless good to prepare for death. Do this every last Sunday of the month. The text "Preparation for Death" at the end of this guide will help you do this more easily.

4. What a faithful Christian should do every year

People have the habit of rejoicing in worldly joy on their name day, and there are few who think of God and His great blessings on that day and truly thank Him for them. It is ungrateful to God who is the Lord of our life and our greatest benefactor.

My dear Christian, do not be so ungrateful, but spend your name day holy and quietly. Remember that you received great grace from God that day because by receiving the Sacrament of Holy Baptism, He accepted you among His children and among the members of the holy Church. He opened Heaven to you, which you will surely enter if you will only live according to His holy law.

Pray that day with special fervor and love. You can find suitable prayers for your name day in the book *Pasture for the Soul.* These are: *Prayer on the day of your name day*, *Prayer to your patron saint*, and *Renewal of Baptismal vows.*

If you are not able to meditate and pray much that day because you are a worker, renew your good intention before God that you would spend the whole day in prayer and in holy meditation if you could. Then commit to pray those prayers on Sunday instead of praying them today.

On the first Sunday after your name day do what is recommended here. You will also do right if you go to confession and receive the Eucharist that day.

It is recommended to you in this guide to examine your conscience every day, every week and every month, and to think about how you spent the past day, week, and month. Therefore, it is even more recommended to you that on your name day, when another year of your life starts, you carefully consider how you spent that past year. After you have completed questioning yourself and reflecting, ask God with a sad, broken heart that for the sake of Jesus' suffering and His merit, He would forgive you your sins and give you grace to always love Him more thoroughly and to act according to His holy will, so that after this life, which so quickly passes, you would gain the eternal life.

Because you see, my dear Christian, how quickly the years of your life pass by, remember on your name day that your last year of life will come soon. The year you begin today might be your last. Therefore, spend this day *preparing for death* with a special piety.

5. What a faithful Christian should always do

My dear Christian, always love God above all and your neighbor as yourself for God's sake. Never forget God's presence and always like to pray.

Out of love for God, always strive to live in His grace, and fear sin more than all other misfortunes.

Always avoid the company of worldly people, and even more of wicked and licentious people. Guard yourself carefully and avoid places where worldly people like to go. These places are comedy theaters, casinos, dancing halls, places where people speak and live indecently, taverns or pubs, etc.

When you speak, remember that God hears you; therefore, carefully guard against all those sins that a person commits with *the tongue*. These sins are gossiping, slandering, lying, cursing, fighting, using angry and insulting words, reprimanding, mocking, using impure words, etc.

Faithfully maintain the purity of your state of life in thoughts, words, views, and actions. Immediately reject every temptation against this beautiful chastity. In times of temptation, lift up your heart to God and ask Him for help. Commend yourself to the intercession of the most pure Virgin Mary.

Following the example of the righteous Tobit be careful not to do wrong or injustice to your neighbor in any matter.

Do not do to your neighbor what you do not wish, by reason and faith, to be done to you. What you want people to do to you, do to your neighbor. Do it not for your own profit or for your honor, but for the sake of Jesus who said that what we do to our neighbor, we do to Him.

When you are examining your conscience in the evening and you find that you have done no spiritual or physical good to your neighbor, consider whether you *could not* or *did not want* to do anything good. If you could not, you have no sin. However, if you did not want to do good, you sinned. Regret your sin and promise your benevolent Jesus that you will no longer commit the sin against love for your neighbor.

When someone does something bad to you, be patient. Try to do something good for this person out of love for God and your neighbor, and comfort this person and keep his kindness.

As much as your conscience allows try not to give anyone the opportunity to grumble and be angry against you. When there is something unpleasant or difficult in regard to a certain matter or work, strive to endure it yourself instead of giving it to your neighbor.

Do not argue at all, but prefer to stop and keep quiet. Always beware of all offensive, harsh and gossipy words.

Furthermore, do not believe immediately if you hear something evil against your neighbor.

Enjoy visiting patients and caring for them. Get to know Jesus in the person of the patient: *"Do not hesitate to visit the sick, because for such things you will be loved."*

Faithfully fulfill not only the commandments of God, but also those of *the Church*. Do not follow the example of careless and neglectful Christians who do not fulfill them well. *"If he refuses to listen even to the church, then treat him as you would a Gentile [...]."*

Avoid and protect yourself as much as possible from all sinful situations and you will also beware of sin.

Always live in the spirit of penance. Suppress what you see, what you hear, what you taste, and desire, and your will at every opportunity. Forbid yourself a permitted pleasure or enjoyment from time to time, so that you get used to abstaining from what is forbidden. Jesus wants to bring us to His kingdom in His own way, that is, along the path of constraint and denial.

Prefer to withhold your own will and, as much as you are allowed and able, rather act according to the will of others than according to your own.

Always trust in God, in the intercession of the Blessed Virgin Mary and all the saints, and commend yourself to them. Consider their examples and imitate them faithfully.

(You will find here some special tools for more ordinary temptations, which you can faithfully use, so that with the help of God's grace you will more easily guard against sin.)

If you have temptations against *faith*, remember that everything that the holy Catholic Church teaches is revealed by God who is eternal Truth. The Holy Spirit enlightens the Truth, which Jesus promised to give to the Church and preserve it until the end of the world.

If you have temptations against *hope*, are too afraid of God's justice and almost give up, consider God's grace, which is greater than all His works, because *"God is love"*. Consider the merit of Jesus Christ, which is infinite, and firmly believe that you will be saved if you truly strive to love and serve God and avoid sin as much as possible.

If you have temptations against *the love of God*, remember that God is infinitely good, wise and holy. Everything He does is perfect, but because of our poor intelligence we cannot always understand why God does something. Reflect and sincerely believe that God is infinitely benevolent to all things, and especially to people, although we sometimes do not recognize His benevolent intentions. In addition to being worthy of all love in itself, He is also worthy of being infinitely loved because He is unimaginably benevolent to us and to all things.

If you hear evil talk that is against the love for your neighbor, or if you are in danger of using evil words, repeat these words in your heart: "O my God, I love you above all things, and my neighbor, for your sake, as myself."

If you are tempted and in danger of committing a sin against purity of thoughts, words or actions, say: "O my Jesus, the Groom of Pure Souls, create a pure heart in me! O Mary, Virgin most pure, ask Jesus for me."

If worldly people want to lead you into dangerous places and worldly follies, do not listen to them in any way, but consider that there are countless souls in hell, who due to a short sinful joy are now condemned to eternal suffering. Consider what the teachers of the Church say: "Whoever wants to rejoice with the evil spirit in this world, will not rejoice with Christ in Heaven."

If you have temptations to do injustice to your neighbor, e.g., to cheat the neighbor out of something, to steal from him, to save for yourself what is his, etc., remember that an unjust sin is not forgiven as long as the injustice is not remedied. Say to yourself: *"What profit is there for one to gain the whole world yet lose or forfeit himself?"*

If vain thoughts rise in your heart, remember that you are dust and ashes before God. Remember the humble Jesus, the Son of God, who, taking the form of a slave, lived among men only out of humility. Give all glory to God and say in your heart: "*Not to us, Lord, not to us but to your name give glory* [...]."

If you are in danger of sinning by intemperance in eating or drinking, remember the words of Jesus: "*Whoever wishes to come after me must deny himself, take up his cross, and follow me.*" This means that a person must act against his evil desire and do as if he would not have it within himself. Remember as well that Jesus starved many times, as is stated in the Scripture, and that in His suffering He was fed with tears.

If you are prone to anger and impatience, consider these beautiful words of Jesus: "*Take my yoke upon you and learn from me, for I am meek and humble of heart* [...]."

When you feel laziness in fulfilling your daily duties or in God's service and prayer, remember Jesus' words that one must work while it is day. When night falls, no one can work anymore. Whoever does not work is an unworthy servant and will be cast out into the outer darkness, where there is weeping and gnashing of teeth. Consider also the words of the holy apostle James that "*faith of itself, if it does not have works, is dead,*" "*even the demons believe that.*"

Therefore, strive to remember God and His holy words in all temptations and dangers, so that you will overcome them more easily and remain faithful to God.

May God grant you grace, my dear Christian, to fulfill this guide of the Christian life faithfully and in action. You may find it difficult from the beginning. However, never give up right away. Even if you will not be able to fulfill all of these rules right away, trust in God and ask Him to grant you His holy grace and help, and you will be able to fulfill them more and more easily. Strive to love God sincerely, and everything will be easy for you because His love will give you strength.

Now I say this with St. Paul: *"Peace and mercy be to all who follow this rule* […].*"*

III.

PREPARATION FOR DEATH

"Put your house in order, for you are about to die; you shall not recover." Consider, my dear Christian, that these words are also meant for you to prepare for your own death, so that you will leave this world pleased and enter a blissful eternity.

The best preparation for death is living a beautiful Christian life. Experience teaches us that a person mostly dies as he lived. Strive to live beautifully and according to Christian rules, in God's grace and love, and God will not leave you at the hour of your death, as He is faithful and His grace is infinite. However, if you dwell in sinful habits, you are in great danger of becoming eternally miserable. Do not rely on the idea of converting on your deathbed and do not delay conversion. Without God's grace you will not be able to convert. You will make yourself more and more unworthy of this grace and will not find it in the end. Think about the horrible words that Christ directs to all those who live in disobedience and delay their conversion: "[…] *you will look for me, but you will die in your sin. Where I am going you cannot come."* Moreover, you are in constant danger of dying a sudden death and appearing before the judgement seat of Christ with all your sins.

A beautiful Christian life in God's grace is *in general and always* a preparation for death. *A special* preparation is done as follows:

1. Remember God and truly reflect before Him what state your soul is in. Ask God to give you the grace to know yourself properly, and to speak to you through your conscience so that you will know the state of your soul. Say to Him with God-fearing Samuel: "*Speak, Lord, for your servant is listening.*" Afterwards faithfully listen to the voice of your conscience because it is the voice of God. Do not seek to make excuses and minimize your wickedness, but judge yourself harshly so that you will not be condemned by God. Consider especially what would cause you the most fear and mental distress if God would announce to you that you will have to die *today* – perhaps some injustice that you have done to your neighbor in regards to his property or his good name, and which you have not yet rectified. Perhaps there is some sinful habit that you still have, even though you have promised God many times that you would abandon it. Perhaps the company you are keeping or a friendship is not pleasing to God. Perhaps some kind of morally corrupt deed you have not yet rectified due to neglect. Perhaps some promise that you have made to God or a neighbor, you have not yet fulfilled due to negligence. Or you have some debt that you could have paid off, but you keep delaying it, etc. Consider the state of your soul and conscience. Then firmly decide with God's help to rectify without delay everything that you find wrong about yourself, and to turn away everything that you realize would make you miserable if you died not doing it.

2. Consider also, my dear Christian, if your domestic affairs and worldly chores are in such a state that you would not be afraid of death if it happens to you *today*. Make a real effort to bring all your temporal affairs and chores to such a state, and always keep them in such a state, that you would be ready at any time to stand before your Judge and give answer about your temporal affairs. In this way, you will be equal to those good servants

about whom Jesus says: "*Blessed are those servants whom the master finds vigilant on his arrival.*" "*You also must be prepared, for at an hour you do not expect, the Son of Man will come.*" If you think that a will would be necessary after your death, it is good to prepare one and keep it.

3. As it is the duty of a Christian to reconcile with God by worthily receiving the holy Sacraments when the time of death comes, so it is beneficial for you to go to confession and receive the Eucharist in this monthly preparation if you are able to do so. However, even without it, you can do this preparation for death. If you receive the Holy Sacraments in this preparation, put yourself on your deathbed in spirit, make a confession and receive the Eucharist, as you would wish to receive these Holy Sacraments at the end of your life for the last time.

Spend the day of preparation for death in solitude and silence, meditate, read, and pray all day. Perform the prayers you find here with special devotion. In addition to this, you can also find suitable prayers for this day in the book *Pasture for the Soul,* e.g., *Prayer to the crucified and dying Jesus for a happy death* on page 522. You can find a suitable meditation for this day in the *Meditation about the Four Last Things.*

Litany as a Preparation for Death

Lord, have mercy on me in my last hour.
Christ, have mercy on me in my last hour.
Lord, have mercy on me in my last hour.
Christ, hear us.
Christ, graciously hear us.

Heavenly Father, Almighty God, have mercy on me in my last hour.
Son of God, the savior of the whole world, have mercy on me in my last hour.

Holy Spirit, true God, have mercy on me in
  my last hour.
Holy Trinity, one God, have mercy on me in
  my last hour.
Saint Mary, ℟. *intercede for my happy last hour.*
Holy Mother of God, ℟.
The Virgin of all virgins, ℟.
All holy angels and archangels, ℟.
St. Abel, ℟.
All who are righteous, ℟.
St. Abraham, ℟.
St. John the Baptist, ℟.
St. Joseph, ℟.
All holy patriarchs and prophets, ℟.
St. Peter, ℟.
St. Paul, ℟.
St. Andrew, ℟.
St. John, ℟.
All holy apostles and evangelists, ℟.
All holy disciples of the Lord, ℟.
All holy innocents, ℟.
St. Stephen, ℟.
St. Lawrence, ℟.
All holy martyrs, ℟.
St. Silvester, ℟.
St. Gregory, ℟.
St. Augustine, ℟.
All holy bishops and confessors, ℟.
St. Benedict, ℟.
St. Francis, ℟.
All holy monks and hermits, ℟.
St. Mary Magdalene, ℟.
St. Lucy, ℟.
St. Barbara, ℟.
St. Catherine, ℟.
All holy virgins and widows, ℟.

All the saints of God, ℟.
Be merciful to me. Have mercy on me, O Lord.
Be merciful to me. Save me, O Lord.
From your wrath, deliver me in my last hour, O Lord.
From wretched death, deliver me in my last
 hour, O Lord.
From all sin, ℟.: *deliver me at my last hour, O Lord.*
From too much fear, ℟.
From despair, ℟.
From insolent hope, ℟.
From all the temptations of the evil spirit, ℟.
From all the power of the wicked enemy, ℟.
From eternal damnation, ℟.
Oh, my Jesus. After your birth, ℟.: *give me a*
 happy last hour.
After your hard and poor life, ℟.
After your sorrow and your tears, ℟.
After your agony in the garden, ℟.
After your immense mortal pains, ℟.
After your endless suffering, ℟.
After your five wounds, ℟.
After your death on the cross, ℟.
After your burial, ℟.
After your glorious resurrection from the dead, ℟.
After your marvelous ascension, ℟.
And according to the grace of the Holy Spirit, ℟.
Poor sinner, ℟.: *I ask you, please here me*
That in my last hour You look graciously upon me, ℟.
To keep Your holy grace for me, ℟.
To forgive all my sins, ℟.
To confirm me in the holy Catholic faith, ℟.
To grant me constant confidence in Your holy
 promises, ℟.
To pour burning love for You into my heart, ℟.
To grant me true repentance for all my sins, ℟.

To give me true Christian patience and a spirit of
  humility, ℟.
To protect me from all evil thoughts, ℟.
To grant me complete surrender to Your holy will, ℟.
To grant me a heartfelt wish to see You in Heaven, ℟.
To bring me to eternal heavenly joy, ℟.
That you want to listen to me, ℟.
O Jesus, Son of God, ℟.

Lamb of God, who takes away the sins of the world,
  spare me, O Lord.
Lamb of God, who takes away the sins of the world,
  have mercy on me, O Lord.
Christ, hear me.
Christ, graciously hear me.
Lord, have mercy on me in my last hour.
Christ, have mercy on me in my last hour.
Lord, have mercy on me in my last hour.
Our Father ... Hail Mary ...

Prayer

O Lord, my God. Hear my prayer and be merciful to
my soul when it departs from this world. Forgive me all
my sins, deliver me from all punishments, and take me
to the eternal, heavenly abode, which Jesus Christ, your
Son, our Lord, who lives and reigns with You, has prepared for me in the unity of the Holy Spirit, God forever
and ever. Amen.

*(I also ask the Mother of God, my guardian angel, St. Joseph,
and St. Barbara to intercede for me for my fortunate last hour.)*

O Mary, most pure virgin and most holy mother of
Jesus, you stood in unspeakable sorrow under the cross
of your loving son, on which He was dying in terrible
ordeal. I am wholeheartedly asking that you intercede
at the hour of my death. For my entire life, I have been
asking for your intercession with God on my behalf. I

am particularly asking you not to leave me in my last hour. At the hour of my death, intercede on my behalf even more because the evil spirit will try even harder to trick me and prevent me from eternal salvation. Ask Jesus to grant me the grace to leave this world in His holy love and in heartfelt regret for my sins, and to stand before His judgment seat. Hail Mary, Mother of God, pray for me, a poor sinner, now and in the hour of my death. Amen.

O my faithful guardian angel. The benevolent God entrusted me to you to protect my soul and my body for my entire life. How faithfully you have hitherto protected me in all dangers. How many times have I received your faithful and loving care. How many mental and physical dangers you have saved me from, which I was not aware of. For all this, I thank you, my holy heavenly guardian, and I praise the merciful God who gave me such a caring guardian. I am asking you, O angel of God, protect me just as faithfully in the future as you do now, especially in my last hour, when this soul, whom God entrusted to you for protection, will shortly depart from this world. Expel then, with God's help, the evil spirit, so that it does not overcome me and that it does not take God's grace from me. And then accompany my soul before the face of God. Amen.

O Venerable Saint Joseph. Among all the saints God chose you to be the guardian of His beloved son Jesus and His most holy mother, the Virgin Mary. Therefore, I trust in your intercession on my behalf in life and in death. Your life was holy, innocent, and completely pleasing to God. Beautiful and honorable was your death. The Son of God, in his marvelous humility, was completely obedient to you as long as He lived. At your death, He faithfully stood by your side. In the same way, your most pure bride, the Virgin Mary, stood by you in your last hour. O most beautiful, most holy death!

I am begging you, venerable St. Joseph, intercede with Jesus that He grant me a happy last hour, that He and His most holy Mother would stand by me then, that He would preserve me in His holy grace, and take me to Heaven after my death. Amen.

O pure bride of Jesus, virgin and martyr, Saint Barbara! How faithfully and tenderly you loved Jesus. Out of love for your heavenly Spouse you were not afraid of terrible suffering nor of death. I beg you, holy Virgin! Intercede for me so that I may receive great love for Jesus in life and in death, and ask for my happy last hour in the grace of God. I especially ask you to intercede with Jesus that He would grant me grace not to die without the holy sacraments, but to receive the holy Eucharist as much as possible when my last hour approaches. Ask Him as well that His loving words would fulfill in me: "*I am the living bread that came down from heaven; whoever eats this bread will live forever.*" Amen.

ACKNOWLEDGEMENTS

Reviewed by:

Very Rev. Fr. Timothy Ferguson
Ms. Lenora McKeen
Rev. Monshau, OD
Dcn. John P. Vidmar

www.ingramcontent.com/pod-product-compliance
Lightning Source LLC
Chambersburg PA
CBHW060904140726

47996CB00001B/109